John Man is a historian and travel writer with special interests in China, Mongolia and the history of written communication. His *Gobi: Tracking the Desert* was the first book on the subject in English since the 1920s. His other books include *Alpha Beta*, on the origins of the alphabet, and *The Gutenberg Revolution*, on the cause and impact of printing. On China and Mongolia he has written *Genghis Khan*, *Attila the Hun*, *Kublai Khan* and *The Terracotta Army*. In 2007 he was awarded Mongolia's prestigious Friendship Medal for his contribution to Mongol–UK relations. His latest book, *The Leadership Secrets of Genghis Khan*, will shortly be published by Bantam Press.

Praise for *Attila the Hun*:

'Shatters the clichés . . . As one's guide into this mysterious world, one could not wish for a better storyteller or analyst than John Man . . . His Attila is superb, as compellingly readable as it is impressive in its scholarship: with his light touch, the Huns and their King live as never before. There is something fascinating and new on every page' Simon Sebag Montefiore

'Attila is known as a savage but there was much more to this great warrior. Man takes his readers on a thrilling ride alongside the man who marauded across Europe, striking terror into the hearts of entire nations' *The Good Book Guide*

'Racy and imaginative . . . sympathetically and readably puts flesh and bones on one of history's most turbulent characters' *Sunday Telegraph*

'There are moments when this book reads a little like a real-life *Lord of the Rings* . . . Meteoric and momentous . . . fascinating reading' *Guardian*

'The warlord's thunderous rise to infamy is enlivened by Man's constant asides, comments and comparisons. His obvious flair for conversational history and clear ability to get the most from well-informed modern sources drives the narrative along at a pace Attila himself would have been happy with. Man is a one man Time Team' *Western Daily Press*

'More like a piece of travel writing than history, as the author shares his imagination and enthusiasm for what he has found in modern day Hungary . . . the powerful heart of this study is Man's fine reconstruction of the battle on the Catalaunian Plains' *Newdirections*

Praise for *Genghis Khan*:

'Absorbing and beautifully written . . . a thrilling account of Genghis Khan's life, death and his continuing influence . . . a gripping present-day quest' *Guardian*

'A first-rate travel book, not so much a life of the Khan but a search for him . . . Man has scholarly gifts as well as acute intelligence and a winning way with words. This is a fine introduction to the subject, as well as a rattling good read'
Felipe Fernandez-Armesto, *Independent*

'A fine, well-written and well-researched book' *Mail on Sunday*

'Compelling . . . Man's perspective is as clearsighted and invigorating as that of the Mongol horsemen he travels with . . . this is an eloquent account, not only of a fascinating historical figure and his people, but of the resonance of history itself'
Waterstone's Books Quarterly

'Enthralling and colourful' *Independent on Sunday*

'This is a great story' *Spectator*

THE GREAT WALL

JOHN MAN

BANTAM BOOKS

LONDON • TORONTO • SYDNEY • AUCKLAND • JOHANNESBURG

TRANSWORLD PUBLISHERS
61–63 Uxbridge Road, London W5 5SA
A Random House Group Company
www.rbooks.co.uk

THE GREAT WALL
A BANTAM BOOK: 9780553817683

First published in Great Britain
in 2008 by Bantam Press
a division of Transworld Publishers
Bantam edition published 2009

This book is a work of non-fiction.

A CIP catalogue record for this book
is available from the British Library.

Addresses for Random House Group Ltd companies outside the UK
can be found at: www.randomhouse.co.uk
The Random House Group Ltd Reg. No. 954009

The Random House Group Limited supports The Forest Stewardship Council
(FSC), the leading international forest certification organisation. All our titles
that are printed on Greenpeace approved FSC certified paper carry the FSC
logo. Our paper procurement policy can be found at
www.rbooks.co.uk/environment

Typeset in 11/14pt Sabon by
Falcon Oast Graphic Art Ltd.
Printed in the UK by CPI Cox & Wyman, Reading, RG1 8EX.

2 4 6 8 10 9 7 5 3 1

CONTENTS

MAPS

A NOTE ON SPELLING

Most Chinese words in this book are names, and all except for the occasional very well-established one are transliterated using the modern system, pinyin (as opposed to the old one, known as Wade–Giles). In pinyin, most letters and diphthongs are roughly as in English, but some have their own pronunciation. These are the main ones:

Consonants:
c as in rats
q as in church
x is between s and sh
z as in suds
zh as in fudge

Vowels:
e as in the US pronunciation of nurse
ie as in yeah
ue as in a contracted form of 'you were' – y'were
eng as in sung
ei as in gay

Commonly, pinyin omits the tones that help define the Chinese character. In Mandarin, there are four tones, indicated with accents on the vowel (the first, in diphthongs):

First (high, level) tone: ā ē ī ō ū
Second (rising) tone: á é í ó ú
Third (falling-rising): ǎ ě ǐ ǒ ǔ
Fourth (falling) tone: à è ì ò ù

Even so, pinyin cannot always specify the exact sign, so for the sake of Chinese speakers and translators I add the Chinese signs, except for proper names, which are so numerous that to give Chinese signs for all would be too cumbersome.

ACKNOWLEDGEMENTS

My thanks:
– to those who eased the way in China and Mongolia: Y. Badral, Three Camels Lodge and Nomadic Expeditions, Mongolia; Batbolt, driver, Choibalsan; Cheng Yinong and Emma, Beijing; Cheng Dalin, Wall expert, Beijing; Goyotsetseg Radnaabazar ('Goyo'); Prof. Dr G. Jorigt, Mongolian Language Institute, College of Mongolian Studies, Inner Mongolia University; Li Yafen, Jinshanling; Ling Qin, School of Archaeology and Museology, Peking University; Luo Hong, driver, Dunhuang; Shagai, driver, Dalandzadgad; Franck Pelagatti, Paris; Shou Weijong ('William'), Beijing; Song Guorong, Yongchang; Sun Chingching ('Christina') and Xu Jie ('Eric'), guides, Lanzhou; Prof. Tsogt-Ochir Ishdorj, Mongolian Academy of Science; Ms V. Urzhingkhand, Chingisin Dalan, eastern Mongolia; Wong Qinglin, Dunhuang; Xu Zhaoyu ('Michael'), Hai Tian Travel Service, Lanzhou; the staff of the Yanguan Museum; Zhang Min, Badaling; Zhou Wangping, Jinshanling;
– to those who helped the flow of information: Rafe de Crespigny, Faculty of Asian Studies, Australian National

University; Robin Darwall-Smith, Magdalen College, Oxford; Prof. Glen Dudbridge, University College, Oxford; David Harris, Mount Barker, South Australia;

    – and, as always, to those who made the book happen: the team at Transworld – Doug Young, Simon Thorogood and Sheila Lee; Malcolm Swanston and Jonathan Young, Red Lion Maps; Gillian Somerscales, for superb editing; and Felicity Bryan and her wonderful staff.

INTRODUCTION
THE WALL OF CHINA
DOES NOT EXIST

If Hollywood ever makes *The Great Wall: The Movie*, it might open with this single, uncut, aerial tracking shot, in Imax:

EXT. EARTH ORBIT. DAY
Below us, as the earth turns, India vanishes off-screen left, and east Asia swings into frame. We're

FALLING TOWARDS CHINA.
LCD displays flicker:
Altitude: 15 . . . 14 . . . 13 kilometres.
Speed: 3,000 . . . 2,750 . . . 2,500 kilometres per hour.
Colours emerge: the green of the fertile south, the burned brown of the desert north, Tibet's white highlands.
Altitude: 8 . . . 7 . . . 6 kilometres. Speed: 1,500 . . . 1,250

kph. Now two great rivers stand out, and north of them a dark, wavy line cutting across the whole region, from deserts to our left, over mountains to the blue Pacific. Height: 1 kilometre; speed: 1,000 kph. We level out over a river and stark brown mountains, and

ZOOM IN

on the dark, wavy line, which is not a wavy line any more, but the Wall, immense, a river of stone 7 metres high, wide as a road, reaching to the horizon in both directions, with a watch-tower every kilometre. Soldiers on the battlements are running to the towers, where they are starting warning fires. Beyond, a nomad horde assaults the Wall, to no effect. We turn along the Wall at the speed of sound. From each tower in turn, flames and smoke leap, as if unzipping the desert. We overtake the dots of flame. On our right, a great chain of snow-capped mountains flickers past. On the left, more mountains, austere ones of dark rock. They close in on either side. We pop through the gap, always above the Wall, then weave through more mountains to a vast, muddy river. The Wall edges the river, veering into a semicircular turn. Now the landscape changes. It's greener. The Wall begins to zoom and twist round and over mountains. We follow in an exhilarating roller-coaster ride. In the distance to our right, beyond the mountains, a huge city. It's past, and the Wall runs onwards, up, down, left, right – more mountains, a lake, a final leap up and over, and ahead is a fortress where the Wall plunges into the sea.

ZOOM
upward into blue sky.

CUT.

That's how it might begin. It would indeed be wonderful, with all those expensive, impossible computer graphics. It would, I think, seduce an audience. They would believe, because they have seen the images of the Wall near Beijing, which looks pretty much like a bit of the Wall in this epic opening. They would believe, because it confirms so much they think they know about the Wall: the only man-made structure visible from space, it runs in an unbroken line of stone across north China, it was built to keep the barbarians at bay, etc., etc.

They would believe. But they would be wrong, because the sequence is almost entirely rubbish. A more accurate title for any film that began this way would be *The Great Wall: Errors, Lies and Assorted Idiocies*.

No, it cannot be seen from space. That quaint idea came from an even quainter one, stated as fact by Robert Ripley, the American illustrator who made himself a millionaire with his cartoon feature *Believe It Or Not!* This specialized in making extraordinary claims, some true, some as fantastic as headlines in a downmarket tabloid – Astronomers Discover Pearly Gates, Nun Gives Birth to Puppy: that sort of thing. The feature became an industry, syndicated, turned into radio and TV shows and films, reproduced in books. As a child, I had one of Ripley's books. It showed a man lifting weights with his eyeballs, which I totally believed. In the 1930s, when

Ripley's feature took off, he had 80 million readers. You can still see reruns of the films on the Sci-Fi Channel, which is where most of the outrageous claims belong, including the one that called the Great Wall 'The mightiest work of man – the only one that would be visible to the human eye from the Moon'. This statement was, of course, founded on no evidence at all, since it was made 30 years before anyone had been in space, 40 before the lunar landings. This didn't prevent its becoming sanctioned by use: so much so that the eminent Sinologist Joseph Needham, author of the magisterial multi-volume *Science and Civilisation in China*, stated that 'the Wall has been considered the only work of man which could be picked out by Martian astronomers'.[1] The Chinese were delighted with the idea, and included the moon version (though not Mars) as a 'fact' in textbooks until the first Chinese space flight in 2003, when their astronaut, Yang Liwei, admitted he couldn't see anything of it from orbit. It was too narrow, too similar in colour to its background. Many cities, yes, even airport runways; the Wall, no. So believe it: you cannot see the Wall from the moon, let alone Mars.

Where does that leave the close-ups? The view of the Wall itself? Surely we should believe in that, as almost all those who see the sections outside Beijing believe. Here the Wall is as astounding as the hype suggests, a roller-coaster of masonry riding ridges over mountains as chaotic as crinkled tinfoil. It zooms, it drops, it doubles back in Z-bends, it vanishes into valleys, it reappears on distant peaks. This is an object that seems as easy to

[1] Needham, *Science and Civilisation*, vol. 4, part 3, p. 47.

define as Buckingham Palace or the Eiffel Tower. You see it, you climb it, you snap it, and there you have it, pinned down and anatomized. 'I climbed the Great Wall', it says on the T-shirt. You have a vague sense that this is a tiny part of a greater whole that stretches for thousands of kilometres, as the pamphlets claim. Statistics batter you into acceptance: 6,000 kilometres long, a zillion bricks, enough to build a wall (or two) right around the earth. You also believe it is old, as old as China herself, as timeless as the pyramids.

The weasel word in the last paragraph is 'it'. The Wall is not an 'it'. It's a 'them', walls in the plural, and they do not form a continuous line. They are in bits, which appear on good maps like fragments of DNA in a scientific diagram. Up close, very few of them look like the glorious creation to which tourists go. Tame sections give way to wild ones – crumbling, overgrown, barred to walkers – and wild ones vanish into gaps made by roads and reservoirs. You cannot join the dots even of this, the Ming Great Wall, and come up with a unity. And these divided sections are nothing against the other walls, those that rise, fall and vanish as you journey westward. All across north China, as mountains give way to terraced hills and arid plains and finally desert, walls of various sorts keep you company. And out there, where tourists seldom go, majestic brick and stone give way to earth: sometimes a rough barrier blasted by wind and washed by rain into camel's humps or saw-teeth, sometimes no more than a gentle bank a metre or two in height, sometimes nothing at all.

And all of these bits overlap each other in time. The sections you see around Beijing are only the most recent manifestations of an ancient urge – recent in two ways, for these are twentieth-century restorations of an original that is a mere 500 years old. This wall has ancient precedents, some of them directly beneath it. Sometimes a new dynasty would keep previous creations, sometimes not; sometimes they would rebuild right on the same spot, sometimes not. A few sections come down to us unsullied, survivals from the very first Great Wall over 2,000 years ago. Some are the worse for wear after 500 years. And there is much more to the Wall than wall: fortresses and barracks, guard-towers and beacon-towers, ranging out ahead of and behind the main Wall in a sort of stretched-out halo.

How can such a muddle be measured? Why should we settle on 6,000 kilometres as its length? We shouldn't. Estimates vary from 1,684 miles (2,694 kilometres), according to *Time* magazine at the time of Nixon's visit to China in 1972, to 50,000 kilometres, according to the Xinhua News Agency in 1979. All are meaningless: there are so many bits, some rebuilt many times over, that no one has yet defined what is meant by the one-and-only Great Wall. Even on the mainstream sections, do you count only those bits that survive today? In which case, what about the gaps? Do you count twice, three times, four times the bits used over and over again by different dynasties? What of the non-walls – the embankments, like those I will introduce you to in Mongolia? And if the length remains unknown, so must the volume, much of which is not stone but earth. Exit, therefore, the idea that the Wall could provide stones enough to circle the globe.

All these bits and pieces, overlapping in time and place, make a nonsense of a singular 'it'. Really, the Chinese term for the Wall, vague and paradoxical, is a far better representation of reality, because it emerges from a distant past, when every city had its wall. 'Walls, walls, walls, and yet again walls, form the framework of every Chinese city,' wrote the Swedish historian of Chinese art Osvald Sirén. 'They surround it, they divide it into lots and compounds, they mark more than any other structures the basic features of Chinese communities . . . There is no such thing as a city without a wall. It would be just as inconceivable as a house without a roof.' So fundamental was the connection between walls and cities that one word covered them both, and still does. This, to a westerner like me, is a paradox – one word, two different meanings – but there it is, in OUP's standard concise dictionary: *Chéng* (城): '1. city; 2. city wall.' It may seem odd at first glance, but synecdoche – using an essential part to stand for the whole – is common enough in English: 'per head of population', 'all hands on deck'. The Wall, of course, is rather more than a city wall; so Chinese adds an adjective, not 'great' but 'long'. Several Chinese guides were perfectly happy to tell me that the Chinese for 'the Great Wall', *cháng chéng* /长城 , means Long City. 'And Long Wall?' I asked. Yes. It could also mean Long Cities, or Long Walls, plural. They see no contradiction here. Nor is there, if you perform a thought experiment: peel back a city wall in your mind, stretch it out, put farms and garrisons along it, and there you have it – Great Wall(s) = Long City/ies.

Yet there is a singularity, which allows us to speak of the Wall as one. It exists not on the ground but in the mind. This

Wall, this 'it', is rooted in the mind-set of Chinese leaders down the ages. It is an idea that gives a boundary to the Chinese sense of identity. In history, it divided the ultra-civilized China of farms and cities from the ravenous barbarian nomads of the north, whose constant raids threatened to tear China apart. And it defined the nation's timescale as well. The original Wall was built on the orders of China's First Emperor, the one who first unified the nation, the one whose vast mausoleum near Xian is guarded by China's most famous tourist attraction, the Terracotta Army. That's the starting point for the notion that for over 2,200 years China has been protected by a curtain of stone, like the one north of Beijing, running all across China, from the western deserts to the sea. Thus was the tide of barbarian assault held back; thus was China unified.

There is as much myth as history in this. No one, until quite recently, was interested in trying to untangle the two (a task in which modern historians claim they are engaged). No one, for example, wrote the history of the northern frontier from the point of view of the 'barbarians' themselves, who had their own highly sophisticated and effective way of life. Myth and history, undifferentiated, produced a solid consensus that every-thing south of the Wall was superior, everything north inferior. Had it not been for the Wall, China would have been infected, assaulted, overtaken, undermined, destroyed. The Wall, in brief, defined the nation, which is why it has been adopted as the nation's symbol, ringing in 1,000 million pairs of ears – as it no doubt will often enough during the 2008 Olympics – in the opening lines of the national anthem:

Arise, ye who refuse to be slaves!
With our very flesh and blood
Let us build our new Great Wall!

Yet historically this adulation is quite a new idea, and so is the myth. Until recently, wall-building was a controversial activity, an action of last resort, often condemned as useless. Moreover, the two sides – north and south, settled and nomad – were never totally divided. They were intertwined in a love–hate relationship that involved trade, diplomacy and intermarriage. The Wall was never the barrier it seemed or was claimed to be. Many times nomad armies rode over and through it, and as many times Chinese armies invaded to quell them. Four north Chinese dynasties were founded by tribes from Mongolia and Manchuria, and two of them ruled the whole country – and to those two, the Mongols and the Manchus, the Wall was no deterrent. Between 1279, when the Mongols conquered all China, and 2007, China was ruled by 'barbarians' for 356 years out of 728. Seen from this perspective, China's rulers have been as much 'barbarian' as Chinese, and for half the time there was no need for the Wall at all, because China ruled on both sides of it.

The truth is that the Wall was only partly inspired by the threat from the nomads. It served many other purposes: it defined spheres of interest, marked a frontier, and confined unruly populations where they could be controlled and taxed and turned into workers. Ambitious leaders built walls as potentates built palaces, keeping their people cowed by displays of power and fearful of alien threats.

That the Wall was not all it has been cracked up to be is clear from the attitude of the nomads themselves. They raided at will, never taking the Wall seriously; the greatest of the nomad nations, the Mongols under Genghis Khan, took no notice of it at all. Neither it nor any of its several offshoots get a mention in the Mongols' foundation epic, *The Secret History*. To Genghis and his armies the Wall, or walls, might as well not have been there. Nor do Mongolians see anything 'great' about the Wall today. To them, it is the White Wall, because that was the colour the Chinese soldiers painted it, and of no more strategic significance than a First World War trench to a tank.

To tackle this vast and complex subject, I travelled from Wall's end to Wall's end, and from top (in Mongolia) to bottom (Lanzhou, the capital of China's Gansu province). The travel was highly selective, dependent as much on chance as choice. At the time, the experiences were both astonishing and baffling, because every site threw up new pieces of history, overlapping with others. I relied on many helpers: as well as Mongolian friends, these included guides, drivers and experts, including the one man who has explored more of the Wall than anyone else. His name is Cheng Dalin. A small, amazingly fit man in his sixties, with twinkling eyes and eyebrows like caterpillars on a trampoline, he told me some of his story in his little Beijing apartment. We were with his soft-spoken son Cheng Yinong, a specialist in medieval towns, who was going to accompany me along the Ming sections of the Wall from Beijing to the sea.

Cheng Dalin came to the Wall by a combination of

chance, talent and commitment. In the 1950s he was in sports college, training as a sprinter and a weightlifter. He injured himself lifting, and turned to medicine. Meanwhile, China's relationship with Russia went sour. War threatened. A higher power decided that the nation needed war reporters. War reporters had to be very fit, so Cheng and several of his fellow students were sent to join the state news agency, Xinhua. There he found a niche as a photographer, specializing in landscapes – a role in which his fitness was an asset, since he found himself walking in remote places carrying cameras. Among his subjects was the part of the Great Wall that ends in the Pacific, Old Dragon's Head, which at that time was badly dilapidated. He wanted to call attention to its condition, and to do that his photographs would have to have captions. That in turn meant doing his own research.

'So he got some books,' the younger Cheng said, when we were alone much later in our trip. 'My father is very strong-minded. He wants everything to be the best. He was not happy with what he found, so he began to develop his own views. Then, with his pictures and text, he published his own book. But he was not a scholar, so experts did not take him seriously. Some people said he should stick to photography. But my father did not listen. He tried harder, did more research. Of course, he had his own work in the agency as well. He ran a department. I think he has much ability – father, sportsman, medic, photographer, scholar, leader.' But he kept going back to the Wall, making countless trips to remote spots, sometimes with little Cheng carrying the cameras. 'So many cameras! Seven of them, for colour, for wide-angle, for black and white, large format . . . and the tripods, and films.'

The result of all this labour was many articles in the *People's Picture Magazine*, publicizing different sections, then a book on the Wall, backed by Xinhua, translated into English and published in Hong Kong – but not in China proper, because Cheng lacked the right academic credentials. Cheng's *Great Wall of China*, published in 1984, is hard to find now, but it and its author gave me what I needed to start with: passion, contacts, guidance, encouragement. No one knew the Wall and all its sub-branches better than Cheng, who had documented his life's work in an archive of 10,000 card-indexed pictures.

'So,' I asked him, 'you have travelled along all the parts of the Wall?'

'No! Impossible! Even now, after thirty years, I have still covered no more than eighty-five per cent.' He paused. 'What can you do, do you think?'

What indeed, in less than a lifetime? I had little choice. I would have to portray the Wall as a living force, taking today's Wall as my starting point, delving into history to explain the present. With Mongolian travelling companions, I would indulge my bias towards the much-abused 'barbarians', the Mongols in particular, because it was the ever-looming barbarian menace, real and imagined, that infused the Chinese mania for wall-building. I would have to be ruthlessly selective. I would try to use my experiences as doorways into history. With the right help, I would be like a portrait painter, using broad strokes to suggest an immense and complex entity.

I

EARTH

1

THE FIRST EMPEROR'S
LESS-THAN-GREAT WALL

FROM THE TOURIST LITERATURE YOU WOULD THINK THE FIRST
Great Wall, built around 214 BC, sprang into being from
nothing as a massive stone rampart. The bits I had seen –
a low hump across fields north of Guyuan, a battered
ridge outside Yinchuan – were all of earth. So when I read
of a section of stone wall north of the Inner Mongolian
capital, Hohhot, I planned a visit, hoping for something as
massive as today's Great Wall at Beijing.

Northward from Hohhot, the road leaves behind the
broad flood plain of the Yellow River, the sparkling new
high-rises, the seething traffic and the side-lanes clogged
with bicycles, swerving up into the hills of the Yinshan and
levelling out into empty stretches lined with poplars. A
hundred years ago, let alone a thousand or two, this had
been nomad territory, not a field or house to be seen. Now

earth-walled villages baked in the autumn heat. Sunflowers wilted, stooks of straw dotted the fields, piles of grain lay on roadsides ready for threshing.

Jorigt, my Mongol-Chinese companion, began to talk about the changing balance of power between Chinese and Mongols. Jorigt, who grew up speaking only Mongol, learned Chinese as a teenager, then Turkish, then English. He teaches at Hohhot's Mongolian University and knows at first hand the problems that minorities face from the sheer weight of Chinese culture. 'Soon I think, in twenty years maybe, there will be no grasslands any more. Many people come for minerals, and we will lose it all.' He thought for a moment, and gave a brief, bitter laugh. 'Chinese people think minority peoples are barbarians. This is a very wrong idea. City people are very closed, so they fear nomadic persons. But nomadic culture is very suitable for people and for the earth. It is, ah, sensible, no—' he scuffled through a much-thumbed little dictionary '—*sustainable* development.'

And suddenly, at a bend around a hill rough with exposed rock, there we were at the very old frontier between the civilized world to the south and the wild barbarians of the north. A concrete sign proclaimed us to be at 'The Great Wall of Qin Dynasty'. Above, an idealized section of the Great Wall at Beijing, complete with crenellations and dragons, framed the Wall's creator, the First Emperor. It was not so much a portrait as a concrete cartoon – staring slit eyes, grim down-turned mouth, thick neck – that made him as repellent as Jabba the Hutt in *Star Wars* (fair enough, as you will see). A lattice fence with two mock guard-towers led into a valley whose steep slopes were covered with scrub and loose slate. Above us, along the ridge, ran the grey-stone Wall, its detailed structure a mystery from that steep angle. A kilometre or two in, where the Wall dropped steeply, the track crossed it. We parked and walked up beside it, into a hot, gusting wind.

There were several surprises. The Wall, made of chunks of flat, slate-like rock, ran along the hillside. It was quite low, a metre or so on the uphill side, two or three on the other, flat along the top, and with no sign of any defences: none of the crenellations, guard-towers and beacon-towers which are the vanguards and rearguards of the later Wall. Nothing at all like the Great Wall of the popular imagination. Wondering if it had once been higher, I looked around. No rubble anywhere, except a few places where the Wall itself had spilled its guts downhill.

'Jorigt, they say this was built to keep you lot out.' This was unfair. The Mongols hadn't even arrived in Mongolia 2,000 years ago. 'But look. I don't think this was ever high enough to keep *anyone* out.'

He nodded. 'Horses could climb here. Archers could shoot over.'

Yet huge amounts of time, effort, manpower and expertise had been invested in this ineffective structure. The slate was nicely dressed on the outside edge, carefully leaning back a few degrees to counter the slope, a superb example of dry-stone walling. All of the stones were solid, except for the rubble that formed the core, and some were quite big, weighing 100 kilos or so. Local certainly, but not the sort of thing you could find lying about.

On the hilltop above, three tall shapes were silhouetted

against the brightness of the sky. For a moment I thought they were people. But there was no movement. Statues, perhaps? We climbed on upwards until the objects revealed themselves. They were simple pillars, made of slates piled on top of each other – cairns to mark the hill-top, as Mongols honour high places with the stone-piles they call *ovoos*. It was easy to see where the stones came from: a little quarry alongside, which could have been a source for some of the stones in the wall as well. Larger ones also came from nearby, as they still do: from over the hill came the boom and dust of an open-cast rock-mine.

I wondered about the supposedly aggressive barbarian hordes. If this wall had no defences, had they been here at all, amid these slaty hills and unpromising tussocks of coarse grass?

'John Man, look.'

Jorigt pointed. Down in the valley were a herd of sheep and goats, and a cattle enclosure. A distant figure was bent over, attending to something at his feet.

We made our way down, and along a dried-up river-bed, to find a herdsman dressed in a camouflage jacket. He was hauling water from a well, beautifully made, lined with stones cut to form a tube a good 10 metres deep. A smart little Suzuki motorbike stood nearby. Jorigt and he chatted. His name was Li Bin, and he had been herding here for 40 years; before him his father had done the same, as had, perhaps, long before that, families of herders, back for 2,000 years. He offered a mug, and drew a bucket of cool, pure water.

I wondered if the Wall impinged at all on his life. He shrugged at my question, and spouted an official cliché.

'It's a cultural relic.' It didn't interest him in the least. 'It doesn't interfere with grazing. I have to collect those sheep.' He had spotted some of his herd wandering off down the dry river-bed. He straddled his motorbike and started it. 'Come again! I'll cook you some mutton!' And he was off, bumping and swerving after his wayward flock, leaving us to ponder mysteries: What use to China's unifier was an indefensible wall a couple of metres high? What had Jorigt's predecessors been doing when, according to tradition, they should have been ravaging their way across China?

Answers emerge from a time long before that of the First Emperor, as the doyen of Mongolists, Owen Lattimore, proposed in *Inner Asian Frontiers of China*, his analysis of the shifting relationship between an evolving China to the south and the evolving steppeland cultures to the north. To understand the conflicts and rivalries that produced the Great Wall, we have to go back to a time before China was China and before there was such a thing as pastoral nomadism on its borders.

By about 1,000 BC the Chinese heartland, centred on the Yangtze and Yellow rivers, was a well-irrigated garden of competing kingdoms and principalities and city-states – about 170 of them. Imagine scores of statelets fighting and absorbing each other, their borders constantly changing, like a colony of single-celled creatures under a microscope, with occasional larger kingdoms emerging to plant an idea of what unity – 'All-Under-Heaven' (*tianxia*) or 'The Central State' (*zhongguo*) – could mean, if only it could be secured and maintained. Linking these rival entities and infusing the ideal of unity was a way of life: agricultural, urban, literate, and proud of all three.

Centuries of fighting between states that were similar in their ways inspired the fundamental traits of Chinese society: ancestor worship, elitist bureaucracies, respect for literary traditions, great art, the study of philosophy and ethics, diplomacy, advances in weaponry and fighting techniques – and walls. This was an age of aristocrats fighting in ritualized ways, as European nobles did in the Middle Ages, with peasant infantry playing a background role. One popular tactic was the siege; so self-defence demanded walls, mostly made of earth tamped down between planks in layers, one on top of the other. Such 'rammed earth' walls last surprisingly well. Some endure today. In the 1920s one scholar, Li Chi, said that of 748 town walls built between about 700 and 200 BC, 84 were still in use.[1] The records say these defences were necessary as defences against 'barbarians', and the assumption arose later that these barbarians were pastoral nomadic horsemen sweeping in from the northern grasslands. The Chinese see themselves as the bearers of culture, who never fought except in defence of civilization, and then did so against an enemy that was alien in every way, socially, linguistically and racially. That was the way it was. That was the way it had always been, from time immemorial.

Not so, explains Lattimore, because in 1,000 BC there were no pastoral nomads to China's north. The barbarians of the borderlands then were sub-groups of agriculturalists,

[1] Needham, *Science and Civilisation*, vol. 4, part 3, p. 43.

either neighbours eager for better land or migrants who had been driven out of their former haunts and wanted to return. Here, roughly along the borders of present-day Inner Mongolia, irrigation was increasingly difficult. Rainfall was scanty; the people were scattered, streams few, great rivers even fewer. The climate up on the Mongolian plateau is harsh, with winter temperatures plunging to −40°C. Further west lie semi-deserts and deserts, the domains of hunters, fishers and gatherers who were also classed as barbarians until they joined the mainstream. So yes, there were 'barbarians'; but they weren't pastoral nomads, because that completely different lifestyle took time to evolve here. By about 500 BC the marginalized sub-groups, driven from the farmlands, forests and rivers, 'were obliged to develop the technique of controlling herds of livestock'. In short, it was pressure on the fringes of the Chinese heartland that forced the development of a new way of life. 'As this technique developed, the line of evolution towards true pastoral nomadism became steadily more profitable.'

Out on the steppe, there was a life to be made by expert horsemen and herders, independent of mainstream Chinese ways and traditional forms of warfare. Sheep, camels, horses, yaks, cattle and – further north – reindeer, fuelled by grass, can produce almost everything needed for human survival. The keys to this new way of life, the antithesis of everything Chinese, were horsemanship, mobility, an intimate knowledge of pastures, small groups of people, few possessions, mounted archery and no cities. It's a tough life; but for those who could master it, it provided an almost overwhelming military advantage over the rooted communities to the south. The stage was set for the confrontation that would define the history of the northern frontier for the next 2,500 years.

Until the middle of the first millennium BC none of the border people posed any great threat, because they were few and marginalized. The 'barbarians', as the Chinese called all these people on the edge – Chinese and non-Chinese – were simply trying to hang on to the last vestiges of farmland before being forced out on to the steppe: the aggressors were the farmers, spreading to colonize the marginal lands. This was only a part of a slow and much-disputed process that was occurring all around the grasslands, from the Siberian forests of the north-east to the desert oasis communities of the west; but on this borderland it was Chinese expansionism that forced the evolution of pastoral nomadism, Chinese expansionism that created the new threat.

The picture emerging here is exactly the opposite of the image mainstream Chinese have of themselves, which epitomizes an attitude often seen when powerful groups expand. To the vast majority of colonial Americans, Indians were wild barbarians who threatened white bearers of western civilization, seldom indigenous people being driven off their land. Any 'barbarian' response to such encroachment was seen as an attack, a perspective reinforced by the fact that it is the dominant culture that leaves the written records. As Lattimore concludes: 'The whole idea of . . . a movement of people inward on China is a later creation . . . disregarding the fact that the cumulative effect of the "barbarian invasions" was the enlargement of Chinese territory.'

By the beginning of the third century BC this process was nearing maturity, with a consequent hardening of attitudes summarized by the historian Sima Qian around 100 BC. The northern barbarians, who were now equated entirely with pastoral nomads, possessed no civilized traits at all. 'They move about in search of water and pasture,' he wrote, 'and have no walled cities or fixed dwellings, nor do they engage in any kind of agriculture.' Little boys learn to ride on sheep, shooting birds and rats with bows and arrows. When grown, they hunt and fight, herding flocks when times are good, plundering when they are bad. 'This seems to be their inborn nature . . . Their only concern is self-advantage, and they know nothing of propriety or righteousness.' They revere strength and youth, giving the old and weak only scraps. They have no 'polite' names, those names used to avoid the appearance of overfamiliarity. When men die, sons marry stepmothers, widows are taken by the brothers of the slain. In brief, they were the utter opposite of everything the Chinese understood by civilization. Luckily for those living to the south, they mostly lived in small groups, owing allegiance only to their local chief, living in obscurity and dying in unrecorded feuds. There seemed no prospect that they would ever amount to anything like a nation.

The first evidence that a new way of life had emerged survives from the northern border state of Zhou (Chou), where a leader (Wu Ling) 'wore the costume of the Hu [barbarians] and trained mounted archers': that is, he adopted some practices of the steppe nomads – swift movement in open country, tactical manœuvre, ambush, sudden assault, rapid flight – in fighting his neighbours. It worked, for decades. Zhou was not overwhelmed by waves of nomads because it was half nomad itself.

At this juncture, competition between Chinese states forced another twist in the spiral of social evolution. Zhou shared the northern borderlands with two other states, Qi (to the south and west) and Yen (north and east). Suddenly, round about 300 BC, *frontier* walls appear. Another new process was at work: the changeover from small-scale city-states to nation-states. Landed aristocrats and their feudal estates were on the way down; the age of the centralized state had arrived, backed by tough legal systems, huge armies, great irrigation projects, bureaucracies, taxation. These states seemed to need the sort of protection everyone was used to: a city wall, but bigger. So all three states built walls around themselves, along their frontiers, not just against the steppe nomads but also against each other. So did other states. China's heartland, from the borders of present-day Inner Mongolia to south of the Yangtze, was no longer a honeycomb of cities and statelets, but more like a rich housing estate of seven individual properties – all walled.

Walls take a great deal of trouble to erect and maintain, and they are not necessarily the best defence. But if you were a Chinese ruler in the third century BC, building walls showed you were serious about ruling. Walls sprang up as the preferred form of defence because, for the first time in Chinese history, it was possible to organize labour on a large scale. Before, peasants could be supplied for work on city walls because they owed allegiance to a local noble; but they were not available for state enterprises, because the state had no power over the nobles. Now that the nobles were more gentlemen-officials than landed aristocrats – in effect, state employees – they could not draw on the peasants for labour. So the peasants were free to work for the state. These walls, ostensibly for defence, were actually built, with a newly available labour force, to define borders and impose the state's will.

One state, Qin (Chin), began to set itself apart. Qin was centred on present-day Shaanxi, now considered the cradle of Chinese civilization, but then a backwater on the southern edge of the semi-desert known today by its Mongol name, Ordos (an old plural of *ordon*, a palace-tent, after the many Mongol chiefs who used to live there).[2]

A word about the Ordos, one of those places that have acquired a definite article in English. It is the only bit of the Gobi that is south of the Yellow River, which embraces it in an enormous north-reaching sweep, heading towards Mongolia until forced eastward by the mountains that form the edge of the Mongolian plateau and eventually veering south again. Along the way, it turns desert to farmland. These geographical features – the Yellow River Loop and the Ordos semi-desert it embraces – are of peculiar significance for the story of the Great Wall, because they create a tongue of

---

[2] And, incidentally, one of the very few Mongol words to influence English. The Mongol group that ruled southern Russia for two centuries was the Golden *Ordon* – Horde, as it became in English, with a shift of meaning from 'tent-palace' to 'clan' to 'a large (threatening) crowd'.

steppeland reaching down into China. The Ordos is like one of those drawings that seems to be now one thing, now another. Ecologically, it is nomad territory; geopolitically, it is Chinese. Strategically, both sides needed it. As a result it was forever being seized and lost again, depending on the strength of whatever chief or dynasty happened to be in power. Its significance is out of all proportion to the quality of the land, which is mostly arid scrub and deeply eroded ravines cut by the occasional flash floods. When I saw the Ordos for the first time, I wondered why anyone would wish to take it. It was Jorigt (again) who explained. There was more pasture a thousand years ago, and more water. According to tradition, Genghis Khan thought highly enough of it to say that he wished to be buried here. He wasn't, but his so-called mausoleum, a temple in his honour south of Dongsheng, is set next to grassland, a reminder to visitors that pastoral nomads could once do quite well for themselves here. Now, there is not a nomad to be seen, and people don't care about the surface of the Ordos, only about what lies underneath – coal.

Well protected by rivers and mountain ranges, toughened by skirmishing with 'barbarian' tribes to the north and west, Qin expanded southward and then eastward into neighbouring Zhou. War followed war. The main source, Sima Qian, claims 1.5 million were killed in 130 years (a suspiciously round figure, but it is, after all, 'only' 11,500 a year). Qin's ideologues would have approved of Machiavelli, and of Fascism: power was the only virtue. The state hardened itself, ruthlessly turning itself into the most authoritarian of its time. Every official act had to go towards making the state rich, the army strong, agriculture efficient and expansion rapid. Qin, too, built a wall: in the early third century BC, across the southern Ordos, defining its northern boundary with the barbarians beyond.

And so the stage is set for the emergence of the First Emperor, the man who would create a new, unified China and defend it with a wall.[3] This happened with astonishing speed – in a mere fifteen years – and was so extraordinary that for outsiders the empire came to stand for the region, the nation and its whole history: China.[4] The man and his achievement made and scarred the country in equal measure. Some say that the date of his accession, 221 BC, is the most important in China's history, because it is seen as the base-line from which flowed everything that followed, right up to the present day. When Mao remade China in the mid-twentieth century, it was to the First Emperor that he looked for a model. And it is from the towering ambition and brutal policies of the First Emperor that the first Great Wall sprang.

As is often the way with dictators, his character was rooted in an insecure childhood. With admixtures of luck, intrigue, drama and a farcical assassination attempt, he grew into a tyrant, a Stalin figure, obsessed by mistrust, mortality and berserk ambitions to make himself

[3] This is a story I tell in more detail in *The Terracotta Army*.
[4] Chinese themselves have avoided the name, because unification was done with such brutality. Qin/China has bad connotations, which is why they usually speak of Zhongguo, the Central Country or Middle Kingdom.

immortal. Perhaps you have to be disordered to be a dictator.

The story opens in the next-door state, Zhou, with a rich and unscrupulous merchant named Lü Buwei meeting a down-at-heel Qin prince, Zichu, the son of a junior concubine of the heir to the Qin throne.[5] Lü at once sees a chance of advancement, and hatches a scheme to lever the young prince on to the Qin throne. He has a very beautiful consort, with whom the young prince falls in love. Lü generously hands her over. She gets pregnant, and bears a son, Zheng, the future First Emperor. Lü goes to the Qin court, armed with cash, presents and smooth talk, and gets Zichu made heir to the heir. Eventually, after a couple of royal deaths, Zichu becomes king, and Lü his chancellor. Zichu dies in 246 BC, leaving thirteen-year-old Zheng to succeed. Lü and the beautiful queen restart their affair, but Lü, afraid of discovery, passes her on again, this time to a notoriously well-endowed stud, about whom Sima Qian provides an extraordinary detail. Lü sought out the stud, Lao Ai, 'who had a tremendous penis, and made him his retainer. At times he [Lü] would indulge in some wild music and have Lao Ai move about in time with it, with his penis filling up the hole of a wooden wheel.' Zheng, now 21, hears of these astonishing scenes, executes the lover and banishes Lü, who poisons himself.

Meanwhile, rumours abounded that the king was not the son of Zichu, but the progeny of his mother's first lover, the chancellor Lü. Sima Qian says this is so,

[5] These anecdotes are from Bodde's translation of Sima Qian, *Statesman, Patriot and General in Ancient China*.

asserting that his mother had had a suspiciously long pregnancy. Scholars now agree that this statement was a later interpolation to discredit the First Emperor. If so, it worked. Until recently everyone believed young Zheng was a bastard, literally as well as figuratively. Perhaps there was talk at the time. In any event, something drove him to seize ever more absolute power, and undertake astonishingly ambitious projects: a 120-kilometre canal north of his capital; the diversion of the Min river into a network to water the Chengdu plain; and, of course, conquests galore. Over the years, Zheng became increasingly distrustful, ruling that no one should carry a weapon in his presence. He began to drift into paranoia, seeking an escape from his fears in mysticism and dreams of immortality.

In 227 BC there occurred an event guaranteed to make things worse. It is a story well known in China, and a popular subject for film and TV dramatization.

Qin's neighbouring state once removed, Yen, determined to stop Zheng's meteoric rise by killing him. A young adventurer named Jing Ge was chosen for the task. Knowing he had no chance of getting close to Zheng without a good excuse, he approached a renegade Qin general who had fled from Zheng and now lived only for revenge. Jing Ge made an extraordinary suggestion: if he could have the general's head, he would offer this to Zheng as a sign of loyalty. He would also take a map of Yen territory as an additional proof of good faith. These two items would gain him access. Inside the rolled-up map he would conceal a poisoned dagger, with which he would stab Zheng. The general found this an excellent plan, and obligingly cut his own throat.

Head and map gained Jing Ge entry into the Qin court, and an audience with the king. Watched by a crowd of courtiers, Jing Ge unrolled his map, seized the dagger, grabbed the king by the sleeve, and struck. The king leaped back, tearing off his sleeve, and Jing Ge's lunge missed its mark. Zheng fled, with the assassin in pursuit, while the unarmed courtiers stood back, appalled, watching their lord and master dodging around a pillar, trying in vain to untangle his long ceremonial sword from his robes. A doctor had the presence of mind to hit Jing Ge with his medicine-bag, which gave the king a moment's grace. 'Put your sword behind you, king!' yelled the crowd. Even as Jing Ge came at him again, Zheng managed to untangle his sword, draw it and wound Jing Ge in the leg. Jing Ge hurled the poisoned dagger, missed, and fell back as the king struck at him, wounding him again. Jing Ge, seeing he had failed, leaned against the pillar, then squatted down, alternately laughing hysterically and cursing the king. The crowd moved in and finished him off.

It was perhaps an insatiable desire for security in an uncertain world that drove Zheng on. In a series of wars, other states fell: Han, Wei, Chu, Qi and, of course, Yen, the source of the head, the poisoned dagger and the would-be assassin. In 221 Qin became recognizably China, unified from the borders of Tibet to the Pacific, from the Inner Mongolian escarpment and the hills of Manchuria to the South China Sea.

Zheng, until then merely a king, declared himself *huáng dì* 皇帝, often translated as 'august emperor'. A more direct translation makes it sound a virtual tautology, 'imperial emperor'. In fact, both terms had many traditional religious echoes suggesting divine creative power, but the two had never been used together before. In taking this title, Zheng declared himself emperor, god, sage and ancestor all in one. Moreover, he was to be just the first, the beginning, the *shǐ* / 始 . His heirs would bear the same title, unto the ten-thousandth generation of Qin emperors. Many books call him by his full title: Qin Shi Huang Di. I'll stick with 'the First Emperor'.

Power made him a terrifying figure. He seems to have been physically unattractive – high, pointed nose, slit eyes, pigeon breast; stingy, cringing, graceless, according to Sima Qian: not much like the Jabba the Hutt caricature on the 'Qin Wall' north of Hohhot, but equally unappealing. Certainly he was moody, easily angered, unpredictable, traits that he shared with other tyrants. Hitler and Stalin come to mind. But of the strength of his personality and vision there is no doubt. He knew what unity meant, and he asserted it with ferocity.

Out went the old kingdoms; in came three dozen centrally controlled commanderies, divided into about 1,000 counties. Former ruling families – 120,000 of them is Sima Qian's unlikely figure – were all moved to the Qin capital where the First Emperor could keep an eye on them. Their weapons were collected and melted down to make bells and twelve vast statues, each weighing 29 tonnes. China's varied coins, weights, measures and scripts were collated, simplified and imposed nation-wide, the standardization of the script perhaps the key change that ensured the unity of Chinese culture. From now on, vehicles had a standard gauge, presumably so that they would fit ruts made in roads. You can see the ruts today on the stone floors of many old gateways, like Cloud Terrace beside the Great Wall near Beijing. Qin law became China's law, with the retention of some extremely nasty methods of execution (tearing apart by chariots, cutting in half at the waist, boiling to death in a cauldron).

Labour now became available on an unprecedented scale. Peasants had always been subject to forced service in their own kingdoms; now they were called up nation-wide, creating a workforce of several million (from a population of about 20 million). A national system of roads arose, including an 800-kilometre north–south highway across the Ordos. The emperor started on a huge palace, whose front hall, or perhaps its courtyard, was to be about 700 metres by 115 metres – 80,000 square metres. Scholars have doubted these figures, but current research suggests that the site was about this size, though the building was probably not finished in his lifetime. He was certainly able to commission such immense structures, as shown by his mausoleum, on which he had begun work as soon as he came to the throne at the age of thirteen. The square hill of earth near Lintong, in foothills 40 kilometres east of Xian, is the size of the Great Pyramid, and seems likely to contain an underground palace, guarded by his most famous creation, the Terracotta Army. The clay warriors number perhaps 7,500 (though only 1,000 have been excavated and restored). This astonishing array of full-size figures, all different, all originally painted in bright colours, vanished from history until discovered in 1974. Since then archae-ologists have unearthed many other pits and treasures –

bronze birds in a water-garden, one-third-size bronze chariots, collections of stone armour – all enlarging the scale of the First Emperor's schemes. Sima Qian says that the tomb contains rivers of mercury, mapping the geography of his empire; and indeed surveys have revealed the presence of mercury vapour seeping from underground.

Unprecedented power and wealth allowed the emperor to indulge his determination to break with the past and build for an eternal future in this world and the next. A magician told him an elixir of immortality could be found on mystical islands in the Pacific. Off went an expedition, which was never heard of again (though legend says its members settled in Japan). When a foolhardy scholar accused him of abandoning tradition, the emperor's chief minister, Li Si, replied that tradition was no longer of relevance in the new China. All historical and philosophical records should be burned, and 'those who use the past to criticize the present' should be put to death, along with their relatives. Another adviser told him he would discover the elixir of immortality only if he kept himself aloof from his fellow men. So he ordered all the roads joining the 270 palaces in and around his capital to be walled or roofed. No one was to know his whereabouts, on pain of death. When complaints about his violence and cruelty arose, he supposedly had 460 'literati' killed – buried alive, according to a later interpretation. For all these events we have to rely on records written at least a century afterwards, so the truth remains hidden. Perhaps the Burning of the Books and the Burial of the Scholars were not the destructive acts that later ages believed. So far, the only direct evidence comes from the earth: the tomb, the Terracotta Army, the palace foundations, the roadways. These show that we should not doubt his grand vision and his ruthlessness. When his son Fusu remonstrated, the emperor banished him to the northern borders, to which our attention now turns.

All this provides a context for the last and supposedly greatest of the First Emperor's projects, the Great Wall. Conventional wisdom proclaims this to have been the most massive state enterprise since the building of the pyramids. When I started researching, therefore, I was expecting to find fascinating details of how the Wall was built, of the stone hauled overland from distant quarries, of the millions who died putting it in place. But those eager for historical truth are confronted, frustratingly, with a near-blank, a mere few lines in the only source, Sima Qian's *History*.

The project, like the north–south highway, was under the command of Meng Tian, one of the First Emperor's top generals. In 221 BC, just after unification, Meng Tian was given an army and sent north into the Ordos, not because the inhabitants were much of a danger but because the First Emperor wanted to secure his 'natural' border along the Yellow River. To do this, Meng Tian drove out two minor barbarian tribes.

Then, as if by sleight of hand, Meng Tian built the Great Wall. This is all Sima Qian has to say on the matter:

Qin, having completed its unification of the empire, despatched Meng Tian to lead a force of 300,000 men and advanced north, expelling the Rong and Di barbarians and taking control of the region south of the Yellow River. He set about constructing the Great Wall, following the contours of the land and utilizing the narrow defiles to set up frontier posts. It started in Lin-dao [south of Lanzhou, in Gansu province] and extended to Liaodong [the peninsula in China's north-east corner], extending for a distance of over ten thousand *lǐ*. Crossing the [Yellow] river, it followed the Yang mountains, twisting and turning as it proceeded north. Meng Tian remained in the field for more than ten years, residing in Shang Commandery [the northern part of the area covered by the bend of the Yellow River].[6]

There is another later passage which repeats this information,[7] reducing the army to 100,000 and adding that Meng Tian built 44 fortresses 'overlooking the [Yellow] River' and manned them with convicts.

Now the problems start. Reading most non-specialist sources, you get the firm impression that the First Emperor built the Great Wall as it exists today north of Beijing. That is the suggestion contained in the Chinese name for the Wall, *wàn lǐ cháng chéng* / 万里长城 , often translated as 'the 10,000-*li* [5,000-kilometre] Great Wall'. Five thousand kilometres sounds roughly like the distance between central China and the coast, if you double the direct route with a few twists and turns.

But hold on. When you look at the Chinese, it's not

---

[6] Burton-Watson's translation.
[7] Chapter 110, on the Xiongnu.

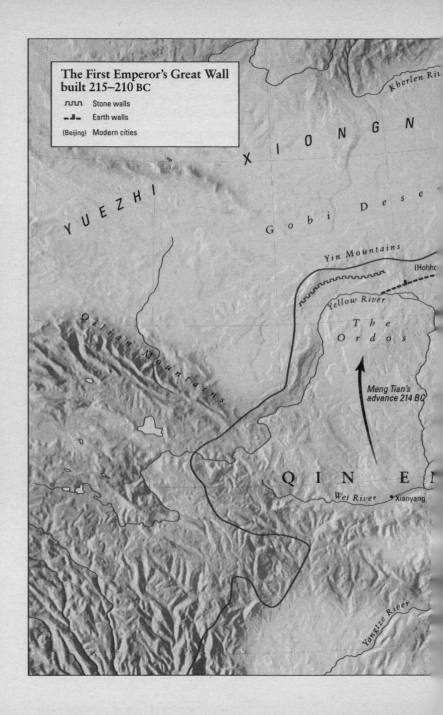

The First Emperor's Great Wall
built 215–210 BC

ᴨᴨᴨ Stone walls
‑‑ᴊ‑ Earth walls
(Beijing) Modern cities

Kherlen Riv

X I O N G N

Y U E Z H I

Gobi Dese

Yin Mountains
(Hohho

Yellow River

Qilian Mountains

The
Ordos

Meng Tian's
advance 214 BC

Q I N   E

Wei River   •Xianyang

Yangtze River

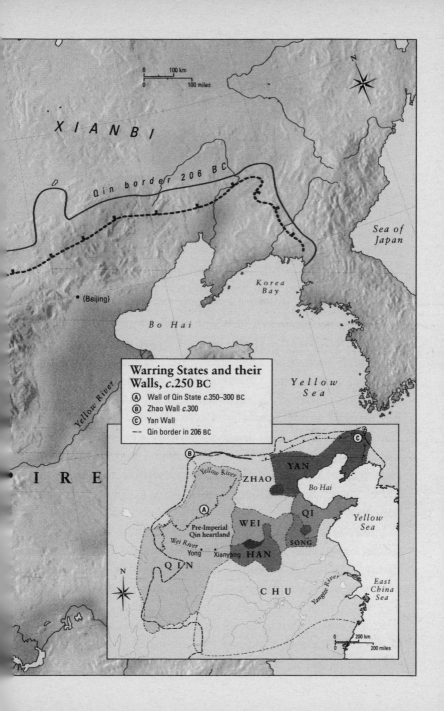

XIANBI

Qin border 206 BC

D

(Beijing)

Korea Bay

Sea of Japan

Bo Hai

Yellow Sea

Yellow River

I R E

Warring States and their Walls, *c.*250 BC

Ⓐ Wall of Qin State *c.*350–300 BC
Ⓑ Zhao Wall *c.*300
Ⓒ Yan Wall
-- Qin border in 206 BC

Yellow River

ZHAO

Ⓑ

YAN

Ⓒ

Bo Hai

Ⓐ

WEI

QI

Yellow Sea

Pre-Imperial
Qin heartland

SONG

Wei River

Yong Xianyang

HAN

QIN

CHU

Yangzi River

East China Sea

0   200 km
0   200 miles

0   100 km
0   100 miles

clear-cut. The word *wàn* / 万 does not mean the exact number 10,000; it is a frequently used synonym for 'very large number'. The First Emperor's throne room or court-yard could seat *wàn* people. In an age when myth served for history because there was no means of cross-checking claims, armies and casualties hardly rated a mention unless they could be counted by the *wàn*.

If we don't know how long it was, do we know where it went? Let's say we have the Wall, of some vague but im-pressive length. You would think its path would be clear. Far from it. According to Sima Qian's account, the Wall crossed the Ordos and went on over the Yellow River – but why in that case would Meng Tian have chased out barbarians to the north? Or did it run along the north of the Yellow River, the stone bit that I saw with Jorigt? Or somehow both, one after the other? Then again, Sima Qian says that, after crossing the river, the Wall wound northward to touch a mountain north-west of Hohhot. But no wall winds *northward* here. Besides, Meng Tian is also said to have built fortresses along the Yellow River, the western frontier of the Ordos, which may or not have been part of the wall. Scholars have twisted themselves in knots trying to make sense of all this, reaching no firm conclusions.

Later developments do not help. If there had been a single Great Wall, the First Emperor's term for it would surely have become fixed to it. Not a bit of it. There were plenty of other long (i.e. great) walls in Chinese history, a profusion which makes it extremely hard for scholars to sort out which wall is being talked about. And the Great Wall itself had other names: the 'frontier-post' (*sài* / 塞)

and the 'barrier' (*zhàng* / 障), both of which were also used to refer to other walls. Much later, the Ming called their Great Wall the 'border wall' (*qiáng* / 墙), to avoid confusing it with the First Emperor's structure, although in places the two overlapped. To be blunt, the First Emperor's Great Wall simply lacks continuity in geography, language and time, which makes it almost impossible to track today; and therefore it is almost impossible to come to conclusions about its original length or construction.

All I can do is suggest a scenario. The pre-First Emperor Qin wall crossed the Ordos, pretty much where one section of the Wall runs today. Upon unification, Meng Tian overran the Ordos, chased out two tribes and colonized his conquest, securing land up to the old, unfortified Zhou stone wall that Jorigt and I saw. That became the new Qin frontier. That's why it is labelled as such today.

It seems that almost everything believed about the First Emperor's Great Wall was wrong. He never built a *stone* wall at all. Whatever was built from scratch was of rammed earth, not stone, and most of it has now vanished or been incorporated into other, later walls. The stone section labelled so impressively the 'Qin Great Wall' was in all probability built by the king of Zhou around 300 BC, 80 years before Meng Tian hijacked it and made it the (unfortified) Qin frontier.

Nor did the First Emperor build a single Great Wall from scratch. What he did was to repair and join up a collection of little walls, which, considering they added up to 2,500 kilometres in length, was quite enough to keep a workforce of over a million labourers employed between his accession and his death. It seems that the First Emperor's Great Wall, if we are talking about one structure built on his orders, is a figment of later imagination, made to seem solid by confusion with later and earlier walls, and given spurious historical roots by Sima Qian's vague words.

2

THE WALL'S EVERYWOMAN

ONCE, HISTORY WAS LARGELY TO DO WITH KINGS, QUEENS and ruling classes; now, historians try to see things from the point of view of ordinary men and women. In the case of the first Great Wall, this is impossible. The few records were for kings and about kings. The great historian Sima Qian had his own royal agenda in support of the successor dynasty, the Han, and spoke little about ordinary people. We can dig up relics, analyse the historical forces, portray the policies of this or that emperor – but who is there to tell us what it was actually like to create this monumental artefact? Who to portray the agony of being uprooted, enslaved, separated from friends and family and forced to labour on it, perhaps dying in the process? No one. China has no history of the building of the first Wall. Nor was there a Chinese Homer to turn its creation into an epic.

The human brain abhors a vacuum. Driven by evolution to make sense of the world, we cannot live in an intellectual void, so we fill it with stories that explain ourselves to ourselves. The stories do not have to be literally true. Their truth is more complex: they capture folk memories, they dramatize a shared past, they give a sense of identity. Historians try to do the same thing by teasing fact from fiction; but they cannot replace those other storytellers who retell myths, legends and folk tales, writing novels and making films, for they tell us who we are and where we come from with greater emotional force. In China, much more than in the West, history and myth overlap.

Myth, legend, folk tales: those are virtually all we have to recall the suffering imposed by the First Emperor. And most of these are lost, or reattached to later walls.

> Don't you just see below the Great Wall,
> Dead men's skeletons prop each other up?

These lines probably stem from around 48 BC, when a writer, Jia Quanzhi, recorded: 'Songs of the Great Wall have never ceased up to now.' But by then the Qin Wall had given way to its heir, the Han Wall, and the press-gangs, the forced labour, the inevitable deaths had all merged together in a single stream of consciousness:

> The Great Wall how it winds and winds,
> Winds and winds three thousand leagues,
> Border towns full of young men,
> Homesteads full of widowed wives.[1]

[1] Waldron, *The Great Wall of China*, p. 196.

That one is from the early third century AD, but it could have been written any time in the 1,500 years after 200 BC. And yet, for all the suffering of the people, there is hardly a single name.

So here comes the shade of a young woman, stepping on to an empty stage. Her name is Meng Jiangnu, and you hear about her everywhere. She is the girl whose tears caused the Great Wall to collapse. But there's more to her than that. She is a many-sided Everywoman, who grows from a passive victim of officialdom into a tragic heroine. She loves, she suffers, she undertakes a great journey, she endures many dangers, she has her revenge on the state's ultimate symbol of power, she stands up to the emperor, she refuses to compromise, she chooses death over dishonour. It sounds like a pitch for a Hollywood movie, which is one reason why the story has lasted so well – and why it exists in so many versions. It has been retold for centuries in plays, poems, novels, dances and operas.[2] There is a 20-part TV series. Meng Jiangnu is so much part of the fabric of Chinese culture that her story is widely believed to be true.

Here is one version, a composite drawn from different sources:

The Tears of Meng Jiangnu
Once upon a time there was a kindly old bachelor, Meng

[2] One poem, with many Buddhist interpolations, was discovered on a broadsheet in a temple in Lanzhou in the first half of the twentieth century. A translation by Joseph Needham and Liao Hung-Ying was published in 1948 ('The Ballad of Meng Chiang Nu Weeping at the Great Wall').

Yuanwai, who lived in Songjiang prefecture south of the Yangtze River. One year a wax-gourd plant in his garden climbed up the wall on to the roof of the house of his neighbour, old Lady Jiang, where it bore a large fruit. When the gourd ripened and fell from its stem, it cracked open, to reveal a delightful baby girl. Both of the old people laid claim to the lovely child so they agreed they would both raise her. Meng asked Lady Jiang to move into his house, and the three lived happily as one family. That is how Meng Jiangnu – Meng and Jiang's Daughter (*nü* / 女) – got her name.

Meng Jiangnu grew up clever, beautiful and accomplished. She was well versed in calligraphy, painting, music and chess. She also showed great proficiency at embroidery and medicine. Both families loved her very dearly.

At this time the Great Wall – the 10,000-*li* Wall of the First Emperor – was beset with difficulties. A new section would rise only to be followed by the collapse of an old one. This situation presented an opportunity to a treacherous court official, Zhao Gao, who wanted to do away with those who were loyal and honest.[3] He proposed to the emperor that the Wall could be made stronger if they buried a man for every *li* of construction. Ten thousand men! This was clearly impossible. So the official suggested that one particularly renowned and clever scholar in Suzhou, Fan Xiliang by name, would be

[3] Zhao Gao, the epitome of evil, was real. He was the First Emperor's senior eunuch and mastermind of the plot that levered a younger son on to the throne after the emperor's death, thus bearing responsibility for the dynasty's collapse.

sufficient for the job, because he was equal to 10,000. This suggestion was readily accepted, and imperial envoys were sent out to fetch Fan Xiliang.

Fan, however, got wind of the plan and, disguising himself, made his escape. After several days' travel he arrived at a certain village in Songjiang prefecture, and, seeing a garden with its gate half-open, he sneaked in to spend the night. The house happened to be Meng Yuanwai's.

The next morning, when Meng Jiangnu was strolling in the garden, admiring the flowers and catching butterflies, she came upon the clever young scholar. Startled, she turned back and told her father of her discovery.

Impressed by Fan's good looks and talents, her father proposed that the young man become his son-in-law. Fan gracefully declined the offer. 'As a fugitive,' he said, 'I have no prospects.' Meng, however, would brook no objections.

And so the home was decorated with red candles, and the wedding ceremony got under way.

But just as Fan Xiliang and Meng Jiangnu were kneeling to heaven and earth, imperial envoys broke in and trussed Fan up with a rope. Meng Jiangnu flung herself upon her bridegroom, weeping.

As the officials dragged him away, Fan said: 'My lady, don't grieve too much. Once I am gone there will be little chance for me. Do not have any hope of my return!'

When Fan arrived at the Great Wall under guard, he was faced with a dreadful sight – a sea of labourers, emaciated and in rags. At the foot of the wall bodies were scattered here and there together with heaps of broken skeletons. Fan said to himself: 'I would die willingly if my death could really save the lives of ten thousand others.' Within three days he was buried alive in the foundations of the Great Wall, a human sacrifice to cruelty and ignorance.

Meng Jiangnu pined for Fan Xiliang day in and day out, in such torment that she could neither eat nor sleep. When three years had passed and nothing had been heard from her husband, she decided to look for him. She would bring him some winter clothes, to make sure he could survive the harshest conditions. Slinging her bundle of clothes on her back, Meng Jiangnu set off on her long, lonely journey.

It was dusk when Meng Jiangnu arrived at Hushu Pass. As she had no money for a room at an inn, she decided to go through the pass and continue her way by moonlight. But the two sentries at the pass would not let her through without paying a toll. The penniless lady took off her apron and offered it to the guards, who were still not satisfied.

'The road to the Great Wall is rough,' said one. 'How can you get there without any money?'

Meng Jiangnu replied: 'Since I am determined to find my husband, high mountains and great distances will not stop me. By walking forward step by step I'll arrive at the Great Wall some day, even if it is ten thousand *li* away. I don't mind having no money. Like people in ancient times, I'll play a bamboo flute and beg. A steel rod can be ground into a needle by perseverance.'

One of the sentries, on discovering that she could sing, asked her to sing a song as an alternative to the toll charge. Meng Jiangnu had no choice. She chose a song of flowers in winter, which described her separation from her husband and her firm resolve to find him. As she sang, she wept piteously. The guards were deeply touched. But just as they were about to let her go, the superintendent of the pass came up. 'Why go to the Great Wall, my dear? Better stay here and marry me.' Of course she refused, and he ordered the two guards to lock her in the guard-house so that he could force her to comply. The sentries, feeling deep sympathy for the girl, were greatly disturbed. One old soldier brought her some food, deliberately leaving the door unlocked to give her a chance to flee. Then, when she was clear, he set the guardroom on fire to divert the attention of the superintendent and help her make her escape.

By the time Meng Jiangnu reached the other side of the pass she was hungry and exhausted, her back was bent and her legs were no longer able to support her. She staggered a few steps further and collapsed by the roadside in a dead faint. When she came to, she found an old woman tending to her. The old woman gave her a bag of dates, saying they would help relieve her hunger. Meng Jiangnu ate one and immediately felt strong and in high spirits again. As she was about to rise to express her thanks, the old woman vanished. The dates from this angel completely revived Meng Jiangnu, and she continued on her way with a spring in her step.

On reaching the bank of the Yangtze River a few days later she was dismayed to find no bridge or ferry to take her across. 'Dear husband,' she cried. 'I've endured untold hardships, only to find that a river bars my way. Oh, what shall I do?'

In heaven, the Jade Emperor heard her cries, and sent

two angels down to earth to help her. The two fairy maidens descended slowly to Meng Jiangnu. With a shake of their arms they each unfolded one of their long sleeves for Meng Jiangnu to cling to, and asked her to close her eyes. For a moment she heard the wind whistling past her ears, and then she found herself on the northern bank of the river.

Days later Meng Jiangnu came to the edge of the Yellow River. She looked anxiously at the tumbling waters, and spotted a rush mat that had drifted to the bank. Could it be that the angels had come to her aid again? With trepidation she seated herself on the mat, which mysteriously floated her across the river.

Meng Jiangnu later came across an old male angel, who told her that the Great Wall was still far away and that he would help her. He held up a stick in his hand and it immediately turned into a horse. Meng Jiangnu mounted, and no sooner did she crack the whip than the steed leaped up into the sky and galloped across the white clouds.

At last Meng Jiangnu arrived at the place where the Great Wall was being built, and began enquiring after her husband. The answers she got were varied. Some said he was at the eastern section of the wall, while others said he was in the west. Finally, a foreman on the project told her the truth. 'Fan Xiliang died three days after he came to the Great Wall. There is no point bringing him winter clothes now. You'd better go home right away.'

Meng Jiangnu burst into tears and cried out: 'To be reunited with my husband I have endured any amount of hardships and perils, only to find he has no need of clothes! Must I now go home alone to face a life of desolation?'

As Meng Jiangnu continued to wail, the sky grew dark and the ground caved in beneath her feet. She fainted several times in her sorrow and grief. Clinging to the Wall for support, she struggled to her feet. In her grief, she dashed her head against the Wall and a section 20 kilometres long collapsed with a crash.

Meng Jiangnu fell unconscious again, and dreamed of Fan Xiliang. 'Indeed,' he said in her dream, 'my bones are buried in the wall, mine and those of many others. To find mine, you must bite your finger and use your blood to test them. Those that remain unstained with the drops of blood are the bones of others, and those that soak them up are mine.' She awoke, to find him gone. Before her lay a mountain of bones where the Wall had toppled. She bit her finger and let her blood drip on them. The crimson drops rolled off every skeleton but one, which absorbed them all.

With care Meng Jiangnu wrapped the bones of her husband in his winter clothes and held the parcel to her breast. But just as she was about to set off on the journey home, a group of horsemen arrived. The leader was the treacherous official Zhao Gao, who demanded angrily: 'Who is that girl who dared to damage the Wall? Seize her and take her to the court!'

There, the First Emperor, fascinated by the girl's unmatched beauty, ordered her to discard the remains of her husband and stay with him as a lady of his court. Meng Jiangnu responded with a tirade against his brutality. 'You have caused the death of tens of thousands, and now the death of a husband who was worth ten thousand men. My lord, you have forgotten the people. In a great ruler, this is foolishness and self-indulgence!'

A horrified silence fell. Zhao Gao was the first to speak: 'The girl should be beheaded for insulting the monarch!'

Then the First Emperor spoke. 'Her crime will be pardoned if she will agree to stay.'

Meng Jiangnu bowed. She would comply, but under certain conditions. First, a gold coffin with a silver lid must be made to contain the remains of her husband, which were to be buried in a tomb on the shores of the Eastern Sea; second, all the officials and officers of the court must go into mourning for him; third, the emperor should personally take part in the funeral procession.

Pleased with Meng Jiangnu's submission, the First Emperor agreed.

Meng Jiangnu, dressed all in white, escorted the hearse carrying her husband's gold coffin down to the coast of the Eastern Sea for burial. When the funeral ceremony was over, she knelt down before the tomb and prayed: 'Fan Xiliang, my husband, wait for me!' Then she rose, and cast herself into the foaming sea.

To this day, a tall reef stands high in the water off Old Dragon's Head. This is the grave of the courageous widow of the Great Wall, who will live on for ever in the memory of the people.

There are endless variations on the tale. Sometimes the parents are married, with families of their own; the husband's name varies. Sometimes the gourd doesn't fall – her parents split it open to find her. Her husband isn't a runaway; there is no proposal to bury 10,000 workers, nor any treacherous official; perhaps she and Fan marry because he sees her bathing in a pond, and she has sworn to marry whoever sees her body. She dreams of her press-ganged husband calling out 'Cold! Cold!' to inspire her to bring winter clothing; in one poem,[4] she sees his ghost, knows he is dead, yet still must deliver warm clothes to him:

> Weeping, weeping, he entered her chamber
> Stooped over the bed, with tears falling,
> 'I am freezing to death,' he seemed to say,
> 'Quickly make for me a padded gown.
>
> 'Suddenly I felt faint, and fell to the ground.
> 'Thus was I buried in the Wall as it was a-building.
> 'So tonight I your lover come to make you this dream.
> 'Neglect not my words like wind passing in the air.
>
> 'Continue to be filial to the old parents,
> 'And fetch back my bones and spirit of your husband.'

She may have a treacherous servant, who steals from her; she defeats robbers; she scolds the emperor only when she is about to cast herself into the sea; there's sometimes a final episode in which Meng Jiangnu and the Dragon King of the Sea raise a storm to confound the First Emperor.

[4] Needham and Liao, 'The Ballad of Meng Chiang Nu Weeping at the Great Wall'.

Yet the basic elements remain constant: the setting – the time of the First Emperor, as the Great Wall is being built; the First Emperor and Zhao Gao as villains; Meng Jiangnu as the foundling; the husband seized on their wedding day; her long wait, her decision to bring clothes to him, her journey, her discovery of his death; and then – the crux – the weeping that destroys a section of the Wall. Then the First Emperor's anger, which turns to lust; his offer of marriage, or of a life as one of his concubines; her tirade, followed by acceptance if he holds a funeral, and the resolution, her tragic, heroic suicide in the sea.

The story grew as the need for it evolved, acquiring onion-skin layers of incident, some magical, some pseudo-realistic, all filling the need to explain the mystery of the Wall's origins, all serving to embed the story of Meng Jiangnu ever more deeply into Chinese consciousness, firmly fixing her in the time of the First Emperor.

But its roots lie much further back than the First Emperor and his Great Wall.[5] A chronicle known as the *Zuo Zhuan*, written probably in the fifth and fourth centuries BC, tells a very short story about a man called Qi Liang, from Qi (present-day Shandong), who died in a battle with a neighbouring state some 200 years previously. 'When the Duke of Qi returned, he met Qi Liang's wife at the outskirts of the city and told her to mourn her husband [i.e. with all the correct observances].' This would have nothing to do with our subject, except that a Han Dynasty source (Liu Xiang's *Shuo Yuan*, at the end of the first century BC) repeats the story and adds this:

[5] According to Shou Hou, 'What Is the Origin?'

'When his wife heard the news, she cried, and her wailing shook the city wall and caused a corner of it to crumble.' That's the seed of our tale – a first-century BC flourish on a fifth- or fourth-century BC anecdote.

No connection yet either with the Great Wall or with the First Emperor.

And no mention of Meng Jiangnu. Not for 700 years.

No one knows her origins, but by the Tang Dynasty (AD 618–907), she has appeared in the tales and so has the Great Wall, possibly under the influence of a spate of endemic warfare and wall-building during the previous dynasty, the Sui. She is recorded in a ballad written on the cave walls in Dunhuang, far in the Chinese north-west, in which she takes clothes to her husband on the Great Wall. During the Song Dynasty (960–1279), the story took shape in almost its present form, with the First Emperor firmly in place as the villain – partly because he had long been cast as the evil genius of Chinese history, and partly, no doubt, because his presence vastly improves the story: Meng Jiangnu now has a powerful opponent. But there may be another force at work, a political agenda. Under the Song, China was united again, and it suited the Confucian mindset to tell a tale of how *not* to assure unity – by oppressing the people, engaging in vast and expensive enterprises, and ignoring the guidance of the Master.

There was a final stage still to go, for it was not until the fourteenth and fifteenth centuries that the Ming created the vast stone fortification that forms the popular image of the Great Wall. Only then did the eastern end, Old Dragon's Head at Shanhaiguan, acquire its imposing fortress and battlements. It is here that Meng Jiangnu casts herself into the sea (never mind that there is no high point suitable for a suicidal leap). Now at last all the elements are in place, assembled over 2,000 years: a sixth/seventh-century BC death mentioned 200 years later, a first-century BC legend about a weeping widow and a tumbling wall, the link with the Great Wall around AD 700, the First Emperor's appearance four or five hundred years later, and finally the amalgamation of two walls, the earthen Qin and the stone Ming.

The popularity of the story was assured, at least among ordinary people. Indeed, it captures such very deep truths about Chinese society that it was presented as literally true in at least one history book in the late 1940s. Meng Jiangnu is popular because she is subversive. She stands up to authority, and gets her way. Of course, in the end, she cannot prevail, which has always been the way with the people *v.* the government.

For the same reason, government has not always welcomed her. In the 1970s she became embroiled in the battle between Mao and his greatest political opponent, Lin Biao, who accused Mao of being as brutal as the First Emperor. Mao struck back, comparing himself to the First Emperor as the nation's unifier, the man bold enough to centralize the state and forge a China strong enough to keep out foreigners, like the northern barbarians or, in his case, the Russians. In this view, Meng Jiangnu was seen as a symbol of those who would destroy the Communist government by toppling its symbol, the Great Wall. She had become a 'repulsive counter-revolutionary', like Lin Biao.

Today she is back in favour, because she is part of

folklore, which is deemed good because it is part of China's intellectual and artistic heritage. Besides, her story is bound up with the Wall, and the Wall is all the rage. Who these days is going to deny a tale that is good for tourism?

If you drive 5 kilometres east from Shanhaiguan, away from the fortress that guards the Wall's eastern end, you come across a car park and some tacky souvenir shops. Behind them is a temple devoted entirely to Meng Jiangnu.

When I arrived, in the company of my friend and guide William Shou and our driver Mr Zhou, it was lunchtime. Beside the car park was a restaurant. We were the only customers. That wasn't surprising. It was a drab place of stained plastic tables, with one depressed waiter. Mr Zhou liked his food. He ate like an athlete and was built like a wrestler, and he was not about to hang around for a bad lunch. He also had a hidden talent.

'I am a driver, but I am also a chef,' he said, and marched into the kitchen. He seized the least dirty wok, chose a knife the size of a cutlass, zapped on the gas and began to dice ingredients, while William reviewed the story we were about to experience in the temple. I can't remember what happened to the waiter. He must have left us to it.

'So the First Emperor, when he saw her, wanted to make her his concubine, because she was very beautiful. But she cursed him, and refused, so she remained chaste.' Carrots, peppers, egg, onions, pork, cucumber, Sichuan beef paste, soy sauce, sugar (yes, sugar), all mixed in a blur and ended up on our plates. 'Then she jumped into the sea.' I hadn't quite taken aboard the theme of chastity, but it is an important one.

Chaste Lady Temple, as it is known, has an ancient lineage – a pre-Song (eighth- or ninth-century) foundation, a late sixteenth-century restoration – but the touristic 1993 reconstruction also includes a garden, relics and a series of stilted tableaux. In this version, swallows bring the gourd-seed from which she springs. Here she stands in a shrine, like a sort of Chinese Virgin Mary. The story unfolds: the wedding scene with the couple 'immersed in happiness', exchanging keepsakes; the husband's abduction; the 'Husband-Seeking Rock', worn into a staircase of footprints up which she climbed to keep a lookout for her lost love (yes, a real rock, as real to believers as a Splinter of the True Cross); episodes on the journey – including one I have never heard of anywhere else, an escape from a crocodile – and the encounter with the emperor. The final scene has her standing on a cliff, with the emperor and courtiers watching in horror. Overlooking the garden is a statue of our heroine, facing her chosen fate with fierce, calm dignity. She wears a headband that makes her look like a warrior. The plaque states the message of her suicide: 'Plunging into the sea to remain chaste.'

Well, obviously no one is meant to take all this literally. But there is an unquestioned bedrock assumption: that the First Emperor built the first Great Wall of stone; that this is the foundation of China as China, and the birth of its greatest symbol. To question this would be like denying the Flood to a Christian fundamentalist. There are some things best unsaid.

3

A THREAT FROM THE NORTH

SO THE FIRST EMPEROR'S GREAT WALL TURNS OUT TO BE – IN part – two walls, one of earth across the Ordos, the other the stone one that I visited with Jorigt, neither of which originated with him. Were these the defence systems they are cracked up to be? I don't think so, because Meng Tian had driven out the locals and there was no real threat.

At least, not yet.

True, there had been countless 'barbarian' raids over the previous 1,500 years; but they had not been made by pastoral nomads, and the areas from which the raiders had come had long been tamed and assimilated. So the whole notion of barbarian hordes assailing the First Emperor and his role as China's saviour was a myth. But it would not remain so, for something new and very threatening was emerging to the north: the first unified nomad empire.

These long-vanished people are notorious in China. To westerners, they are both unknown and yet oddly familiar: unknown because scholars generally refer to them by their Chinese name, Xiongnu (Hsiung-nu in the old Wade–Giles orthography, pronounced 'Shung-nu'); but familiar because, after they were scattered in AD 119, some of them drifted westwards and *may* – I emphasize 'may' because there is no proof – have become the Huns, who came out of the unknown void of Central Asia in the late fourth century to tear at the flanks of the Roman empire.

We know that they were there, because Meng Tian is said by Sima Qian to have 'struck terror into the Xiongnu people' when he built the first great Wall. Later, it was the Xiongnu who were regarded as the inspiration for the Wall. But the key word is *later*. Right then, in 221 BC, they were not the power they would become. It was not they who had to be chased from the Ordos. What was going on?

To understand we must look north of the Qin border, to the Mongolian plateau, the wastes of the Gobi and the grasslands that roll northward to the Siberian forests. There, in response to the growth of unified states in China, the Xiongnu were in the process of unification. The First Emperor was a contemporary with the first known Xiongnu shanyu (chief), Tumen, which means 'Ten Thousand' in today's Mongol, as it presumably did also in whatever unrecorded mixture of early Mongol and Turkish the Xiongnu spoke. (Both Mongol and, as we saw in chapter 1, Chinese use ten thousand as a 'large number' word, rather as we talk of zillions. It is an odd but meaningless coincidence that the First Emperor built a Ten-Thousand-*li* wall between himself and a man called Ten Thousand.)

Tumen was simply one tribal chief among many. The two Ordos tribes chased out by Meng Tian, the Rong and Di, were buffers between Qin and the Xiongnu. When the First Emperor seized the Ordos, he became a direct threat to the Xiongnu. So Tumen pulled his people back, and spent years building up a secure power base beyond the Gobi. It was not the First Emperor who was threatened; precisely the other way around. As the complete lack of defences on the 'Qin' wall north of Hohhot shows, no one south of the Yellow River feared a barbarian invasion from the steppes *until after the Wall was built*. Conventional wisdom has to be turned on its head. It was the Chinese who were the aggressors, the nomads who would have been the victims, if they hadn't fought back.

Only after the First Emperor died in 210 BC did the Xiongnu emerge as a threat. The driving force was not Tumen but his heir, Modu,[1] who did for the Xiongnu what the First Emperor had done for China. He too had insecurity built into him as a child, if Sima Qian is to be believed. His father preferred a younger son, so sent off Modu to a neighbouring tribe (the Yuezhi of today's Dunhuang, in western Gansu, of whom more later) as a hostage. Wishing him dead, Tumen launched an attack, expecting Modu to be killed. Instead, the prince staged a dramatic escape, stealing a horse to gallop back home,

---

[1] As he is in Chinese (Mòdú / 冒頓). He is also spelled Moadun and Motun.

where his father greeted him with forced smiles and a gift to match his status: his own body of troops. It was a fatal gift. Modu determined to make every one of his men guilty of the crime he was planning. First he drilled them into total obedience. 'Shoot wherever you see my whistling arrow strike!' he ordered. 'Anyone who fails to shoot will be cut down!' Then he took them hunting. Every animal he fired at became a target for his men. Then he shot at one of his best horses. The horse died in a hail of arrows. But some hesitated, and they were executed. Next, he took aim at his favourite wife. She died, and so did the waverers. Then it was the turn of one of his father's finest horses. This time, no one held back. Now Modu knew all his men could be trusted. Finally, 'on a hunting expedition, he shot a whistling arrow at his father and every one of his followers aimed their arrows in the same direction and shot the shanyu dead'. Next in line were his stepmother, his younger brother and his father's officials.

Whether all this is true or not, there is no doubting Modu's effectiveness. His nearest neighbours, the Xianbi to the east on the other side of the Gobi, started to test his ambitions, asking first for a famous horse, then for the Xiongnu chief's favourite wife, then for the Gobi itself. This was too much for Modu. 'Land is the basis of the nation! Why should I give it away?' He attacked and seized the Xianbi state, then turned westward and southward, advancing to the edge of Tibet – and then back into the Ordos, from which the tribes who were now his vassals had been driven just over a decade previously.

He had an easy run south, because the Ordos was suddenly wide open. It shouldn't have been: after Meng

Tian's victory, soldiers and colonists had moved in by the ten, if not the hundred, thousand. But there had just been the most astonishing change. The First Emperor had set off on one of his tours to check out his empire. Searching along the Pacific coast for the elixir of immortality, he fell ill. His final act was to write to his son, Fusu, the one he had banished northward to serve with Meng Tian, telling him to take power. But, in a plot to put a younger son on the throne, the letter was suppressed and replaced by one ordering both Fusu and Meng Tian to commit suicide. Fusu did. Meng Tian, unable to believe what he read, did not; but there was no escape. He was imprisoned by the plotters and, facing inevitable death, chose to take poison. Sima Qian gives him a fine death, which he chooses freely for having built the Great Wall.

> 'What crime have I before Heaven? [he said.] I die without fault!' After a long time he added: 'Indeed I have a crime for which to die ... I have made ramparts and ditches over 10,000 *li*, and in this distance it is impossible that I have not cut through the veins of the earth. This is my crime.' He then swallowed poison and so committed suicide.

But Sima Qian has his doubts. He was quoting some other lost source, which accused the general of offending against the traditions of *feng shui*, wind and water, the practice of geomancy that claims to understand the influences exerted on any structure by its geographical situation. 'What did his crime have to do with the veins of the earth?' Sima Qian asks himself. Nothing at all. Yet he concludes that the general did actually deserve death for other crimes – he had conscripted forced labour for the Wall and failed 'to alleviate the stress of the common people, support the aged, care for the orphaned, or busy himself restoring harmony among the masses'. In brief, he had not been a good Confucian, any more than his lord and master, the First Emperor.

With the First Emperor in a paradise of his own creation, attended by his terracotta warriors, rebellion broke out. Murders, executions and uprisings multiplied, until in 206 BC the regime fell. Along the northern borders, the army and the colonists fled, giving Modu his easy run south. The First Emperor's stone wall north of the Yellow River might as well not have been there. Modu's new empire now reached right down to the earthen frontier-wall, which cut across the southern and eastern Ordos.

And there it was not Qin that faced him, but a new dynasty, the Han.

The First Emperor's brutality had been his nemesis, for it had inspired a rebellion, eventually headed by a man who had been born a peasant, Liu Bang. Liu had fled from farm work and become a low-grade patrolman. One day, some prisoners he was escorting escaped. Fearful that he would be punished for their flight, Liu Bang released the remaining captives and fled himself, becoming the leader of a band of robbers. As such, he joined the rebellion against the First Emperor's heir, rising to fame and fortune when the rebellion overthrew the Qin empire. There followed a four-year civil war, from which Liu Bang emerged victorious. In 202 BC he proclaimed himself emperor and established the Han Dynasty. By 200 BC, therefore, the two rival empires confronted each other, Xiongnu v. Han China. You would think this confront-ation would have been simple to define. The poor but acquisitive nomads wanted to invade; the Chinese wanted to stop them, and the Wall helped them do so.

But it wasn't like that. The fact is that the relationship between the two societies across the Great Wall was highly complex. On both sides were people who were adapting to the demands of frontier ecology, on one side by including herding in their farming, on the other by including farming in their herding. What looked like a hard and fast border defined by the Wall was in fact both vague and porous. Xiongnu raided southward with impunity. Generals switched allegiances with remarkable ease and frequency. Local 'Chinese' commanders were often 'barbarians' born and bred, who took service with the Han regime to better themselves. Others were former merchants, who had cordial relations with Xiongnu partners. One at least was a Xiongnu who joined China and then, recaptured by his own people, served with them again.

If the Wall's prime purpose was not to prevent invasion – which it couldn't anyway; minor raids were frequent – its main function could only have been to serve China's internal political purposes: to define itself, to declare its identity to itself – and to keep its own people in line: to stop them setting up their own little fiefdoms in alliance with the Xiongnu, and thus tearing apart the unity that had just been so hard won.

Proof of this came while Liu Bang, the rebel who made himself Han's first emperor, was still establishing control over his realm. He sent one of his closest aides north to hold the Wall frontier, only to have him surrender to the Xiongnu and join them. Together, the new allies advanced southward, reaching the city of Taiyuan, some 225 kilometres south of the Great Wall. Forced to confront this combined invasion and rebellion, Liu Bang almost lost everything. The Xiongnu surrounded his army, and might have inflicted a severe defeat, but Modu pulled back. It seems he was not after territory. It was his *ally*, the former Han general, who wanted his own realm; rebellion, not Xiongnu invasion, was the greater threat. Clearly, the Xiongnu and the Han served their own interests better by preserving a shaky peace in their own spheres than by waging open war and expensive invasions to take over each other's territory.

In order to prevent local warlords emerging, Liu Bang had to keep the frontier well guarded. In several frontier provinces, he crushed rebellion after rebellion, but he 'did not venture beyond the frontier'. If there were forays into the steppe, they were not to take it over, not even to undermine the Xiongnu's ability to raid, but to counter the constant centrifugal tendency by which generals could become upstart warlords, groups on opposite sides of the frontier allies, fraying the borderline and endangering the cohesiveness of the Han state.

In these circumstances, the Han emperor could rely on his own people only if they could be allowed to serve their own interests, finding wealth and status as Chinese subjects. This meant maintaining a working relationship with the 'barbarians', which was done by means of letters written on strips of bamboo. In 198 BC the Han emperor and the Xiongnu shanyu agreed a peace treaty, declaring themselves to be brothers. A Chinese princess was sent off to Modu, along with silk, wine and grain. This was the first instance of a Chinese princess being used to bind non-Chinese people into the Chinese sphere, the idea being that her son – in effect, the emperor's grandson – would in due course become king of her adoptive realm; and, as Sima Qian wrote, 'whoever heard of a grandson attacking his grandfather?' In return, Modu promised not to invade.

No such luck. Appeasement seldom works for long. It didn't with the Vikings or the Nazis. It certainly didn't with the Xiongnu, for Modu could not stop some of his chiefs indulging in raids across the Wall, nor was it in his interests to do so. And clearly, as is the way with dictators, he was always on the lookout for ways to increase his power. After the death of the first Han emperor, when the empire was run by his widow, the empress Lü, Modu even tried his hand at diplomacy, in a famously crass way. In 192 BC he wrote to her in mock-self-deprecating terms, apparently suggesting a marriage alliance. 'I am a lonely widowed ruler, born amidst the marshes and brought up on the wild steppes in the land of cattle and horses . . . Your majesty is also a widowed ruler living a life of solitude. The both of us are without pleasures . . . It is my hope that we can exchange that which we have for that which we are lacking.' The sub-text is a veiled threat: *You're past it, old girl; why not let me take over?*

In fact, Empress Lü was an extremely tough-minded

lady. When her husband died, a son by his favourite concubine was in line for the throne. She solved the problem in brutal fashion. First she dealt with the concubine by ordering guards to cut off her hands and feet, put her eyes out, make her dumb by destroying her larynx with poison, and toss her to the royal pigs. Then she showed the result to the poor girl's son, who went insane and died. By the time Modu wrote, she was in full control, and gave Modu a brush-off. The idea of marriage was ludicrous, wrote the regent. 'Both my hair and teeth are falling out and I cannot even walk steadily. The shanyu must have heard exaggerated reports. I am not worthy of his lowering himself. But my country has done nothing wrong, and I hope that he will spare it.' It may sound like a plea for mercy from a potential victim, but that was not Lü's style. I think the sub-text reads: *I might be old, but if you want China, you'll have to take it*. That was not Modu's aim at all. His bluff called, he sent an envoy to apologize and resume the treaty of friendship signed six years before, with its lucrative exchanges.

Modu recognized, however, that wealth flowed from China only because war and peace remained in precarious balance. China followed the path of appeasement – *hé-qín* / 和親, 'peace and friendship' or 'harmony and intimacy' – only because the Han saw the Xiongnu as unstable, uncontrollable barbarians. To get gifts, he had to act the wild man; to avoid provoking retaliation, he had to act the diplomat. It was a tricky balancing act, but if it could be managed he would have his cake and eat it. So the raids continued, even one large-scale invasion which took a force of '85,000 carriages and cavalry' to defeat. And so did the peace process. In a letter to the Han court in 176 BC, Modu acted contrite. The invasion was not his fault. He blamed one of his unruly subordinates, who acted 'without asking my permission'. But the emperor also had to take some blame. He, Modu, had sent an envoy, but had had no reply. Still, he was prepared to be generous. He had punished the wayward general by sending him off westward, where 'through the aid of Heaven' he had been successful, extending Modu's empire into present-day Gansu and Xinjiang, driving out the inhabitants, the Yuezhi, the tribe with whom he had once been lodged as a hostage. The territory thus acquired included the Gansu Corridor, the way west along the good grazing grounds at the northern edge of the Qilian mountains. Now, he wrote, 'all the people who live by drawing the bow are united'. Our peoples should make peace, he suggested, 'such as they enjoyed in former times'.

What choice did the Han have? As the emperor's officials agreed three years later (diplomacy being a slow and careful business), the shanyu, riding on a wave of victory, could not be attacked. His empire stretched from the Pacific to the Aral Sea. Moreover, any lands taken could not be held. They were 'all swamps and saline wastes, not fit for habitation'. Better to make peace, and preserve it with a steady stream of gifts (one delivery included an embroidered robe lined with patterned damask, an embroidered and lined under-robe, a brocaded coat, a sash with gold ornaments, ten rolls of embroidery, 30 rolls of brocade and 80 rolls of silk).

This would have been humiliating for the Chinese, but for the spin they put on their own policy. They were being not weak, but magnanimous, as befitted a superior culture. Moreover, all this generosity had a hidden agenda: not just to buy peace, but to undermine the hardy Xiongnu by addicting them to luxuries. As one statesman and scholar, Jia Yi,[2] wrote, 'Our markets beneath the Great Wall will surely swarm with the Xiongnu . . . When the Xiongnu have developed a craving for our rice, stew, barbecues and wine, this will have become their fatal weakness.' Hence the occasional Chinese princess journeying across the Gobi to join the shanyu's court. Border markets thrived.

A eunuch who had switched sides, Zhonghang Yue, warned the Xiongnu against dependency. 'From now on, when you get any of the Han silks, put them on and try riding around on your horses through brush and brambles! In no time your robes and leggings will be torn to shreds and everyone will be able to see that silks are no match for the utility and excellence of felt or leather garments.' Same with Han foodstuffs. 'Throw them away, so that the people can see that they are not as practical as milk or *kumiss* [mare's-milk beer]!' He was an embittered character, this eunuch, because he had been sent against his will to accompany one of the Chinese princesses, and he was eager to see the Xiongnu as the embodiments of noble savagery and his own people as softened by luxury. As he told a Han envoy, the Xiongnu are simple, straightforward and strong. Their customs may seem barbaric,

---

[2] Jia Yi (201–169 BC), famous for his essay *The Faults of Qin*, quoted by Sima Qian in his biography of the First Emperor (in *Records of the Grand Historian*).

but they are practical. So what if they marry their stepmothers? It helps the clans survive. In China, families drifted apart and ended up killing each other. And the Chinese lacked spirit. All that farming, all that building – they exhaust themselves, they have no aggression. 'Pooh! You people in your mud huts – you talk too much! Just because you wear hats, what does that make you?'

He would have been gratified to know that corruption never took hold. The Xiongnu remained as tough as ever. 'They scale and descend even the most precipitous mountains with astonishing speed,' reported one envoy. 'They swim the deepest torrents, tolerate wind, hunger and thirst . . . If they ever suffer a setback, they simply disappear without a trace like a cloud.'

But, as is the way with extortion, the price for keeping the peace rose, and still the raids continued. One Xiongnu 'raid' in 166 BC was in effect an invasion – 140,000 horsemen, who got within 150 kilometres of the Han capital. There was a sort of stability, but only because the Han kept on paying. Things could not go on like this. As a minister wrote to the emperor in about 160 BC, the Xiongnu are arrogant, insolent plunderers, 'yet each year Han provides them with money, silks and fabrics'. This was the reverse of the natural order – emperor at the top, vassals below. 'Hanging upside down like this is something beyond comprehension.'

Someone had to do something.

4

WAR OVER THE WALL

THE MAN WHO TOOK ON THE XIONGNU WAS THE HAN Emperor Wu (140–87 BC). Wu was a monarch of genius – autocrat, statesman, strategist, artist – with a court to match his own brilliance, and a reign long enough to allow both to flourish: 53 years, a tenure unmatched for the following 1,800 years. His despotic ways almost matched those of the First Emperor, and his achievements – his laws, institutions and conquests, sealed by the western extension of the Great Wall – would mark China from then on.

It took Wu a while to find his feet, because he was only fifteen when he succeeded to the throne, but almost at once he focused on two matters: extending his domains and finding a final solution to the Xiongnu problem. First, he needed allies – tribes to the west, beyond the Xiongnu, so that he could open a war on two fronts. No one had yet penetrated the expanses of Central Asia, but there was at least one tribe which would surely hate the Xiongnu: the Yuezhi, the tribe expelled by the Xiongnu from the Gansu region three decades previously. Where they were no one knew, but once contacted the tribe would surely make a valuable ally.

In 138 BC Wu sent off a 100-strong expedition headed by a leader noted for his strength, generosity and charismatic leadership: Zhang Qian by name, he was to become one of the nation's most romantic figures, a hero of exploration. He set out with instructions to persuade the Yuezhi to return, become allies of the Han empire and help destroy the Xiongnu. This highly dubious venture foundered almost at once when Zhang was captured by the Xiongnu: an event that began a series of adventures which turned him into a sort of Chinese version of Lewis and Clark, the explorers who crossed the United States in the early nineteenth century. He was treated well by the Xiongnu – perhaps because he had a Xiongnu companion, Ganfu – and stayed with them for ten years, taking a local wife; then he escaped, with his wife and Xiongnu companion, and resumed his journey westward. Two thousand kilometres further on, he found the Yuezhi, who were in Uzbekistan on a long migration to north-west India,[1] and had no interest in returning over the Pamir and Tian Shan mountains, not to mention the Taklimakan desert and the Desert of Lop. Instead of going home with

---

[1] Where they would eventually settle and build the Kushan Empire (first to third centuries AD).

this bad news, Zhang continued his explorations, visiting many of the great cities of Central Asia, even picking up information about India and the eastern Roman empire, before finally returning home after an absence of thirteen years – still with his Xiongnu wife and the faithful Ganfu.

By this time, events had moved on. Emperor Wu could do without the Yuezhi. But the information about peoples and established trade routes that Zhang brought back would change his country's history, turning attention westward to rich civilizations of which the Chinese had had no previous inkling. In particular, he told them of wonderful horses raised in Ferghana, the fertile valley of what is now eastern Uzbekistan. Tall, standing 16 hands high, these 'celestial horses' – or 'blood-sweating' horses, as they were known, from the pin-prick wounds caused by local parasites – were just what Wu needed to strengthen his cavalry. Such tempting prospects would inspire China's penetration – conquest, some call it – of Central Asia. From the seeds planted by Zhang sprang both the great trade routes joining China and the West, and their defence: the future Silk Road and the Great Wall's western extension.

Without any barbarian allies, Emperor Wu had got off to a poor start against the Xiongnu. In 134 BC the Han court backed a plot to destroy them. A merchant pretended to defect to the Xiongnu and claimed he would murder the top men in a certain town 100 kilometres south of the Great Wall. This would allow the Xiongnu to pillage with impunity. It almost worked. The merchant returned, killed a condemned prisoner, hung his head outside the wall, and sent a message saying it was the governor's. It was, of course, a trap – which the Xiongnu realized 50 kilometres from the town, as Sima Qian relates with his usual flair for the dramatic. The shanyu, leading 100,000 troops, noticed that, although the fields were full of animals, there was not a single person in sight. Growing suspicious, he attacked one of the beacon-towers, perhaps to see if it was manned or not. By chance, an official who knew of the planned ambush had taken refuge there.

> The shanyu . . . was about to put the defence official to death when the latter informed him of the Han troops hiding in the valley [300,000 of them, if we are to believe Sima Qian]. 'I suspected as much!' exclaimed the shanyu in great alarm, and proceeded to lead his forces back to the border. 'Heaven was on my side when I captured this defence official. In effect, Heaven sent you to warn me!' And he awarded the defence official the title of Heavenly King.

That was the end of any peace process, and the start (after a four-year pause) of a period of all-out war that would last for fourteen years.

Once again, please note, the increase in violence was initiated not by the 'barbarians', but by the Chinese. 'Peace and friendship' could have gone on working, with the occasional raid, expensive appeasement and the eating of much humble pie. But this was not the kind of stability Wu could accept. No emperor of a unified China could claim the Mandate of Heaven and at the same time tolerate as neighbour a 'barbarian' ruler who saw himself as an equal, and who was liable to launch raids whenever he felt like it. The only answer was to set the boundaries of China wider. In Lattimore's words, Wu needed 'a closed economy, a self-sufficient world, and an absolute Frontier'. It was in pursuit of this absolute that Wu escalated the rumbling rivalry into full-scale war.

But this was not, by nature, a frontier of absolutes. It was (and is) a collection of transition zones; of desert, scrub, gravel, good pasture along a few rivers and bad pasture fed by seasonal runoff. Strategic requirements came up against two problems. The first was the grasslands of Mongolia, which started just north of the Yellow River and ran eastward. The other was the oases – 26 independent tribal areas – of the Central Asian badlands, which lay westward. The difference between them was this: the steppe could not be conquered and held; the oasis kingdoms could, because they were self-sufficient. Once the Chinese had taken them, moreover, they could run them like their own cities, whereas nomads could benefit from them only by giving up nomadism. The war aim that Wu adopted, therefore, was to 'cut off the right arm' of the nomads (the west, since the dominant direction for nomads was southward) – i.e. to pick off the tribal kingdoms one by one and garrison them in order to deny them to the Xiongnu. With the Western Regions in Chinese hands, it would be possible to isolate, invade and destroy – if not to hold – Xiongnu lands.

There were two keys to success in this venture, both lying closer to the Chinese heartland. The first was the Ordos, the steppe enclave embraced by the great bend of the Yellow River. The second, starting only 150 kilometres beyond the Ordos, was the narrow stretch of land running westward through what would later be known as Gansu. The Gansu Corridor, also known as the Hexi (*hé xī* / 河西 , 'river-west', i.e. west of the Yellow River) Corridor, is another geopolitical keystone, crucial to understanding not just the Wall but much else about China's relations with Inner Asia from the second century BC onwards. The Corridor is hemmed in by the Qilian mountains to the south and deserts to the north, with icy rivers from the Qilian's snowy heights forming fine pastures down the middle. It was through this bottleneck, only some 25 kilometres across at its narrowest point, that nomads galloped to invade north China from the west. From now on, barbarian kings and Chinese emperors imbibed a great truth with their mothers' milk: *Whoever wishes to rule China must rule the Gansu Corridor.*

In summary, to close off this open frontier, Wu had only one option: total, all-or-nothing commitment to a range of strategies, all interlinked, all leading step by inevitable and very expensive step to the Great Wall. He had the manpower (a population of 50 million, a million-strong conscript army, some 10–13 million available for forced labour). He had the firepower. He needed horses by the tens of thousands, and these would have to be raised in China, or bought, or stolen. There had to be an enduring relationship with the oasis kingdoms to the west, which meant great expenditure on gifts, especially silk. There had to be invasions of Xiongnu lands, and a conquest. Trade goods had to flow. There could be no occupation of the steppes, but the newly conquered borderlands had to be secured; this meant garrisons, which would have to be fed, which meant sending in colonists to grow grain. And there would have to be fortresses, and overnight places, and houses, and lookout points, and an administrative apparatus to supervise the whole thing, all operating like an enormous Long City – or, as we call it, a Great Wall. This was the iron logic that drove Wu's decision not simply to refurbish the First Emperor's wall, but to extend it westward.

The ensuing war was catastrophic for both sides. Repeatedly, the opposing armies thrust into each other's territory. A dozen times – almost every year – the Xiongnu went on the offensive. Sources speak of 20,000 horsemen here, 30,000 there (though as usual the figures are suspiciously round and suspiciously large). Thousands were robbed, hundreds killed. Sometimes, 'senior officials' died, occasionally a governor or a commandant. Almost every year, too, the Han launched an offensive, with anything from 40,000 horsemen (129 BC) to 100,000 (124 BC). In 127 BC they retook the Ordos, capturing 'several thousand enemy and a million sheep', then sending in 100,000 colonists to reclaim farmland along the Yellow River, up to the outer Great Wall, the stone one north of the watercourse. The 124 BC attack probed 350 kilometres northward, snaring 15,000 Xiongnu captives and 'several million' animals; another 19,000 Xiongnu casualties were notched up the following year, 30,000 more in 121 BC. Han, too, suffered appalling losses: tens of thousands of dead, 100,000 horses lost in 124–3 BC alone. But eventually, for the Han Chinese, the risk and the effort paid off, because the great campaign of 121 BC snatched from the Xiongnu most of the strategic Gansu Corridor and forced the surrender of 40,000 Xiongnu, who were forcibly resettled south of the Great Wall.

At this point the Xiongnu should probably have withdrawn, like the true nomads they had once been. That's what they had done in the past, vanishing like smoke across the Gobi. Now, however, they were not as nomadic as they had been. Their new territories in Gansu included many cities, and their fortresses controlled the Gansu Corridor. To prevail here they would have to beat the Han at their own game; and to attempt that was to court disaster.

My guide, Xu Zhaoyu, or Michael, as he called himself, knew where to go. Michael was the best guide in Gansu. I know this because he told me, several times, and proved it often by revealing a knowledge of history which was astonishingly detailed given that he looked like a teenager. Actually he was over 30.

We headed north-west out of Zhangye, which guards the Gansu bottleneck, to see something he wanted to show me. Autumnal corn lay drying in the fields, the radio blared pop songs – No. 1 was *ta bu jidao*, 'She doesn't know (I love her)' – and all was well with the world. We turned down a farm track, until rough ground forced us to park by a field of chilli peppers. Michael led the way past an empty earth-walled compound and through cornstalks awaiting harvest.

Ahead loomed a sand-dune, dotted with camel thorn and red willow bushes, above which rose an earthen wall. This, Michael explained, was once a Xiongnu fortress city, their advance base, dominating the Gansu Corridor. We climbed, and the full thing came into view: eroded walls making a huge square, 250 of my paces on each side, with the stub of a guard-tower in the north-east corner.

A river used to run through here, Michael explained: the Black Water (Hei Shui). It is one of those that run down from the heights of the Qilian mountains, and it still flows, though with a different course. The Xiongnu must have thought they were there for keeps: fine farmland, their own river, a stranglehold on trade through the Corridor. But they had reckoned without Emperor Wu and his brilliant young general Huo Qubing. Huo had been made a commander in his teens, and was still only 22 when, in 119 BC, he and four other generals were given 50,000 horsemen each and sent off to solve the Xiongnu problem for good and all.

It was Huo who assaulted Black Water fortress. He at once saw the weakness of the Xiongnu position: there were no defences right across the Corridor, and the fortress was utterly dependent on its water supply. So he diverted the river, isolated the town and destroyed it. Emperor Wu was so delighted with the victory that he sent Huo a huge flagon of wine. Huo said that it was his soldiers, not he himself, who deserved the wine, so he poured it into a spring to share it with all his men. I can't think that the gesture was enough to make him popular – he was noted for his utter contempt for the lives of his subordinates – but it was enough to enter folklore; the town of Jiuquan ('Wine Spring') 150 kilometres north-west of the fort recalls his act.

Huo was as implacable as a Rottweiler. Wu offered him

a mansion to settle down in, to which Huo replied: 'The Xiongnu have not yet been wiped out. How can I settle and start a family?' He then advanced another 1,200 kilometres northward to reach Lake Baikal, almost the northern frontier of Xiongnu territory; but though he claimed to have slaughtered vast numbers of the enemy, he failed in his aim of crushing them entirely and the shanyu eluded him. He died on his return, aged just 24, supposedly after drinking water from wells the Xiongnu had poisoned by dumping dead animals in them. More likely it was the plague.

His grave, 50 kilometres west of Xian, honours him in a fascinating way. Emperor Wu had his tomb-mound raised close by his own, itself a considerable accolade. In addition, though, the tomb became the focus for something entirely new in Chinese art: monumental rock sculpture. Don't be put off by a dragon and a tiger made of some artificial hedge-like stuff. Set out in the pavilions and arcades around Huo's 40-metre tomb-mound are seventeen lumps of roughly carved boulders weighing many tonnes each, all of granite quarried from the Qilian mountains some 500 kilometres away. Actually, the whole mound was probably an evocation of the peak where Huo died. The mound is swathed in firs today, but originally the statues were scattered over the bare flanks. Mostly of animals – fish, tiger, elephant, boar, frog, ox, horse – they seem unfinished, as if the subjects were suggested by the shape of the boulder and are struggling to escape from its rocky embrace. Three seem to be magical carvings – a monster holding a goat in its jaws, a masked figure hugging a small bear, a human head with a hand raised as if to say 'Stop!'

One statue is of particular importance. Usually described as 'a horse trampling a barbarian', it seems to be an obvious symbol of Huo's achievement. But that idea comes from the man who first described the statue in 1914, the French ethnographer and art historian Victor Segalen. In fact, there is no trampling going on. This superb composition in 3.8 tonnes of granite portrays a horse simply straddling a heavily bearded 'barbarian', who has a bow in his left hand and an arrow in the other. It is as if the horse and barbarian are in some sort of formal relationship, superior and inferior, a static portrayal of an ideal, now that the Qilian mountains and the 'barbarian' inhabitants of the western regions had been brought inside the empire. In any event, as the historian of Chinese carving Ann Paludan points out,[2] this is the first example of stone animals of the kind that line the approaches to later imperial tombs.

The ruins of the Black Water fortress would make as good a memorial, for they were the very image of desolation. Sand had piled up against them and flowed down the inside. At the south-east corner, a dune had risen higher than the walls. I climbed it, and saw that someone in authority had made an attempt to recall the significance of the place with a silly little pavilion and a plaque: Ancient Ruined City of Black Water. But it was not its history that was recalled. 'This is the most mysterious sand-dune in history,' it announced, rather poetically. 'It is shaped like a big whale. No matter how the wind blows, it has not moved in 2,000 years. It is as if it is waiting for

[2] In *Chinese Sculpture: A Great Tradition*.

something. Who can solve the problem, and say why it is still here?'

Below was a shattered gateway, leading to a courtyard covered with sand and rubble. Beneath my feet, it looked like the surface of Mars. Further off were the remains of interior walls – houses, storerooms, offices: reminders that thousands once lived here.

I wondered about the rubble. Surely the Xiongnu would have built with rammed earth? Oh, said Michael, it was reoccupied by the Yuan and then the Ming.

'But if they used brick and tiles, where are they?'

'Taken for building material.'

That put a different complexion on the place. Built about 160 BC, destroyed in 119 BC, reoccupied God knows how often until finally abandoned in the seventeenth century – it had to be a potential treasure trove for some ambitious archaeologist, someone who might be able to confirm my tentative hypothesis: building a fort here to control the Gansu Corridor was a strategic error. It was not the best place. It's too far east to keep in ready contact with the tribal lands in Xinjiang. The very best position lies 160 kilometres to the west; but that was realized only 1,500 years later, by the Ming. Meanwhile, Han strategists opted for a forward base yet further west, where the trade route – the future Silk Road – divided to run north and south of the Taklimakan desert.

Military victory was not enough. Something had to fix the frontier, define what was China and what wasn't. That something was, of course, the Wall. So Wu picked up where the First Emperor had left off. In the centre and east, old walls were repaired and sections linked. In the west, new bits of the Wall arose, running from Lanzhou northward then west over the border of what is now Xinjiang. To build and man it, four new administrative areas sprang up, two of them, Gan and Su, straddling the narrow middle section. Eventually, these two gave their joint names to the province of Gansu. Its origins explain Gansu's odd thigh-bone shape, 1,500 kilometres long, fat at either end with an extremely narrow waist of only 60 kilometres (not quite coinciding with the narrowest point of the Gansu Corridor).

Wu's push west went into overdrive. In theory, it all fitted together beautifully. The borderlands would be colonized. The colonists would make deserts bloom, and feed themselves, and provide labour for an extension of the Great Wall, which would protect the soldiers, the traders, the farmers, the administrators. The far western oasis kingdoms would fall into line, as China proved itself the dominant power. Silks would be sent, and horses received. China would not only be unified; it would be secure at last – and eventually, surely, richer than ever. What greater legacy could an emperor leave?

This, the influx of 119 BC and afterwards, was the real beginning of the modern Wall as both artefact and defining symbol of China, running all the way from the western deserts to the Pacific. It became a sub-culture, the 'long city' suggested by its Chinese name – indeed, several 'long cities', given its various branches. Soldier–farmers began to arrive by the hundred thousand, supplementing volunteers, conscripts and convicts. Families followed, bringing the total number of settlers to an estimated 1.5–2

Qin: 3rd century BC
The First Emperor's Wall

Not much remains of the wall built in 214–210 BC by the First Emperor to guard north China. A spurious portrait on a spurious bit of wall, a few kilometres of restored stonework, a modern plaque, a few low mounds. Mostly, though, this symbol of the newly unified Chinese nation is a wall of the mind, built of words in books and tourist brochures.

Left: *The First Emperor, Qin Shi Huang Di, stares grimly down from a modern wall at the start of a remnant of his grandest creation north-west of Hohhot.*

Below: *Lacking battlements and only a metre or two in height, the wall itself seems to have been more of a border than a defence. The post-like objects on the hilltop are not people, but pillars made of rocks piled up to mark a summit.*

Han: 2nd century BC – 3rd century AD
THE WAY WEST: START AND FINISH

When the Emperor Wu (141–87 BC) of the Han Dynasty extended his empire westward, the rammed-earth wall he commissioned stretched almost 1,000 kilometres, from Lanzhou, the capital of Gansu province, to Yumenguan (The Jade Gate Pass) on the edge of Xinjiang's wastelands.

Left and below: *North of Lanzhou, little of the wall remains. This switchback remnant, hemmed in by rolling hillocks, dirt tracks and tiny fields, is near Yongdeng. These pictures give some idea of the depth of soil that provided the material for the rammed-earth wall, and today provides farm workers (inset bottom left) with excellent crops.*

Above and right: *At the Han Wall's far western end, sandwiched layers of earth and dried reeds have survived the intervening 2,000 years remarkably well. Up close (right), the reeds look as though they had been harvested and dried yesterday.*

Below: *All that is left of a thriving border-town is the stark core of Yumenguan's fortress. Eroded by wind and the rare downpours, it is now protected from the few tourists by a fence and a 20-yuan (£1.30/$2.50) charge.*

A Young General, A Great Victory, A Lasting Memorial

The most brilliant of Emperor Wu's leaders was Huo Qubing, who became a general while still a teenager. He was largely responsible for defeating the Xiongnu in several campaigns. In one of his many battles, he destroyed the Black Water fortress, near Zhangye, in the narrow Gansu Corridor that leads west. That was in 119 BC, when he was only 22. He died two years later, and was rewarded with a lavish tomb: a mound and a dozen granite statues, something entirely new in Chinese sculpture.

A corn-field (background) acts as reminder that this was once a place well supplied with water from a nearby river. The odd pagoda in the distance caps the adjacent dune (right).

The rain-washed, wind-blown walls of Black Water fortress are flanked by an enormous dune dimpled by the feet of the few visitors.

Above: *In 1914 Huo Qubing's tomb-mound was bare and ignored, the huge granite sculptures scattered (including its most famous one, centre). Today, it is rebuilt and tree-covered, with formal gardens and its sculptures on display for tourists.*

Right: *The tomb's best known sculpture – tentative in line, but beautifully designed – is usually seen as a horse, representing China, 'trampling' a Xiongnu. In fact, the horse is simply astride the barbarian warrior. What it really means is anyone's guess.*

Han: 2nd century BC – 3rd century AD
A MYSTERY MOUND IN THE GOBI

The 'Wall of Genghis Khan' (as it is often called on maps) runs across southern Mongolia and Inner Mongolia. In fact, it is not a wall and has nothing to do with Genghis Khan. It is actually a mound of desert earth that is scarcely visible except when it catches a low sun or wind-blown snow. Locals call it a 'ridge' or 'road'. Though it runs for several hundred kilometres, its purpose and date remain unknown. My own theory is that it marked the Han Dynasty's northern border, and that it was built after the defeat of the Xiongnu, some time in the second century AD.

Left: *A nearby pile of stones turned out to be the remains of a long-abandoned kiln.*

Below: *A tortoise-like rock on a plateau – possibly an ancient volcanic plug – the sides of which, from a distance and at dusk, I mistook for a wall.*

Above: *A woman begins the process that will turn the milk of any of Mongolia's five domestic animals into curds, cream, yoghurt and/or cheese, all of several different consistencies.*

Right: *Bayas poses on the 'wall' (or ridge, or road, or whatever it is). Beside him is an ovoo, a pile of stones, the traditional way of marking a high spot – one that is only about half a metre above the surrounding desert.*

Below: *My UAZ 4 X 4 sits on top of the 'wall'. Travelling west–east along the ridge, we have just crossed our own tracks, made as we headed south the previous day, entirely unaware that what we sought was almost invisible except to those who know it.*

LEGENDS FLOATING FREE FROM HISTORY

Two modern statues and a painting recall three Great Wall personalities. Though widely seen as real people, they have only the most tenuous connection with historical fact. Zhaojun was an imperial concubine sent off in 33 BC beyond the Wall to marry a barbarian ruler – and civilize him, according to legend. The Roman represents a legion which is wrongly supposed to have come to China about the same time as Zhaojun left. Meng Jiangnu, whose tears for her dead husband 'caused the Wall to tumble', is the Wall's star: humbly born, long-suffering, and brave enough to challenge the emperor and commit suicide rather than submit to him.

Right: *Zhaojun, who carried civilization (symbolized by her lute-like pipa) to the wild north. The painting is by the modern woman artist Liu Fufang.*

Below: *This lumpish Roman dominates the approach to Yongchang, in Gansu province, where his legion supposedly settled.*

Above: *In the nearby 'Roman' village, my guide Mr Luo sits beneath a pseudo-Roman folly built to lend credibility to an unlikely tale.*

Below: *This modern statue of Meng Jiangnu shows the character she has acquired over centuries: tragic, heroic, steadfast. It stands in a temple complex devoted to her Virgin-like cult near Shanhaiguan, near the Wall's eastern end.*

million – roughly equal to the whole Xiongnu population – and all were provided with land, animals and seeds. Where there was water, villages and farms arose. Roads would lead to the Wall, canals would be built to supply it with water (one in Ningxia was 60 kilometres long, with 290 side-channels; another in Xinjiang ran for 100 kilometres).

Emperor Wu, known as the Martial Emperor, had the power to make all this happen. Silk began to flow westward in prodigious amounts. By 111 BC, ten vast caravans a year, each the size of a small city on the move, were rolling west, the beginning of an economic offensive that by 50–40 BC would carry every year anything up to 18,000 rolls of silk out to the west, along with some 3–4 *billion* coins: about 30 per cent of the national cash income, perhaps 7 per cent of the empire's total revenue. In 105 BC a princess was despatched to be wife to the chief of the Wu-sun, 1,500 kilometres beyond Wu's western borders in the Ili valley in present-day Kazakhstan (a ploy of dubious use, since the Xiongnu countered by sending one of their own princesses). Other tribes were knocked into line with military expeditions. By 102 BC, 180,000 more settlers had arrived to build new farming communities along the Edsen Gol, the Lord's River, as it is in Mongol (Ruo Shui in Chinese), a watercourse that flows down north-eastward from the Qilian mountains into the desert. In 101 an army drove westward into the Ferghana valley to capture enough of the 'heavenly horses' to start a breeding programme, and to shock vacillating states into submission. The effort and expenditure bore fruit. The Xiongnu were held in check, their potential allies bribed and scared into alliance with China.

And the Han Great Wall became many things: a defence, a series of safe-houses for traders, a hugely extended barracks, a road for the transport of goods – and thus, as the Chinese implies, a very long city.

But this immense effort, which drained the Han economy, took some time to take effect. In 103 BC a Han force of 20,000, which had advanced 1,000 kilometres across the Gobi, was surrounded and massacred. Sporadic Xiongnu raids continued. In 99 BC another campaign ended in total catastrophe. One army, attacking westward, killed 10,000 Xiongnu (who counted, I wonder?) yet lost 60–70 per cent of its own men. A second army, 5,000 men with wagonloads of food and arrows, struck northward for a month across the Gobi and the Mongolian heartland, aiming (I imagine) to attack the Xiongnu capital. It was not a big force for so ambitious a project. Perhaps the general, Li Ling, was confident that his repeating crossbows, with arrows carried by the hundred thousand in his wagons, would carry him to victory. But even these terrifyingly effective weapons, the ancient equivalent of machine guns, were no match for 30,000 Xiongnu horsemen, reinforced by another 80,000 from neighbouring tribes. Li Ling staged a fighting retreat over grasslands and desert to the Gurvan Saikhan (Three Beauties) range. Perhaps he fled into these dark, rocky hills and dry valleys because he needed water – there is at least one river that flows year-round through a ravine, now known as Vulture's Gorge, so shadowy that its winter ice never melts. Anyway, he and his wagons were trapped. 'The enemy was lodged in the hills, surrounding him on all sides and shooting arrows like drops of rain,' according to our source,[3] which speaks of half a million arrows being shot in one day. The surviving Chinese – only half of the number that had set out – fled, outmanœuvred and with no arrows left, through a narrow valley, while the Mongols tossed rocks down on them, blocking escape until night fell. That night, Li Ling took ten men and galloped clear, only to be hunted down and forced to surrender. Just 400 of his men, armed with clubs made from the spokes of their wagons, made it back home. All those men, all those horses, all those repeating crossbows blown away like a dust-devil whipped into non-existence by a Gobi wind. Two years later, 70,000 cavalry and 100,000 infantry, in two armies, had no better luck.

To cap it all, the Xiongnu showed no sign of collapsing under the strain of their new-found wealth. Enriched with gifts from China and tributes in people and cattle from vassal tribes, the ruling class had built a sophisticated and varied life for themselves in the mountains of northern Mongolia and southern Siberia, with the trappings of the settled ways of the Chinese. Archaeologists have revealed that one town, near present-day Ivolga in Siberia, was well fortified and counted among its inhabitants carpenters, masons, farmers, iron-workers and jewellers. Some houses even had underfloor heating, Roman-style. To the west, beyond the Great Wall, the Xiongnu, having

[3] *Han Shu* ('Han Documents', known as the *History of the Former Han*), written by Ban Gu and his sister Pan Zhao in the second half of the first century AD.

expelled the Yuezhi, controlled some 30 city-states in the Western Regions, mainly in today's Gansu. In three great annual festivals, subjects flowed to the capital, bearing trade goods, slaves and gifts.

Xiongnu notables buried each other in style, as a Mongolian mining engineer named Ballod discovered in 1912. He was surveying the pine-covered Noyan Uul hills 100 kilometres north of Ulaanbaatar, looking for gold, when he came to a mound with a hole in it. He dug down, found bits of metal and a few traces of gold, and realized he had stumbled on a burial mound, which had been robbed at some indeterminate time. Revolution and world war delayed any response, but in 1924 the great Russian explorer Petr Kozlov, returning from Tibet, heard about Noyan Uul and set a team to work. He unearthed a huge Xiongnu royal cemetery, 10 kilometres square, containing 212 burial mounds. Grave-robbers had taken most of the gold, but left enough bits and pieces to suggest the acquisitive, un-nomadic ways of the Xiongnu upper class: silk-covered wooden beams, silk-lined birch coffins, patterned felt, lacquered wooden bottles, horn spoons, bronze bridle decorations, jewellery, silver plates, embroidered carpets, wonderful tapestries adorned with animal motifs and portraits. A shard of pottery recorded the maker, the painter and a date corresponding to 2 BC. Nor was this the only burial ground. Another necropolis (containing a large first-century BC tomb, presumably imperial, with three smaller ones) is currently being excavated by a French–Mongol team in Gol Mod, 450 kilometres west of Ulaanbaatar. It includes bits of a chariot: apparently the shanyus liked to travel in style, Chinese fashion, across their domains.

All these wars, all these losses on both sides, stated hard truths about the nature of the Great Wall frontier. So long as both sides remained unified, neither side could win. Han and Xiongnu were like two equally matched sumo wrestlers, locked together, neither able to gain an advantage. And what role did the Wall play in this great-power rivalry? Absolutely none, in itself. Sima Qian records many invasions, large and small; never does he mention that the Wall stopped one.

The Wall did many things: it proclaimed the frontier, it employed thousands, it prevented defections, it displayed the might of the emperor. What it could not do on its own was keep out the barbarians. Nothing would while they still existed.

5

THE WALL GOES WEST

I HAD HIGH HOPES OF LANZHOU, GANSU'S CAPITAL, BECAUSE it had once been a major Silk Road city and a cornerstone of the Han defence line running up to the Gansu Corridor. Merchants struck north from here, protected by the Wall and the Zhuanglang River, heading for the Corridor and points west. Apparently it had a great museum, with experts to consult.

But no. Lanzhou's 3 million people had pretty much buried the past and the museum was closed for renovations. The city's extraordinary setting, straddling the Yellow River and cradled by very steep mountains, holds pollution as a bowl holds water. There was a limit to my interest in its iron bridge (the first over the Yellow River, 1910; built by Germans, actually) and the modern (1987) Mother-and-Child statue in pink stone, a symbol of the river nurturing the people. What I wanted was the Wall, as I told my guide, a strapping, broad-faced girl by the name of Sun Chingching.

'But you can call me Christina,' she said. She spoke in formal, phrase-book sentences, with endearing frankness. 'My English name was given me by my English teacher because I am a Christian. I believe in God. So he called me Christina.'

There was no trace of the Great Wall in today's city, but Christina rose to the challenge. She got on the internet, phoned friends and reported back. There was some wall left, after all. We would drive north with an old school-friend who knew the area.

Next day she appeared with a slim, studious young man. 'His name is Xu Jie. But you can call him Eric. We call him Eric because he has a warm heart. He likes to help people.' No, I didn't understand the logic either, but it was true. The two together made a perfect team.

Northward, peach trees gave way to gaunt red-brown hills, fog to clear skies, hideous suburbs to the Lanzhou–Wuwei expressway – new, of course, and not on my map.

Eighty kilometres on, we turned into a little place called Yongdeng, where Eric picked up a schoolfriend, a nine-year-old cousin and an aunt, Miss Li, a homely figure in a smart black jacket. It was quite a party, six of us and the driver. We all squeezed into the car, bumped up a side-road, and parked by a railway line. Miss Li led the way across the line and along the grassy edges of little ploughed fields, talking about the Wall. There wasn't much left – Christina passed on Miss Li's words – because local people didn't know much about it. There used to be more, but it had been knocked down and ploughed into fields. Miss Li showed me a coin, and began its story. Her father had found it beside the Wall, with many others, but . . .

She broke off, because there it was, marking the edge of a field along the top of a ravine, guarding nothing but bone-dry, tussocky hills. It was in terrible shape, all gap-toothed bits and pieces, sometimes no more than a metre and a half high, sometimes three metres. Grass sprouted on the top and in odd, eroded corners. It ran for no more than a couple of kilometres. I am sure it had survived only because ploughing it under would have put half the field into the ravine.

We wandered along, like a class of schoolkids on an outing, then descended through a gap into the ravine. It was a storm channel, which might have once acted as a moat, deterring intruders descending from the barren hills. Nowadays, storms were clearly rare, because someone had put a small field down there, now harvested and neatly dug for autumn.

It struck me as pathetic, in the original meaning: a sight full of pathos, a quality that arouses pity. People came here now only to tend fields. The Wall was vanishing year by year, and no one cared.

'Did your teachers bring you here to visit?' I asked Eric's friend.

'No. No one knew it was part of the Great Wall. We just called it a "border wall".'

And here was I, expending a good deal of time, energy and money to track down this ruin. I felt as if I had stumbled on the last remnants of a species heading towards extinction.

'Is this all there is?' I asked Christina.

'On the internet, it said there was more. It is near. Shall we look for it?'

Certainly we should. We dropped off Miss Li and her niece, drove a few kilometres, asked the way, walked up a narrow lane into fields of tomatoes and lettuces, asked again. Well, there was once a bit of the wall three or four *li* that way – an old man pointed – but it's all gone now. On the other hand, now he came to think of it . . . and he gave the driver some instructions.

'People don't know about history,' mourned Christina, as we returned to the car. 'They just want to make lots of money. They destroy old things, and build new ones.'

'The trouble is,' I said, 'that it's only earth.'

'I think it is very important to us.' She donned her formal role as guide and guardian of China's traditions. 'It is a symbol of our national spirit. But I think people round here, they do not agree with me.'

We manœuvred backwards, past a tractor–trailer so completely covered with straw that it looked like a mobile haystack, and continued on our way beside fields, along a canal, and through a village. It was rather a fine village, with a concrete road, new houses and well-kept fields. We stopped at a school, the Ma Jia Wan Primary School, built in 1996. This was promising, because the back wall of the compound was actually a bit of the Great Wall, 4 metres high, solid, and neatly topped with new tiles. Surely there was more. Two men with catastrophic teeth and glasses as big as headlights gave more directions. On we went. Beneath our wheels, concrete gave way to dry mud.

And there, suddenly, was a sight to make the day worthwhile: right beside the track stood a single isolated but very solid piece of wall, rearing up in the shape of two giant fins that looked as if they belonged to some buried stegosaurus. True, there were hoe-marks at the base, where someone had gathered barrows of earth. But at least here someone cared, for a plaque, set up in 1981, stated that this was indeed part of the Han Great Wall. You could see the striations where, over 2,000 years before, workers had built up their layers of rammed earth. It would not last for ever, but this little section clearly had some way to go.

Even odder than the wall was its setting; for here the track ran through a muddle of ravines and holes and little cliffs, with every flat surface, even the floor of what looked like a dry river, turned into pocket-handkerchief fields, all neatly hoed. The wall was part of the jumble, apparently diving into the ground then reappearing further on. Then, as I climbed about this warren, I saw we were on high ground. Off to one side was a basin of open farmland that rolled over to grey hills about 500 metres away, and in the middle of it were some farm workers.

We made our way over to them to chat. They were tending a family plot marked out by raised earth borders which also carried little irrigation channels bringing water from a nearby well. They were gathering carrots – big, fat ones. A grandmother with a blue beret took on the role of spokesperson, while a dozen others stopped hoeing to gather round, intrigued by the arrival of a westerner. It was the end of a sunny afternoon, and they were cheerful.

I praised the carrots, and asked about the harvest.

'It is good. This is the second harvest. First, we grow wheat, then we grow carrots. You can try one.'

And they did all this by hand?

'Yes, all by hand.' She wiped a huge carrot with a cloth, and handed it to me. 'The fields are too small for machines.'

And what about the Wall? I asked through a crunchy mouthful. Was there more of it once?

'Several years ago, there was more,' Christina reported, 'but—'

She checked herself, and asked more questions. There was a quick flurry of conversation. These people knew about the Wall, and its significance. 'She says it was the rain. It was not destroyed by the people, because the government forbids them. They are not allowed to gather earth from the Great Wall. Please, she says, take more carrots, if you like.'

From here the Wall used to run on northward, guarding against a flanking attack from Tibet. It then headed west, to the famous passes (*guān* / 关) of Yangguan and Yumenguan, beyond which lay the hideous wastes of the Taklimakan desert. Now, finally, in the first century BC, the Wall had something like its present-day dimensions.

Imagine the Wall as a line of watch-towers, at intervals of 2–5 kilometres – not today's drab grey blocks, but shining in the desert sun, plastered and whitewashed (hence the Mongol name, the White Wall) – linked by ramparts. Each tower, containing a single large room, was a world in itself for the half-dozen men posted there. It rose about 10 metres, with a parapet at the top, and also a pole, with pulleys for raising coloured flags or fire-baskets to send warning signals. If you were lucky, your tower had a stairway, but in most cases you climbed to the top with a ladder, or by using crude footholds and a rope. Below each tower stood stacks of brushwood with which to make signal fires, along with reed torches and piles of dung, used both for repairing plaster and for fuel. Equipment was kept in little store-houses: four axes, four hammers, a drum, 500 arrowheads, 40 javelins, water jars, spare pipes, four medicine containers. Kennels for the

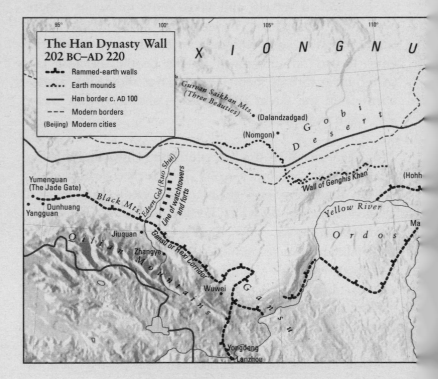

tower's two dogs. And all this, down to the way wood-piles were stacked, was subject to rigorous inspection. The other side of the Wall, sand was piled up and raked so that any nocturnal spies would leave footprints.

On either side of the Wall at irregular intervals were beacon-towers, some tall, some squat. These served several purposes. All were observation-posts, of course, with those out in front of the Wall acting as advance warning of an assault, while others behind the lines were rearguards, to send news of an attack that had over-whelmed forward sectors. Some were also command

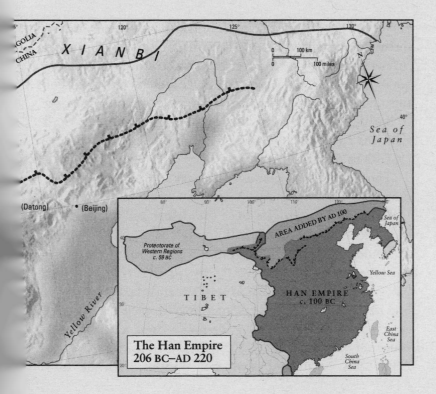

posts, or safe-houses for travellers. Further back still, separated from the Wall itself by 30 or 40 kilometres, stood the company HQs, strongholds surrounded by their own walls, set in compounds 50–100 metres square, with store-rooms for grain, weapons and clothing.

Such was the character of the section of the Wall that ran from Lanzhou for 1,000 kilometres to the most extreme western gateways, Yumenguan and its smaller sister Yangguan. These Han dynasty outposts, on the very edge of the black hole of the Taklimakan, would be my next destinations.

Have you ever noticed that mirages appear only in the direction of the sun? Only sunwards, on the desert road to Yumenguan, beyond flat, grey wastes, did the quivering air reflect sky, a sky beaten of all colour by the heat. For this view, you pay 30 yuan for a man to unhook a strand of barbed wire, giving you access to a dead straight road that was paved as a business venture. It carries adventure tourists to the Wall's end, and beyond.

'They go to a geological park. Ravines, gullies, pinnacles,' said my guide, Vicky.

We could have driven over the desert and avoided the toll. This is an empty land. If you fell asleep at the wheel, it wouldn't matter. You would wander safely over the hard sand until bumped awake by tussocks that look like half-buried hedgehogs. As it was we travelled straight, in one dimension. Ahead, something rippled into fuzzy existence – a person? – a camel? – no, a car, which squeezed past so close we almost clashed mirrors.

But this wasteland was not endless. Distant hills

emerged, shaky with the heat, and a beacon-tower, and smoke. The road ran out into gravel. There was a building – a museum, as it turned out – an old railway carriage where drivers gathered for tea, a minibus, half a dozen floppy-hatted tourists and an unnecessary wooden gateway, which framed the Great Wall's last outpost.

Pictures of Yumenguan – Jade Gate Pass, named after one of China's most sought-after trade items – usually show it looking like a stark block of baked earth, a lonely bastion silent against an infinite wasteland. In fact, you have to choose your viewpoint carefully to see it like that, because the smoke you see at a distance is not smoke, but dust from a rock-crushing operation. You're not alone at Yumenguan these days, and you're certainly not awed by silence, because there isn't any.

But one shouldn't carp. In its heyday, as created by Emperor Wu, Yumenguan would have been a bustling, noisy place. In Han times this was the centre of a town of 40,000 people, busy with soldiery, merchants, camel trains, officials, food stalls and shops. A river ran nearby, and still does, making a flood plain of soggy pastures where sheep graze.

The gate tower was hard to get into then, and it still is. There's a fence around it, and a 20-yuan charge, taken by a little old woman who delivered a constant stream of chatter. Inside the 10-metre walls of bare brown earth, she was eager to point out the alternating layers of reed and hemp, the remains of the earth stairway people once used to get to the top, the ragged portals long ago stripped of stonework.

'There used to be a ladder up the wall,' she said. 'Guards climbed up to sound the alarm.'

I loved her walnut face, her smile, her friendly eyes, but she was strangely camera-shy, ducking sideways, or raising an arm, or whipping round her blue headscarf whenever she saw me focusing. Later, I would understand. Right then, I was in a hurry to see the Han Great Wall itself, bits of which lay a couple of kilometres further on in the desert.

There wasn't much of it left. This wasn't surprising; indeed, it was surprising that anything at all had survived, considering that it was built of the only materials to hand – earth and the straw of local grass. A couple of hundred metres of wall and a lone beacon-tower rose from the rough, ash-coloured sand, protected from curious hands by a metal fence. I had never seen a structure like it: the winds of two millennia had gouged into the earthen layers, leaving the straw ones standing proud. It looked like a 2-metre-high layer-cake. You would not think that straw would last so well, but close up, there it was, sticking out in hairy lines as if it had been gathered yesterday.

And small sections of it, a layer or two only, emerged from sandy ridges outside the fence. As I stooped to collect some strands, I heard voices. The tourists had caught up with us. They turned out to be American teachers from Beijing's International School. A grey-haired lady in a patterned shirt and Bermuda shorts followed my example and waved a handful of 2,000-year-old straw in triumph. 'It's amazing!' she said. 'I'm touching history!'

All very interesting, no doubt, but it was too much like studying tombstones. Where, I wondered out loud to Vicky on the way back to the fort, was the evidence of what life had been like out here? She spoke with the driver.

'Do you mean the things that locals find in the sand?'

Things. What things?

'Things dropped by traders.'

His words gave me an idea. Back at Yumenguan, there was the same old lady, chatting with the driver of the tourist bus. She was holding an aged horse with skin like a moth-eaten rug.

'Vicky, ask her about things found in the sand.'

At her question, the old lady manœuvred us away from the driver, leaned forward and whispered.

Vicky, too, became conspiratorial. 'She has antiques. You want to see?'

I nodded. 'She keeps them here?'

'No. At the fort. In a brown cage.'

I was baffled, and intrigued. 'We could stroll over.'

'No, no. She says it is far.'

No, it wasn't, actually. Only 500 metres, which I had walked once already. But we were in a different dimension now, reduced to a huddle of three conspirators. What was she suggesting?

'She says: take the horse.'

If this was a ploy to disguise the real purpose of the expedition, it was a very transparent one. I climbed on the horse and urged it through the gateway towards the fort. For this poor old bag of bones, bottom speed was also top speed. At the end of long shadows cast by the setting sun, we plodded after the old woman, who stopped at, of all things, a metal safe standing on a small rise 50 metres short of the fort. Waiting for me to dismount, she began to remove item after item: strips of bamboo with writing on them, a small dagger, chunks of mineral, a handful of silk. She glanced round warily, though out there we could hardly be discreet, three lonely figures and a horse spotlit on top of a rise. Then, from inside a cloth, she produced a sword, half a metre long and covered in verdigris. Bronze, surely.

'She says: she was feeding the horse, when the horse stepped in a hole, and she found this.'

If it was genuine, it was surely rare and wonderful.

'How much?'

'She says: she will never sell this.'

She wrapped it again and hid it away back in the safe.

'She says: do you want to buy it?'

'I thought she said she would never sell it.'

'She is afraid of the government. But she says she can sell it, maybe. For twenty thousand yuan [$2,500].'

'I'm sure it's worth it. But I can't afford that.'

'I have never seen anything like it. Over a million yuan, I think. She says: how much will you give?'

'I don't have that sort of money.'

She brought out a jade brooch, a little jade lion, a tiny Buddha's head.

'She says: she found all these things on the antiques beach.'

Puzzling about the mention of a beach out in the desert, I took the Buddha's head, which was the size of a pendant and engrained with dirt. She pounced. How much would I give? Five hundred yuan ($62)? For some reason, having taken it, I now felt obligated, if only in exchange for this little adventure.

'I don't want it . . . I don't know . . . I wouldn't give more than two hundred.'

The price dropped to 400 yuan, then 300. She put the head away and, in an attempt to swing a better deal, produced a ceramic horse.

'She says: this is Tang. It is original.'

Oh, sure, a 1,200-year-old horse. At this point, I lost faith in everything. It was all fake, had to be.

'OK, Vicky, tell her two hundred, and that's it.'

So I have my little green Buddha's head, which now goes everywhere with me for good luck. I had no idea whether it or anything else was genuine or not, but I suspect that if I had been less ignorant and richer, I could have picked up something interesting. Had that little sword fallen from a traveller's pack 1,000 or more years before? I came to think it might have done, given what I learned next.

To beat the dark, we raced the setting sun across the desert to the oasis town of Yangguan, skirting donkey carts, piles of grain, poplar trees and a statue of a man apparently addressing the desert, to arrive at the fortress, the exit point for the southern branch of the Han trade route which would eventually become the Silk Road. It used to have the same back-story as its sister, Yumenguan: for those setting out westward, the last stop before the desert; for those arriving, the first outpost of China; apprehension for some, relief for others. People remember the apprehension of parting more sharply, perhaps because goodbyes sear the soul, while welcomes heal it; and it is this feeling that inspired the modern statue of a Tang dynasty (eighth-century) painter and poet, Wang Wei, much admired for his celebrations of nature, who stands here proclaiming the quatrain engraved beside him:

At Weicheng morning rain has dampened light dust,
By the inn, the willows are all fresh and green.
I urge you, my friend, to drink a last cup of wine,
West of Yangguan, you will find no more friends.

But such mournful thoughts do not belong to Yangguan today, because the whole place has had a makeover, turning a shell of dusty walls into a museum and a film studio. A guide, Miss Lu, rushed me around in a little canopied tourist bus, past a mock-up siege engine and Mongol campsite, out to a beacon-tower. The moon was up, lighting a view that explained much that had puzzled me.

In Han times, the softly lit plain before me had been a lake, fed by four springs. That was why Yangguan was here, why it had been famous for its wild swans and fish: fresh water. For centuries, 10,000 people had lived around its shores, protected by the fort and its garrison. People had bathed, swum, collected water and, inevitably, dropped things. Then the springs had faltered, the lake had shrunk back, people had left. By about AD 900 the fortress had fallen into ruin. But over the past century, some had returned, drawn by what they could find beneath the sands.

'We call it the Antiques Beach,' said Miss Lu. 'People could pick up anything. Now it is all fenced off, and they cannot.'

But of course they can and do, as I knew, because I had in my pocket my Buddha's head. If its engrained sand was from the Antiques Beach, perhaps everything in the old woman's safe in Yumenguan was genuine, after all.

The moonlight made Miss Lu poetic. 'Ah, how

prosperous was this area in ancient times!' A few years ago, people came here, and saw only a ruin. It was sad. So a local businessman – 'he was crying, crying to see just a beacon-tower' – decided to raise money, renovate it, build a museum to remind people of its history, and recoup some of his expenses from film companies and visitors.

Back at the fort, Miss Lu opened the museum up for me, and revealed something extraordinary: one of the finest, perhaps *the* finest, of the many collections scattered along the Wall. This part had been open for two years already, but the enterprise was only half complete – 34 million yuan ($4.25 million) spent, the same again to come. This was where the finds from the Antiques Beach now ended up, and clearly there were enough of them to keep local dealers supplied with a few surreptitious jade figurines and the odd sword. Here, beautifully lit, were cabinets of chariot accoutrements, spinning-wheels, chess pieces, bronze statuettes, coins, ornaments, buttons, buckles, beads, slips of bamboo with writing on them, information enough about centuries of habitation for a dozen theses. Models of these sections of the Wall showed it winding eastward, complete with a penumbra of 80 beacon-towers.

Outside again under a glorious moon and star-studded sky, I made a promise to Miss Lu. I said I would spread the word about this place. Yangguan won't ever again be much of a gateway for traders, but it certainly should be for tourists and archaeologists.

What was it like, being sent out to these god-forsaken places to build, live, fight and die? We don't know, because for the four centuries that the Han were in power in this part of China, no one left an account. But it is possible to evoke life from scattered details.

By 100 BC the lines of the western Wall were established pretty much as they remain to this day, stretching from Wuwei to Dunhuang, then forking to Yumenguan and Yangguan. There was also another line of the Wall that broke away, running northward from the Qilian mountains with the Edsen Gol until the river vanishes after 250 kilometres into swamps and salt lakes. Although this counts as part of the Wall, it was in fact a line of 156 watch-towers and 10 forts, ending in the base the Chinese called Qu-yen. Centuries later, there would arise here a great city, Khara Khoto (Mongol: Black City), ruined by the Mongols in 1227; but for now it was the back of beyond, colonized by the Chinese in 107–102 BC to grow food for the Wall garrisons, deny pastures to the Xiongnu, defend traders, control (i.e. count, tax and recruit) the scattered locals and catch fleeing convicts.

For the 800 or so officers and men charged with performing these functions, the bone-dry climate must have made life harsh. For modern archaeologists, it has been a godsend, because long after the Edsen Gol fortifications were abandoned some two centuries later, the sand preserved thousands of bamboo strips as the only written evidence of life in these barren parts. Ten thousand strips – a minute fraction of those that were produced – were gathered in 1927–34 by a Sino-Swedish expedition led by the great Swedish explorer Sven Hedin. Via Beijing and Hong Kong, they ended up in the Library of Congress in Washington DC, where they were examined by the

eminent Cambridge Sinologist Michael Loewe in the mid-
1960s. Thousands of others were also recovered from
Dunhuang and Wuwei, a trove of information it will take
decades to assess.

'Wooden stationery' was made of many different
woods, in many sizes; but overwhelmingly it consisted of
30-centimetre strips of bamboo, which could be joined by
thread to form scrolls. These strips and scrolls, on which
clerks wrote vertically, bound the Wall's officers, men and
families to higher authorities. Most were written to
officers down the line in the next sector, a few to or from
seniors in Dunhuang, or even the national capital. Besides
strips used as labels and travel documents, there are
reports, statutes, accounts, lists of food, numbers of men
coming and going, charge sheets, and all the other routine
items of documentation that armies generate. The strips
would be bound, tied, put in a leather container, addressed
and despatched, with instructions for either first- or second-
class delivery, i.e. either by runner or by horse. All mail was
logged in and out, and the actual time taken for the journey
compared to the official time. A runner was supposed to
cover 11 *li* (about 5.5 kilometres) per hour for short
distances, a little less – hardly more than walking pace – for
longer stretches. One of the strips criticizes a private
for slowness: 'The sector extends for a distance of 80 *li* [40
kilometres], and the scheduled time is nine hours. What is
the explanation for the delay of one hour?'

Overwhelmingly, the content of the strips is what you
would expect from junior bureaucrats: tedious in the
extreme. But it is possible to use the strips to paint a
composite portrait of life on the frontier.

Take, for example, young Xu Zong, 20, section commander. He is a volunteer from somewhere in central China, 50 days' march away, and has been well rewarded. He needs to be, because he already has a considerable family of dependants: a wife, four children, two brothers and two sisters, all of whom help on his 5-acre plantation. He is a low-grade official, paid partly in cash, partly in grain. Not long before this, cash would have been highly suspect. Coins varied, counterfeiters were everywhere. But Emperor Wu had introduced new coinage, which had won universal acceptance. You knew what you could get for one of the 3-kilo strings of 1,000 coins.

Young Xu fields a stream of directives, for this is a time when the Han Dynasty is imposing itself with tough laws. One of his tasks is to catch criminals and deserters. If a deserter is caught, 'a full report is to be submitted, listing [his origins], his given name, surname, age, height, colouring; the clothing he was wearing, and the equipment and baggage he carried; the date of desertion and the number of men involved'. He has to make sure local trouble-makers are duly caught and punished – as happened with two guardsmen, Han Hoyang and Chin Kuei, who got into a swordfight. Chin was injured near the right eye, Han in two places on the fingers of the right hand. Both were 'detained in manacles'. He may also have checked on travellers, like Cui Zidang, who 'states that he is engaged in domestic and private marketing in Qu-yen. I beg to state that Cui Zidang has not been subject to official judicial proceedings, and is qualified to receive a passport.' Cui would then have been given his numbered passport, written on wood split into two parts, one of which was held locally, so that on his return he would be allowed on his way only when an official, like Xu, had matched the two.

Xu's job includes looking after contingents of three types: convicts; conscripts, those men between 20 and 56 serving part of their compulsory two years of service; and volunteers like himself. They arrive in squads, exhausted by their march from the farmlands, ignorant of conditions here, illiterate, resentful, but cowed. They must all be listed, provided with clothing, equipment and food, and allocated to a group, with specific duties: guardsman, pioneer, farm worker. You couldn't trust the convicts and conscripts, of course. Given a chance, they would sell what the state provided and be off to join the Xiongnu. Then he would have to get his clerk to write up what he had done: 'Issued: barley, [1,740 kilos] as rations for 66 pioneers engaged in hard labour for the 5th–8th months inclusive.' Their tasks included digging earth for the body of the Wall and clay for baked bricks (each man to make 80 bricks of standard size, 41 × 18 × 14 centimetres). Meanwhile, others would be preparing the horse-dung plaster or splashing on yet another coat of whitewash. Reed-gathering, tree-cutting (yes, there were plantations then, though there are none now), tending orchards and vegetable gardens, sometimes guarding them against pilferers – the tasks were never-ending, and all subject to checking by seniors. 'One large flag on the tower old and damaged; wall unswept and unplastered,' a carping officer wrote. 'One dog absent.'

Then there were the camels and horses to be fed, and their fodder to be accounted for. As in most guard duty, boredom must have been the greatest enemy, followed by carelessness. The 26 watchtowers in Xu's 40-kilometre section did not have staircases, only handholds and ropes. You could easily lose your footing, as one of his fellow officers did in the high summer of 56 BC. 'On the evening of August 24,' he reported, 'I fell off the tower accidentally and injured my back. After recovery I resumed duties this day, August 31.' Imagine him on yet another boring day, climbing the towers, inspecting heavy crossbows on their mountings – one in reasonable condition had a range of 255 metres – making sure they were well greased, counting the helmets and armour and pots of grease, and wishing himself and his family back south, where there were no bitter winds in winter, where there was grass in summer, and trees to lie under, and fruit, and cool streams.

One of Xu's duties was organizing the roster of patrols along the outer sandbank, hunting for the footprints of would-be intruders. For ten mornings in succession a private would take the dogs out, scanning a few kilometres of sand, almost always returning with the same report: 'No traces of illegal passage by men or horses.'

Then there was archery (with crossbows: 12 arrows to be fired, 6 hits for a pass) and signal practice (with flags and smoke-baskets by day, torches and fires by night). 'Officers in command of posts shall record in writing the date and time of arrival of signals,' so that the same signal could be sent on down the line and simultaneously back up as confirmation that it had been received. Xu would know that the signal would be passed all the way to Dunhuang and Wuwei, where its arrival would be logged.

At some point, someone would arrive from HQ with the records to check how long the whole operation had taken.

Someone always had to be on watch in case of a real emergency. Then you had to remember your codes – each one posted on notice boards 'so that all may know it and understand it' – and know which one to use, depending on the numbers of attackers and their success:

For penetration of defences by 1–10 men:
by day-light – one wood-pile and two flags raised; by night – two torches to be lit.
500 enemy sighted:
one wood-pile, three flags, or three torches.

But:

If the enemy occupy the outer defences of a post and it is not possible to light the stacked wood-pile, by day one flag and a smoke signal should be raised over the post, and by night a signal should be made with a torch, and the next post in line shall light the stacked wood-piles, in accordance with the prearranged codes.

How many times must Xu have tested himself on these rules? (When must I use a wood-pile and two flags, when one flag and a smoke signal?) Did the Xiongnu ever attack, and if so did he get it right? Did he and his family ever return to central China? Perhaps buried somewhere in the sands of Edsen Gol there is a strip of bamboo that will tell of his fate.

* * *

It was the loss of the Western Regions that undermined the Xiongnu. From the settled oasis communities they had derived grain, iron weapons, taxes and manpower. When former vassals turned against them, from about 71 BC, the once great empire went into slow but steady decline. When the empire was at its height, the shanyu had delegated authority to subsidiary kingdoms, whose rulers now worked at making themselves independent. At the centre, successions were disputed, purges frequent, reigns short. In 57 BC the empire split into five rival groups, which settled into two contending factions, led by two rival brothers. The northern brother, Zhi-zhi, defeated the southern one, Huhanye, who in 53 BC surrendered to the Han.

It was a bitter pill to swallow, but, as one of Huhanye's senior advisers put it, 'There is no way for us to restore our fallen fortune. In spite of all our exertions, we have experienced hardly a single day of tranquillity. At present our very security depends on whether we submit to the Han or not. What better course is there for us to follow?' So they did, accepting the usual humiliating terms: homage paid, hostages sent, tribute given, protection accepted. The Han sealed the bond with lavish gifts of grain and cash. In 44/43 BC shanyu and emperor signed a peace treaty, promising mutual aid in the event of attacks, in accordance with which, in 36 BC, the Han emperor helped in the defeat of the northern Xiongnu's leader, Zhi-zhi. In gratitude, Huhanye asked to become the emperor's 'relative' and received not a princess, but a concubine named Zhaojun, who would become famous both as a beauty and as a political key to peace between the southern Xiongnu and Han China. These two events – the defeat of Zhi-zhi and the journey made by Zhaojun – had consequences which I will tell you about in their own chapters.

It was not all peace and friendship, for when the Han collapsed for two decades (AD 6–25) the southern Xiongnu seized back their independence. But in AD 48 the southern Xiongnu resubmitted, this time for good, with all the usual terms: from the shanyu, a son as hostage in the Han court; from the Han emperor, gifts galore – 10,000 pounds of silk, 36,000 cattle, cash (amounting in AD 91 alone to 100 million coins). These Xiongnu shifted further south, mingled with Han colonists and so became part of expanding China, in today's Inner Mongolia and its neighbouring provinces. But they were not totally integrated, because they objected to forced labour and conscription, and often revolted. After the Han dynasty ended in 220 and China collapsed into a muddle of mini-states (third to fifth centuries), one of them was founded by a Xiongnu, the first of several alien regimes.

Were these not the very 'barbarians' the Wall was supposed to keep out? To non-Chinese, yes indeed. But, in Chinese eyes today, no, because these particular barbarians have been magically transformed by living the right side of the Wall. They had become a 'minority': barbarians no longer, but part of the great family of China.

What, meanwhile, of the Xiongnu left north of the Wall? Well aware they were isolated, they tried to come to an accommodation with their powerful southern neighbour, sending tribute and envoys – but to no effect. The Han were willing to talk only about trading points, not diplomatic recognition. Ignored by the Han court, the

Xiongnu reopened the Great Game in the Western Regions, levering several small states back into their fold, threatening to regain control of the Silk Road cities. Once again, the Han had no choice: they had either to retake the Western Regions or to fall back.

Several campaigns into Mongolia, backed by some intense diplomacy in the Western Regions, regained old allies and annihilated the northern Xiongnu. Thousands, mainly Xiongnu vassals, fled to safety south of the Wall – some 200,000 civilians and 8,000 troops in AD 87 alone. Isolated, his supporters ever fewer, defeated in battle, abandoned by allies, assaulted by neighbours, the northern shanyu, as a Chinese source says, 'was not able to hold his position any longer and therefore fled to far-away places'.[1] A new set of barbarians, the Xianbi, took over their lands, and the northern Xiongnu vanished from history into the depths of Central Asia. They were last heard of in the mid-second century. From then on, silence.

Or possibly not. For two hundred years later there emerged from the great sweep of grassland that flows across Central Asia a tribe with a strangely similar lifestyle – tent-dwellers with wagons, supreme mounted archers – and a strangely similar name: the Huns, who, a century later still, would be a major force in the collapse of the Roman empire. Some who like their history simple say that the Huns bounced off the Great Wall and ricocheted westward. Chinese historians make no distinction between the two, and both are 'Hun-nu' in Mongolian. Well, there is some evidence to link the

---

[1] Sima Biao, *Hou Hanshu* (late third century).

names;[2] but no evidence (yet) to show that the Xiongnu and the Huns were actually the same tribe. No one recorded Xiongnu language; no one recorded Hunnish, or Hun mythology. It will take some DNA analysis, I think, to tell whether Attila's genes owed anything to Modu, 500 years before him.

If you had to make a list of images that symbolize China, the chances are that the Flying Horse of Gansu would be near the top. It could also be seen as a symbol of the Great Wall, to which it owes its inspiration, disappearance and rediscovery.

Caught in mid-gallop, with three legs off the ground, the little (9-inch) bronze statue balances neatly on the hoof of the fourth leg, head and tail held high. Why 'flying'? Because the fourth hoof is on a swallow, harbinger of spring, bringer of happiness and good fortune. Speed, balance, beauty, nobility: it has all the qualities associated with the best of horses, the 'celestial', 'blood-sweating' horses that became famous as a result of Zhang Qian's westward journey into their homeland, the Ferghana valley. The making, the burial and the rediscovery of the horse were all a direct result of Emperor Wu's decision to extend the Wall westward; for the Han general with whom it was buried around AD 200 was the commander of today's Wuwei, the HQ for this sector of the Wall and guardian of the Gansu Corridor, from which the Xiongnu had been evicted over 300 years before.

[2] Etienne de la Vaissière in Susan Whitfield (ed.), *The Silk Road*, Serindia, Chicago, 2004.

Usually, all you are told is that the horse was found when the tomb was opened, along with a collection of other bronzes, and that it then became the symbol of China. But there's a lot more to the story, which came out, slowly, in a series of onion-skin revelations by the tomb's official guide and my own, Michael. Actually, there are three stories, each with its own mystery. Working backwards in time, these are The Discovery, The Robbery and The Burial.

The story of The Discovery starts in the autumn of 1969, when everyone was being urged to dig air-raid shelters in preparation for war with Russia (once friends, China and Russia had become bitter opponents; troops massed along the borders; war was very much on the cards). Out on the edge of Wuwei, a bunch of about fifteen locals decided to dig into a mound on which a monastery stands. Named Thunder Terrace, it is a fine fifteenth-century collection of temples, courtyards and gateways. Students used to come here to take their examinations, and it exudes Confucian peace. You can contemplate in the shade of a 1,000-year-old locust tree. You can pay homage to a seventeen-eyed Thunder God and his companions, Fortune, Money and Long Life. You can learn your future from a Daoist (Taoist) fortune-teller, a middle-aged man with a straggly black beard. He has a cup of bevelled wooden slips with writing on them. If you pay a small sum, as I did, he shakes the cup, and the motion shuffles one of the slips clear of the others.

'What kind of fortune do you ask for?'

'I ask a blessing on my work.'

'Hm.' He studied the text. 'It is not going smoothly. Maybe you will meet some problems. But in winter your fortune will turn.'

(Is that how it turned out? The research seemed to be going pretty well. I remember money problems that autumn. They were sorted out by January. So I guess that's 2–1 to the fortune-teller.)

Underneath the monastery is the mound, 6 metres high, just the right size for an air-raid shelter. So the team of locals began to dig. A metre or two in, they hit brickwork; making a hole, they found themselves in a brick-lined chamber, very beautifully made, square at the base and rising to a round, domed roof. An arched doorway hardly more than a metre high led to a passageway blocked with sand; but in the dome itself stood the Flying Horse, together with dozens of other bronze figurines of men, horses and chariots. The un-witting archaeologists put their finds in plastic bags and took them home. But these were clearly important discoveries in an important tomb, so it was agreed that the authorities be told. Proper archaeologists came, retrieved the Flying Horse and its attendant delegation, and started work.

The sand went, the tomb was revealed. Architecturally, it is a masterpiece of dry-stone walling, with a vaulted passageway leading from the outside down to three rooms and another three smaller side-chambers, all of them square at the base, rounding themselves as they rise to form self-supporting domes, locked with keystones engraved with a lotus flower. The burial chamber lies at the end. In one wall, darker bricks form two signs, *xī xī* / 喜喜 , happiness twice over: a symbol of marriage, presumably for the couple buried there.

And here we enter upon the second story, The Robbery. There were no bodies in the tomb, only a few pieces of bone and bits of coffin, along with some kitchenware, some pottery, a few coins – and a hole in one of the chamber walls. The place had been burgled. The crime must have been committed soon after the burial, because the robbers knew where and how to enter. Those digging the air-raid shelter almost 2,000 years later were lucky. Break open any one of the chambers in the wrong place and the whole thing will collapse. So suspicion falls on someone closely involved with the tomb's creation – the chief architect himself, perhaps – returning after several years when the bodies had decayed and people had begun to forget about the place. Whoever the burglars were, they were not family, because they missed the real treasures, the Flying Horse and its associated figurines, standing in another chamber. But why, when removing most of the funeral goods, did they also remove the bodies? Why did they make such a mess of it? Why did they not return to finish the job?

One consequence of the grave-robbery is that the third part of the story, The Burial, remains shrouded in mystery, the man who was interred here almost unknown. Records and the remaining relics suggest his family name was Zheng, and that he was the general in charge of this section of the Wall frontier around AD 200. He would have chosen the spot himself, and the tomb's design, and the objects that would accompany him into the afterlife – including his favourite piece, his own Celestial Horse, a top person's symbol of power, authority and taste. He may also have designed the mound to cover the tomb, and the planting of trees on the top, the great-parents perhaps of the gnarled old locust tree that stands there today in the middle of the temple courtyard.

We are left with the main items of evidence, the Flying Horse and other pieces – and even they have another story attached. They were all taken to the museum in Lanzhou, where they were stored away in obscurity. Then, in the early 1970s, the polymath Guo Moruo (poet, historian, translator, novelist, playwright and archaeologist . . .) was accompanying Prince Sihanouk of Cambodia on a trip through Gansu. They toured the museum, and afterwards Guo Moruo asked to see the storeroom. The moment he spotted the Flying Horse, he recognized it as a work of genius. From then on, it was assured of fame, and China had a new symbol.

6

WALL-HUNT IN THE GOBI

THE GREAT WALL OF CHINA IS NOT ALWAYS GREAT, NOT A single wall, and not all in China. Some of it is in Mongolia. That, at any rate, was what I guessed from my English maps, for in Mongolia there are two objects – one down south in the Gobi, the other in the north-eastern grasslands – both marked with battlemented wall-symbols, both called 'Wall of Genghis Khan'. Mongolian maps, on the other hand, call them Genghis's 'embank-ments' or 'ridges' (*dalan*). I knew they could not be anything to do with him, because Genghis did not build any walls or ridges. Were they remnants of much more ancient structures?

I arrived in late September under a blazing sun, planning to visit both walls (ridges, whatever) with an old friend, Goyo, who is uniquely qualified for such trips.

Born and bred in the countryside, she has a remarkable tolerance for rough conditions; this she combines with an unwavering ambition that shot her from her Gobi home to Guildford, England, with a scholarship to study tourism. Before the first trip, south into the Gobi, the night was spent at her sister's place, a socialist-era apartment amid dingy concrete blocks and potholed roads on the way to the airport. There was no furniture, except mattresses and a couple of chairs. Ulaanbaatar is upgrading fast, but there's a long way to go. I was on the kitchen floor.

We woke early, to find that Mongolia had apparently leaped from midsummer to midwinter overnight. A taxi took us through snow flurries to the airport, with its usual mix of the odd and interesting: two Texans in Stetsons off to hunt ibex in the south Gobi; three Canadians investing millions in a copper-mine that would transform a wilderness into a treasure trove; a Chinese passenger, the sight of whom set Goyo railing against the Chinese in general, which is something of a national pastime in Mongolia. They spit, they buy up property, they 'dig holes' – I think she was referring to mining operations – there are 300,000 of them, they're like a plague. Two impossibly good-looking Russians, Maxim and Irina, were looking for spiritual insights. I would surely be aware that Genghis Khan had known how to tap into the power of the Heartland, the source of Eurasian spiritual power? They wanted to feel it for themselves, and the Gobi was the place.

On the way south, the landscape below could have been Antarctica. If it was like this all the way, we wouldn't be going anywhere. But then, after an hour, it turned out that these extremes gripped only the central part of the country. Down south, the barren expanses were not white but brown and ash-grey, with the occasional squiggle of a car-track. The whole world had turned into a runway, on some part of which we landed, beside a single building, many miles outside the nearest town, Dalandzadgad.

Mongolia is vast, its population tiny, with the result that the country seems to run on the energy created by co-incidental meetings. Coming into Dalandzadgad's airport building was like entering a club. Goyo's brother was there – she didn't know he was anywhere around – and so was a guide she knew. The board of the Mongolian Arts Council was awaiting a return flight. One member had been running George Soros's operation; another was Oyun, whose brother had been Mongolia's leading democrat, the charismatic young Zorig, stabbed to death in still unexplained circumstances in 1998. She had assumed his mantle, and ran the small but influential Citizens' Will party. This has nothing to do with the Wall, but she's very charismatic herself, so I like to mention her whenever I get the chance. I talked with a *New York Times* correspondent, and a geologist, and a bunch of Alaskan national guardsmen – Alaska having apparently adopted Mongolia to strengthen the Coalition of the Willing by doing good works. There was even someone I used to know in publishing 20 years ago.

Meanwhile Goyo had vanished from the hectic social round to look for a car and driver from among the dozen or so waiting for customers outside. She reappeared with a disreputable, weasely looking character called Shagai

(Anklebone, which sounds an odd name, but is not, given that Mongolians use anklebones as dice). He wore a decaying baseball cap and camouflage trousers. I distrusted him at first glance, but he had a Russian UAZ Jeep, which is the mechanical equivalent of a camel, so I said nothing, and we set off into the wilderness in search of the Wall of Genghis Khan.

This was the start of a roller-coaster two days, which were about to reveal how uncertain everything is when you go off into wildernesses in total ignorance – my own, of course, but also in this case everyone else's as well. Every apparent step forwards turned to be a step sideways or backwards. In these circumstances, one should bear in mind William Goldman's capitalized words when speaking of film scripts:

NO ONE KNOWS ANYTHING.

After a breakfast of rice and dumplings, Shagai headed south under a brilliant sky. The heat made mirages shimmer like mist over the plain, reflecting the stark black Three Beauties range, over to our right. There was, of course, no road, only many tracks over the waste. Not *total* waste, I should say: there was the occasional blade of grass, enough for camels, and enough to dust the distant gravel with a pastel shade of green.

A couple of hours later we breasted some ash-grey hills, where shards of dark rock glinted like jewels, and ran down into the little town of Nomgon to ask the way. The only sign of life among the random scattering of houses and round felt tents was some slow work being done restoring a Buddhist monastery. It had been destroyed in 1937, when Stalin's up-and-coming stooge Choibalsan began a purge of monasteries and lamas which, over the next two years, involved the destruction of some 5,000 monasteries and the execution of 20,000 lamas. The half-dozen workers were making their own bricks, and doing a nice job of recreating the Tibetan-style architecture.

'When will you finish?' I asked.

'In two years. We will mark the seventieth anniversary of the destruction.'

No one knew anything of any wall.

Onward, then, along a dry river-bed, and upward through a gorge on to a plateau, then down towards a plain. But then, as we came clear of the hills, suddenly under a crag was a most surprising sight: a spring-fed lake, with children splashing about; water running off down a gentle slope; people working in a field of vegetables – corn, potatoes, cabbages, cucumbers, sun-flowers, onions, watermelons and wonderful tomatoes. All around was almost barren, but the vegetable garden was a reminder that the Gobi is sterile only because there is no water on the surface. There is quite a bit underneath, and where it rises, usually at the base of hills, the desert blooms. Pastoral nomadism is the Mongol way, but it is an option, not a necessity. These families, in their six round felt *gers*, were doing very nicely.

Did they know anything about Genghis's wall?

'Genghis's Ridge?'

No, his *wall*. Or so the map said.

There were doubtful silences. Did we mean his road, perhaps? Or the Yellow Road, the one that led northwards long ago? I was more uncertain than ever. We bought bag-loads of tomatoes and cucumbers, and tried again. One thing for sure, because it was marked on the map: whatever it was we wanted, it lay to the south. Ah, in that case, people ahead would know where to find it. In the hills a few hours away, beyond a grim area of sand and tough little saxaul bushes, there was a Brigade, a sort of local government HQ, which should have a few families and a primary school. We couldn't miss it.

The sand-and-saxaul area turned out to be a sub-wilderness of its own, the Borzongin Gov, the Brown Brick Gobi – an odd name for which we found an explanation later. It was all mini-dunes and gnarled little bushes through which we wove and bumped, sending the occasional family of gazelles bouncing away, white rumps flashing in the setting sun. According to my map – hardly reliable since there was not much to record – we should by this stage have stumbled across whatever it was we were looking for, but now we were out of the sand-and-saxauls and racing over hard gravel towards – was that a wall ahead? It was getting hard to see in the evening light. No, they were hills, dark as coal tips. We followed a track, and came to buildings, three of them. Two were in ruins, one was a barn beside a cattle corral. There was a great deal of dung from sheep and goats. A child's shoe lay beside the track. The place was totally deserted. Everyone was still in summer quarters. There hadn't been anyone here for weeks.

And the sun was already touching the western hills.

What to do? I felt a twinge of apprehension. As I write this, I feel it again, and the memory becomes immediate.

We don't have a GPS, so we can't find out where we are. Mobile phones don't work this far from anywhere. Still, on the plus side, we are in Shagai's hands, and very good hands they have turned out to be. So much for my gut reactions; Goyo had chosen well. Like other good countryside drivers, he handles his Jeep as if he were a horseman, with utter confidence. He has also turned out to be good-humoured, interested in our venture, and witty. He knows these parts – even if not this part exactly – and neither he nor Goyo seems too worried. So I should not be either . . . should I?

Shagai heads east, along the track, in the hope it might lead somewhere, because it has been used quite recently. We weave around and up and down for several minutes; then, to get a view, turn towards a hill. The track leads up past another cattle corral, on the side of which stands a little brick house with a blue door. Beyond it, Shagai parks, pulls out some binoculars, looks around, then hands them to me. We are in a desolation of ravines, rocks and low hills. I check out the house. Locked tight, ready for next season. No people, no animals, no water. Who used the track and why? There is no telling.

We retrace our steps, until we can see back the way we came. Twenty kilometres of sand, saxauls and gathering gloom. Shagai checks out the far distant hills (they are called the Rugged Mountains, I learn later). He mutters something to Goyo.

'There was a flash,' said Goyo. 'It might have been a windscreen catching the setting sun. Or a tent.'

I am sceptical. I don't believe there's a single person as far as we can see in any direction. Thank

God it's a clear evening: high clouds, with a half-moon.

There's nothing else to do but head back across the Borzongin Gov in the hope of finding a family in the Rugged Mountains, or, if the worst comes to the worst, rediscovering the vegetable garden. Shagai's still relaxed. He has faith in his car, and it has two petrol tanks, 85 litres in all, enough to get us to Dalandzadgad, assuming nothing goes wrong. I remind myself this is a typically Mongolian experience. Things can't go *that* wrong. So we have to spend the night in the desert. So what?

Ahead, there is something. A shadow, a long, dark line – which must be ignored, because a sleek fox breaks cover, and Shagai's hunting instincts come to the fore. He chases it, finding hard sand between saxaul bushes, the car shuddering and rattling, until the fox jinks sideways and vanishes. Now the dark line is closer, looking more solid in the moonlight.

'Are you thinking what I'm thinking, Goyo?'

'Might be . . . yes, it looks like a wall.'

Looks like, certainly – a few metres high, solid, long. We pull up beside it. But no, it's natural: a low cliff of rock, at its base boulders which, with a little imagination, turn into guardian animals – a tortoise here, a lion there. I climb on to it. It's enormous, a huge flat surface of rock, with a scattering of boulders, their skins flaking away through millennia of frost and dusty winds. Artificial it certainly isn't, though what it is has me baffled.

I join the other two at the base. There's something else nearby, and this is artificial. It's a tower of some kind, round, half fallen.

'What do you think, Shagai?'

'I think we stay here tonight, and see in the morning.'

We discussed our experiences over tomatoes and cucumbers bought from the plantation. There's a wall marked on the map, but the locals don't seem to know about it. How can that be? Did the mapmakers somehow mistake this rock wall for some sort of Great Wall? If so, you would think the locals would comment on it. But all they mentioned was a Yellow Road.

We give up, and speak of something else that is on my mind.

'Do people die out here?'

Goyo laughs. 'Only in winter.'

'But we could get bogged down if it rains.'

'Well, we would walk. In thirty kilometres, we would meet someone.'

We haul sleeping bags from our packs and cram ourselves into seats to sleep. They're lucky, those two, being Mongolian and a good deal smaller than me. I twist and turn, but can't straighten my legs. Come one-thirty, I admit defeat, reset my sleeping bag on sand in the lee of the escarpment, stretch out in it, and stare up at the moonlit sky.

What an odd series of coincidences brought us here. A good car, a good driver, a good guide. The vegetable garden, which gave us enough fresh food for two days, just in case we get stuck. The advice to find locals, with whom, if we had found any, we would have spent the night. Then the crazy decision to cross the sand-and-saxaul waste to find a family that almost certainly does not exist. All of which led us to this glorious, puzzling place.

Should I worry that if anything happens we will die of

hunger, thirst and heatstroke? No, that's just melodrama. With good weather above, comfortable sand below, and no rain or snow pending, I really can't summon up any anxiety. Tenger, Blue Heaven, the Mongolian sky-god, is on our side.

I woke to sun, with a single cloud moving away from us on the horizon. After a breakfast of more tomatoes and cucumbers, we explored. The rock escarpment, standing 3 or 4 metres above the desert, turned out to be a plateau in the form of a rough circle, about 200–250 metres across, flat, and covered with hard sand and loose boulders. I guessed it was the stub of an ancient volcano. It seemed as desolate as the moon, until Shagai stopped by a rock that been broken down over – what? A hundred thousand years? A million? – into the shape of a tortoise-shell, forming a little cave underneath. He pointed to droppings.

'*Chono* [wolf],' he said. 'New.'

Then there was the tower, which daylight revealed to be something else. It was roughly circular, with thick walls centred on a round area carefully built of smooth-sided stones. Low down on one side there was an arch, filled in with sand. Shagai dug it clear with his hands. It was an air-hole, had to be, and this was a broken-down kiln.

Little bits of broken pottery scattered in the sand confirmed the idea. It had collapsed sideways, spilling its stones into a heap. While the stones that lined the oven were dressed smooth on one side, the others had been left as they were found, random lumps. I circled, counting paces, trying to get an idea of the structure's original shape. Originally, it must have been a dome. There was no sign of cement. Whoever made the kiln knew their business. To make a dome without cement you would need to pile up earth in a neat mound as a support, build the dome over it, drop a keystone in place to make it self-supporting, then remove the earth. The designer also had to plan for the air-vent, and another hole through which to place the pots for firing and remove them afterwards. And what had they used for fuel? Dung, perhaps, and the wood from the saxauls through which we had driven the previous night? Whatever the problems, the products were top-class. The pots were fine-grained, well-shaped, with a brown glaze and good solid bases. I have some pieces still, one of which was part of a perfectly round container 115 mm across, the size of a large cup.

The implications of this find were astonishing. Once upon a time, this place must have been the centre of much activity, with many people working here for some time. Making pots for whom, out in the middle of the Gobi, several hundred kilometres from the nearest town of any significance? And when?

I was right not to worry. Shagai suggested we go west until we came across the tracks we made yesterday, and then head north, back to the vegetable garden. That was exactly what happened. Sand, escarpments, dunes and saxauls fell away behind us, and there were our tracks, passing a hill with two vultures perched on its crest.

'They're sorry to see us go,' I said. 'There goes their lunch.'

'They will be all right,' said Shagai. 'They can kill fully grown gazelles. They hit them with their wings.'

There were other tracks, too; a regular footpath.

'Cows,' explained Goyo. 'They know where to go. You just follow in their footsteps and you find water. You see how safe it is down here.'

In this case, the water was back at the vegetable garden, along with our sources of puzzling information. Things became clearer. There were two roads, the Yellow Road and the Wall Road. First we would check out the Yellow Road, together with a carload of volunteers: a man named Bat, his sister and her daughter. Bat directed us on to a huge expanse of gravel, the sort of landscape Roy Chapman Andrews, the American explorer whose 1920s expeditions found tons of dinosaurs not far from here, called 'a 100-mile tennis court'. We stopped, got out, and stood around.

'This is the road,' he said.

I could detect precisely nothing except gravel. Then, as my eyes adapted, I saw that I was standing in a slight depression, no more than a few centimetres deep, 2–3 metres across. Beneath my feet there seemed to be nothing to mark it out. But there was – if you looked *along* it, to the horizon – the faintest hint of yellow, created by tiny organisms like minute clover, so small they were more like lichen than plants.

'This is a *road*?'

'Oh, yes. Camels made this, coming from China.'

That had to be right. I was standing in something created by the slow pad of a million camels, whose urine and droppings over many years had created their own very extended micro-ecology.

'It goes right across the Borzongin' – where we had been the previous night – 'and over the border into China.'

'And there is no wall around here?'

There was not. The wall was south. Back at the garden was someone who could show us: Gergee, a wrinkled, sunburned 73-year-old with the zest of a man half his age. He wore a newly laundered blue-and-white checked shirt and a smart white sun-hat. He knew exactly where it was, and became a fund of information and dis-information, intermixed. It was definitely a 'wall-road', whatever that was. You could drive along it. But it was also a wall. It came from Beijing, and it was built by a Chinese king who didn't want to see his wife when he was travelling, so he built it to hide her, she presumably travelling on the far side. No, it wasn't much used nowa-days. It ran parallel to the border, east–west, and people only travelled due south. What people? We hadn't seen any. Oh, border guards who went back and forth to a crossing point which opened for traders every once in a while. That much at least rang true. It solved the mystery of the recently used track.

Shagai drove over virgin wasteland, with Gergee point-ing the way to something he wished to show us: low, eroded walls, looking like the humps of half-buried camels. These were the remains of another monastery, also destroyed in 1937. There would be no restoration here. All the roof tiles had vanished, some long ago, the remainder to be used for the rebuilding of the other local monastery in Nomgon. Once, the monks had made their own brick here – and that solved another mystery, the name of this part of the desert, Brown Brick Gobi.

Not far beyond, surrounded by nothing but flat, grey, sandy gravel, was a *ger*, with a herd of horses and a motorbike standing nearby. A blue door stood open. We entered, unannounced and without knocking, as one does. Inside was your typical *ger* interior: old woman asleep on the floor, wood stove burning in the middle, kitchen gear and food hung up on the wall-slatting, including a bloated sheep's intestine, neatly tied off at both ends. 'It's for cream,' Goyo explained. 'If you keep it like that, it doesn't go bad.'

Our host, Bayas, offered a silver bowl of distilled sheep's milk. Milk brandy is the closest thing to nectar I have ever tasted, soft and delicate, without the astringency of vodka. But you have to be careful, because it creeps up on you stealthily. 'Don't be drunk,' said Bayas, as I handed the bowl back, left hand to right elbow, in the proper fashion.

He had the most endearing face, long and lugubrious, with a fine nose and a glittering silver tooth. He used to be a ranger, looking after the environment, because theoretically, as he said and I confirmed with the map, we were in a national park, the Little Gobi Reserve – not that there was any sign of it. He knew the place even better than Gergee, and was happy to lead us to Genghis's Wall. Yes, *wall* (*kherem*), not 'ridge' or 'road', was the word he used. Concentrating on that, fighting the effects of the sheep's-milk brandy, I entirely forgot to ask about the kiln.

With Bayas ahead on his motorbike and pop songs blaring from the car radio, we sped across gravel for a quarter of an hour, an interval in which to ponder the odd way things develop. The 'wall' had changed its nature several times, from wall to ridge to barrier to road and back to wall. A wilderness with little charm and not without danger had become a friendly place in the company of those who look on it as I look on Hampstead Heath.

We stopped on a little rise of fine grey gravel, exactly the same colour and consistency as the surrounding desert. This, to my consternation, was it – the road, the wall: a metre-high bump, though a long one, if I was to believe Bayas. He said it ran from Hohhot, the capital of Inner Mongolia, to Hovd in western Mongolia, a distance of almost 2,000 kilometres. Two things made me pause. The first was that the wall (road, barrier, ridge, whatever) does not point north-west; it curves around until it is heading south-west. Second, Bayas said it dated from Ogedei's time (thirteenth century), which was 300 years before Hohhot was founded in 1575. It struck me that what I was dealing with here was folklore, not fact.

But he was surely right when he said, 'This was never a barrier. Mongolia's soldiers conquered the world on horseback. This would have been nothing to them.'

It looked more like a road to me, 4 metres across and convex, like a Roman highway. I had seen a part of the Great Wall that was a thousand years older – a bulky, rain-rounded ridge north of Guyuan – and there was more to it than this almost invisible bump.

Now we were driving east along the top. The going was good, except in the few places where a torrent from the unnamed hills on our right had washed it away. It hugged a low contour, snaking along the foot of the hills, right towards where we had been only the day before. Good grief, I thought, we must have crossed this non-wall twice, and never even noticed it.

Indeed we had. At one point the car dropped into a

gully, and there, running at right angles along the bottom, were our own tracks. We had come full circle. No wonder we'd missed it. Where we had crossed there was no hump at all, nothing to indicate that the little dip was a cut through the wall, the ridge, the barrier, the road.

What to make of this? Despite the look of it, a road doesn't make sense. Roads lead somewhere, and this one didn't. It is possible that with the foundation of Hohhot in 1575 its denizens could have needed a road to western Mongolia. But why not due north, to the heart of Mongolia? This one ran in entirely the wrong direction. And why build a road at all, when you can go over the desert, as the Yellow Road camels had done for centuries? It would have been an immense, unnecessary expenditure.

If it is not a wall and not a road, what is it?

There's a hint of an answer right at the end of the Mongolian epic about Genghis, *The Secret History*, in a section concerning Genghis's heir, his third son Ogedei. When dying of alcoholism in 1241, Ogedei ticks off the rights and wrongs of his reign. He lists four good deeds and four bad ones. The first of the latter is that 'I was at fault to let myself be vanquished by wine', but his fourth fault is the one we are after: the building of walls. 'Being greedy,' he confesses, 'and saying to myself, "What if the wild animals born with their destiny ordained by Heaven and Earth [i.e. to be hunted] go over to the territory of my brothers?", I had fences and walls built of pounded earth to prevent the animals from straying.' In other words, he wasted huge sums on keeping animals in his home domains so that he could indulge in vast hunts. So might the mound in the Gobi be the remains of his fences and walls? I don't think so. It's far too long, too far south, and across a region far too barren to support much game.

Here's another suggestion. As we know from the commitments made by the First Emperor (of Qin) and Emperor Wu of Han, emperors paid to demarcate borders as well as defend them. Is it coincidence that this non-wall seems to spring in the west from, or almost from, the most northerly prong of the Han Great Wall, the section that ran due north along the Edsen Gol, deep into the Gobi, just 10–15 kilometres from the borders of present-day Mongolia? Coincidence that its eastern end points towards – maybe once reached – the Qin Great Wall north of Baotou, the stone one that Jorigt and I had visited, like-wise was not defensive? Could it be that the Gobi ridge wall is part of the northern border wall as defined by the Han about AD 150, after the Xiongnu had gone, when there was no point in building defences?

I don't know, and nor will anybody else until someone does some research. Just about the only certainty is what we started with: a Wall of Genghis Khan it isn't. Only when on- or under-the-ground evidence is made to fit with history and all the other walls that wander through Inner Mongolia will it be possible to explain this baffling and intriguing – whatever-it-is.

7

THE CONCUBINE AND THE BARBARIAN

IN INNER MONGOLIA'S CAPITAL, HOHHOT, MY HOTEL, WHICH would not have been out of place in central London, or Paris, or New York, had a vast and intriguing bas-relief behind the check-in desk: a woman wrapped in a large fur-lined cloak playing some sort of a lute. She was obviously important, because she was surrounded by dancing girls, soldiers and horsemen. When I asked about her, I was told the hotel was named after her, and that she was indeed important: she had brought peace to China by journeying beyond the Great Wall and marrying a northern barbarian. This is her story.

Defending Han China from the barbarians was expensive, and not only in men and materials expended on the Wall. It was expensive in princesses and concubines. Part of the 'peace and friendship' policy by which the Xiongnu were bribed to stay away involved the occasional delivery of high-status girls to placate the savages who lived north of the Wall. The girls were, of course, just one facet of a many-sided policy, but the handing over of a princess was an act of peculiar significance, not just for the poor girl, but for the court and for the Chinese people. The princesses may actually have had perfectly good lives in the shanyu's court, but that was not how their fate was viewed back home. To ordinary Chinese, who knew nothing of nomad ways, it was a fate worse than death. To send anyone, let alone a princess, across the Great Wall into the hands of the barbarians was the equivalent of sacrificing a virgin to a dragon in European folk tales – except this was for real. Later, a poem was placed in the mouth of the princess Xijun, despatched to the wild Western Regions from the effete comforts of Changan in 105 BC. It recalls the feelings of those she left behind, transposed to her:

> My family married me to a lost horizon,
> Sent me far away to the Wusun king's strange land.
> A domed lodging is my dwelling, of felt is its walls,
> Flesh for food, mare's milk for drink.
> Longing ever for my homeland, my heart is full of sorrow,
> I wish I were a brown goose flying home.

The practice had such emotional clout that it demanded mythic expression, which it found in the story of one particular girl, who was not, as it happened, a princess. Somehow, that only added to the pathos. As often in

Chinese history, the few bare facts were then overtaken by multi-layered fiction. She acquired attributes, passions and relationships that turned her first into a heroine and then into a goddess, celebrated in plays, poems, memorials, a film, an opera and, of course, at least one plush hotel.

Her name was Zhaojun, and her real-life story begins in 33 BC, when the southern Xiongnu and Han Dynasty China were at peace. To recap: two decades earlier, the Xiongnu had split. Two brothers, Zhi-zhi and Huhanye, vied for the throne. Huhanye swallowed his pride and turned to the Han for help. In 51 BC he came to Changan (as the Han called today's Xian) to pay homage, an act for which the Han emperor, Yuan, paid heavily: 12 kilos of gold, 200,000 coins, 77 suits of clothes, 3,600 kilos of silk, almost a million kilos of grain. In 44 or 43 BC, the two strengthened their relationship by signing a pact of non-aggression and mutual assistance, as a result of which, some eight years later, a Chinese army besieged Zhi-zhi's capital and killed him (on which more in the next chapter). In 33 BC the grateful Huhanye came on another state visit, saying that he wished to 'become the Emperor's relative'. He was hoping for a princess; what he got was something rather less – a lady-in-waiting, Zhaojun.

Off she went to Huhanye's court near Karakorum. The emperor died shortly afterwards, as did her new husband. Following Xiongnu tradition, she married his heir, her stepson, by whom she had two daughters. She then vanished from the historical record, though the elder daughter did return to China as a companion for the (female) Han regent.

Her transformation began about two centuries later, and has never stopped. Version followed version, building incident and character to serve one agenda after another, until now scholars list some 250 books, 780 poems and several plays about her.

Here's how the story went in its earliest form:

At seventeen, Zhaojun[1] is already a celebrated beauty, so beautiful that her father refuses all offers of marriage and presents her to the emperor. But her father has no influence at court, and she is one among many. She is put in the Palace of the Concubines, and there she lives for several years, until depression sets in and she ceases to care for herself. No wonder, then, that she is never noticed. When the Xiongnu king comes, there is to be a great spectacle of dancers, musicians and singers. Zhaojun seizes her chance, and appears at her best, wonderfully dressed, her face and figure radiating beauty. When the emperor asks the shanyu if there is anything he would like in particular, the shanyu replies, 'I have treasures enough, but the Xiongnu women cannot compare with the Chinese. Grant me one of your beauties.' At this the emperor asks for a concubine to step forward and offer herself voluntarily. Zhaojun advances and speaks: 'Your humble servant has had the good fortune to find herself in the Palace of Concubines. Alas, alone among them, she was too ordinary to be of interest to Your Majesty. I therefore wish to offer myself to the shanyu.'

---

[1] As often, our heroine had many names. Originally, she was Wang Qiang. Her 'style' or 'courtesy' name was Wang Zhaojun, Zhaojun for short. At court she became Mingfei (Shining Consort).

The emperor is stupefied by her beauty, and filled with regrets, but cannot go back on his word. With a sigh, he lets her go. Her heart, however, stays with China. On her arrival in the wild lands of the north, she remains the image of sadness, and composes mournful songs, lamenting her fate among the swirling sands, the biting winds, enduring an incomprehensible language and fermented milk that ruins her hair. She has exchanged unhappiness for pure misery. In one poem, 'Bitter Nostalgia', she sees herself as a beautiful bird, shut away in a far-off palace, tormented out of her mind, yearning to join the wild geese in their flight south.

> High is the mountain,
> Deep the river!
> Alas, my father! Alas, my mother!
> How long is the road that separates us!
> Oh, how many are the sorrows
> And the cares that afflict my heart!

She has a son, who on the death of her husband succeeds him. She asks him whose traditions she should follow: the Xiongnu's or the Chinese. He says: Do as the Xiongnu do. So she takes poison, and dies.

Already, she has some character. She is no mere victim, but a volunteer, which makes her tragic. She is devoted to her emperor and her country, and she cannot live with her loss. But it is all rather depressing. We could do with a little more drama, which is what was added by the fifth century. Now a new character appears, one of the court painters, the evil Mao Yanshou. Since the emperor can't possibly see all his concubines, and since he wants only the most beautiful as his consorts, it is the job of the artists to paint the portraits of all the girls so that the emperor can choose the most beautiful. Customarily, the girls bribe the painter to upgrade their charms. But Zhaojun has integrity. She refuses to pay. In revenge, Mao paints her ugly. When the shanyu asks for a Chinese girl, the emperor chooses the ugliest – Zhaojun – and discovers his mistake only as she is about to leave. He cannot, of course, go back on his word, and in his fury has all the painters executed.

Even in this version, Zhaojun is still the epitome of passive suffering. Later, therefore, she not only chooses her fate: she does so bravely, for a noble cause. As she says in a letter that she is supposed to have written to the emperor: 'In a thousand years to come, and even ten thousand, it will be remembered that Your Majesty once had a woman who played the role of special envoy in a foreign court beyond the Frontier.' Now she has become the self-elected representative of a superior culture, who, like a missionary, seeks to teach the Xiongnu the ways of civilization, ensuring decades of peace. (Not really. It was peace at the expense of Han dignity, shattered by the wars that led to the final destruction of the Xiongnu in the second century AD.)

Some time in the first millennium she acquires another talent, and an attribute: she becomes a singer, who plays brilliantly and sadly on a pipa, a Chinese lute. The pipa, the instrument of court musicians, had special significance, as the third-century poet Fu Xuan recorded: 'The pipa appeared in the late Qin period. When the people suffered from being forced to build the Great Wall, they played the instrument to express their resentment.'

The final element in the evolving story was the addition of a love interest. The emperor hears Zhaojun playing her pipa. He falls in love with her. It is he who confers upon her the name Mingfei (Shining Consort). The evil Mao defects to the Xiongnu, and persuades the shanyu to demand Zhaojun's hand. The emperor is weak, and must comply. The lovers part, in tears. The Xiongnu withdraw. Zhaojun, the saviour of the nation she has lost for ever, casts herself into the Yellow River.

It is in this form that the story reached maturity, in a drama by the fourteenth-century playwright Ma Zhiyuan entitled *Autumn in the Han Palace*. Ma wrote with his own agenda, which could not be the established one of how Zhaojun civilized the Xiongnu, because China had recently been invaded and occupied by the Mongols. Weakness had led to unprecedented disaster: for the first time, the whole nation was under foreign rule. Beautiful women like Zhaojun get taken over by the barbarians, and China loses her very soul. This was tragedy, pure and simple.

So she entered the world of myth. After the Mongols fell, people reverted to the old theme, saying she had been sent from heaven by the Jade Emperor to make peace between the Chinese and the barbarians. To prove her divinity, people told the story of how, as she journeyed beyond the Great Wall, just as she came to the Yellow River, there was a terrible storm of wind and snow. Calmly she descended from her horse and began to play her pipa. There followed an astonishing transformation.

The blizzard ceased, the sky cleared, and on the plain flowers appeared and the grass turned a wonderful springtime green. All the places through which she travelled became fertile.

She was buried on the steppes, but where exactly no one can say. She has three temples devoted to her, and eight possible burial sites. A village in Hubei (Baoping in Xingshan County) claims to be her birthplace, commemorating her with a temple, courtyard and well. It was said that everywhere beyond the Great Wall the grass withered, except upon her principal tomb, which, in the seventeenth century, settled some 10 kilometres south of Hohhot.

And now that the barbarians – the Xiongnu, the Mongols, whoever – are all part of one big happy family, the agenda is fixed: Zhaojun brought civilization to the wild north. She is very much *persona grata*; hence the opera and the film.[2] The 30-metre hummock is now one of Hohhot's tourist attractions, complete with a pagoda dedicated to the 'friendship between different races and peoples'. A victim of Chinese weakness in the face of alien demands has become a symbol of strength and national unity.

[2] For film and opera buffs, the title of her story is *Zhaojun Chu Sai*, 'Zhaojun Leaves the Stronghold' (*sài* / 塞 being a synonym for the Great Wall).

8

LOSING THE LOST LEGION

IF YOU EVER DRIVE DOWN THE NEW MOTORWAY BETWEEN Zhangye and Wuwei, forget the Wall that you have been following, and turn off to the left about 60 kilometres short of Wuwei. Leave the formidable snowy peaks of the Qilian mountains behind you, and follow the gentle slope down to the town of Yongchang. The approach road ends at a roundabout, in the middle of which is a strange sight: three lumpish concrete statues, the central and obviously Chinese one flanked by two that are equally obviously Roman: a woman and a soldier, the latter with his hand on his armoured chest in a Roman salute.

This is the story of how these two Romans came to be here. It is actually two stories. The first concerns real Romans, and an astonishing suggestion that once upon a time, when the Han were building their Great Wall and reaching out westward, some of them settled in China, not far from Yongchang. The second is the story of the story, of how a historical will-o'-the-wisp arose from nothing, and strengthened, and became an obsession – locally, nationally, internationally. Now, for those who need the story to be true, it is fixed in stone by these statues.

The starting point for both stories was a 1957 monograph by the Professor of Chinese at Oxford, the wonderfully named Homer Hasenpflug Dubs.[1] Dubs was as eccentric as his name suggests, 'well liked, but a bit odd', as a senior member of his college, University College, put it; 'an unexpected addition to the Senior Common Room'. 'No airs and graces,' remarked his obituary, 'Good-humoured . . . had three wives and a daughter . . . rode a motorbicycle . . . no-one who remembers Homer Dubs has a bad word to say of him.' One Fellow recalled 'the tale of how Professor Dubs turned up late to dinner one evening, and went to the Fellow presiding at the head of the table to say he was sorry for being late, but his wife had died half an hour previously.' Dubs was much struck by the possibility that a village near Yongchang had once borne the name by which (he claims) the Chinese once referred to Rome: Li Qian (or Lijian; the spelling varies); and he gave an elaborate and ingenious explanation as to how this could have happened.[2]

---

[1] It was originally a lecture given two years earlier to the China Society.
[2] He based his account on ch. 28 of the first-century text *Han Shu* (see ch. 4, n. 3, p. 74).

Between 110 and 100 BC, there arrived at the Chinese capital an embassy from the King of Parthia [roughly present-day Iraq and Iran]. Among the presents to the Chinese Emperor are stated to have been fine jugglers from 'Li Qian'. The jugglers and dancers, male and female, from Alexandria in Egypt [part of the Roman empire], were famous and were exported to foreign countries . . . When these persons were asked whence they came, they of course replied 'from Alexandria', which word the Chinese, who disliked polysyllables and initial vowels and could not pronounce certain Greek sounds, shortened into Li Qian [by dropping the *A*, and transliterating the second and third syllables, *lexan*, using the *q/ch* sound to replace the Greek *x/ks*, which does not exist in Chinese, and coming up with *lí qián* 骊 (驪) 轩].[3] When they also learned that this place was different from Parthia, the Chinese naturally used its name for the country of these jugglers. No Chinese had ever been to the Roman empire, so they had no reason to distinguish a prominent place in it from the country itself.

To summarize: Alexandria became Li Qian; Alexandria was part of the Roman empire; therefore, by about 100 BC, the Chinese for Rome was Li Qian. If this was so, it wasn't for long. By the sixth century the Chinese were referring to ancient Rome and its empire as Da Qin / 大秦 , Great Qin, as in the dynasty and empire created by

[3] Not completely unlikely. The Chinese for America is Mei: they drop the *A*, find a character (*měi* / 美 = beautiful) to represent the second syllable, and forget the last two.

the First Emperor, and later still as Luo Ma / 罗马, an approximation of Roma.

Now for the next element in the story, which starts in Rome itself in 59 BC, when Julius Caesar, Pompey and Crassus formed a triumvirate, the first of several that governed the empire. Crassus was a property tycoon who craved military glory. In 54 BC he led an army of seven legions, some 42,000 men, against Parthia. The Parthians were mounted archers, the Romans specialists in hand-to-hand combat. They met the following year at Carrhae (now Harran in Turkey). Like the Mongols much later, the Parthians took care to keep their distance and riddle the Romans with arrows, often faking a retreat and firing over their shoulders – the famous 'Parthian shot' at which all mounted archers excelled, corrupted into the English term 'parting shot' in a war of words. The Romans gambled that the Parthians would run out of arrows. They didn't, because the Parthian commander had organized relays of camels bringing new supplies. The Romans' only response was to form a *testudo*, a 'tortoise' of interlocking shields. Still the arrows came, lobbed in high trajectories over the shields, flashing in underneath them into Roman legs, until their feet were nailed to the ground (as Plutarch put it in his life of Crassus). Nearly 20,000 were killed and another 10,000 captured, many of whom were sent over 2,000 kilometres across Parthia to guard its eastern frontier against the Xiongnu. At this point, they drop out of western history . . .

. . . and – so Dubs claimed – into Chinese history, eighteen years later. One of the two rival Xiongnu chiefs, Zhi-zhi, had set himself up on the Talas river in southern

Kazakhstan, just beyond the far borders of the Western Regions, threatening to gain control of the Silk Road. In 36 BC a Chinese commander of the frontier, intent on glory, led 40,000 men westward, laying siege to Zhi-zhi's well-defended capital, with its double palisade of wood, moat and earthen ramparts. Hundreds of armed men crowded the battlements, yelling, 'Come and fight!' Horsemen galloped about, challenging the attackers. A band of foot soldiers drilled in close formation. In the siege that followed, Zhi-zhi was killed along with over 1,500 others, and the city taken.

But it was the group of foot soldiers that seized Dubs's attention. In his translation of Ban Gu's text, the attackers noticed that 'more than 100 foot soldiers, lined up on either side of the gate in a fish-scale formation, were practising military drill'. This, Dubs suggested, was a Roman *testudo* of interlocking shields. In addition, he argues, the idea of a double palisade was a standard Roman design, unknown elsewhere. The Chinese took 145 prisoners, who Dubs guessed were the 'more than 100 foot soldiers', spared because they were not Xiongnu. Dubs's conclusion is that these Romans had escaped their Parthian masters and fled to the Xiongnu, who had taken them on as mercenaries with some interesting military insights, and now found themselves in Chinese hands – not unhappily so, because they had nowhere else to go.

These men were now good frontiersmen, helping to guard the Wall, the narrow Gansu Corridor and the way west. It would have been natural for them to be settled in their own frontier town, named after themselves: Rome, or Li Qian. That's as far as the story goes.

But the threads wind on down the centuries to the present. These Romans, now men in their forties with unrivalled experience, would have married local women and raised families, creating a community with looks very different from the locals. So different, perhaps, that it is possible to see their origins in some of today's 'foreign-looking' inhabitants. That was the rumour. That was what drew me to Yongchang, and onwards, to remnants of the Han Wall, and to the town supposedly built by Romans 1,300 years before China established any other links with the West.

I was with Michael, seeking evidence to back the rumours. He had given me the background, so he was as intrigued as I was. Those statues lent weight to his words. There they stood, the two Romans, with the heavy-duty stone plaque underneath: 'In Memory of Li Qian', challenging anyone to doubt the story.

He questioned a passer-by. Yes, everyone knew that there were people around who 'looked foreign'. We should ask at the local government office, which was just around the corner, up a side alley. There we were greeted by Song Guorong, a man with slicked-back hair and a silver tooth who was, by chance, an expert. He had edited a little book of papers on the subject. It had not yet been published, but he presented me with a proof copy, which was nice of him, because the whole subject was rather sensitive.

'If you want to see a man who looks like a foreigner,' he said, 'you have to register with the police.'

'But why?'

'Because other foreigners come here and make trouble. So many other foreigners! Italians come here and see the local foreigners and call them brothers. People are tired of them, so it becomes more difficult.'

But not *too* difficult, because he immediately telephoned a friend.

'How many have come?' I asked, through Michael, as he put the phone down.

'More than hundreds. They stayed for weeks. There was an Italian film producer, talking about making a film next year. Then a scholar came from Oxford. He looked foreign, like you. Maybe he was your brother? He wanted to research, but there was the SARS scare, you remember, and he couldn't travel anywhere. But you can see. Mr Luo is coming. He looks foreign. He will show you. If you want to discover the truth,' he added, 'you could pay Mr Luo, maybe fifty yuan for half a day.'

Mr Luo, who had apparently been downstairs, was certainly anything but mainstream Chinese. He had hazel eyes, a thick head of hair, heavy black eyebrows, saturnine looks and a supercilious manner that would have served him well if he ever went for a bit-part in a Mafia movie. He was a sharp dresser, too. Black polo-neck, lightweight grey jacket, black trousers, black slip-on shoes.

Mr Luo took us in hand. We would go to his village, Zhelai, where the foreign-looking people were. There used to be many more, he said. They had mostly gone away looking for work in Lanzhou, Beijing, Shanghai. But there were still seventeen or eighteen left.

We set off along a dirt road under the motorway back towards the Qilian mountains.

'Did I tell you,' said Michael, 'that people round here used to like to see cattle fighting?'

'Not any more?'

'No. Now they use tractors.'

I had a vision of farmers jousting with tractors. But he was just commenting on changing agricultural practices.

'Mr Luo, how do people feel about looking different?'

'Before nineteen seventy-eight, they felt bad. Some had yellow hair, which they thought was bad, because people came to see them; so they dyed their hair black. But since China opened up to the outside world, they have become proud.'

As we climbed, terraced fields gave way to big, open country, with glorious views towards the snows and glaciers of the mountains. A beacon-tower stood guard over stubbly wheat, which meant that the Han Great Wall was, or used to be, somewhere around.

'There used to be lots of towers round here,' said Luo. 'But villagers made them into fields.'

Past a stand of yellow poplars, we came to a score of mud-brick houses and courtyards and thatched barns, all of medieval simplicity. This was Zhelai, where people supposedly looked foreign. It was hard to tell, because there was no one around. Bar a distant cockerel, the place was silent as the quite large tomb which we were now approaching. It turned out not to be a large tomb, but a small section of earth wall with a fence around it. 'Li Qian Historic Ruin' said the sign, giving the impression that this was the very wall created by the Romans when they came to live here. It looked suspiciously like any other piece of the Han Great Wall, which you can see running all along the Gansu Corridor parallel to the new motorway. It must once have run right through the village. All the rest having long since vanished under ploughs, this 27-metre slab of rammed earth had been saved by being declared Roman.

The wall was the centrepiece of the village's claim to fame, a claim celebrated by one of the most incongruous pieces of architecture you can imagine. Raised on a low platform of pink granite stood four fluted pseudo-Roman columns, set in a square, supporting an architrave and a flat roof. It might have been copied from a tomb or shrine, but all it shielded was a stele recording that 'Roman troops settled here' and its date, 1994. It stood to the side of a courtyard or parade ground. These days it seemed to be used for winnowing, for chaff blew around the waist-high walls.

Alongside the village, but across a dry ravine in a much more barren area of hard sand and tussocks, were more walls, in better shape: the remains of a substantial fortress or campsite. It seemed a strange place to build a camp.

'In ancient times,' explained Mr Luo, glancing round at the wasteland, and raising his voice over a dusty breeze, 'this was grassland. The ravine was a big river flowing from the Qilian Shan. People called the place Treasure Basin and saw the shape of a sleeping Buddha in the mountains. But the population grew, and so did the numbers of sheep and cattle, and the grasslands died, and the river dried up, so the people left.'

Perhaps that explained why the place was empty?

No, it was not empty. There were still 300 people here,

in 28 families. We would go and see. Buffeted by the wind, we walked back, through clumps of brittle grass that crackled in the breeze like wildfire. Mr Luo promised to find a girl who was the most foreign-looking of them all. Xiao Dan was her name: Little Dan. She would be in the school.

She wasn't, because the school was shut. Mr Luo led the way to her house, which turned out to be a total surprise. In an apparently poor village, a woman, Little Dan's aunt, who looked thoroughly Chinese, ushered us into a tiled compound and then into an airy marble-floored room, with a sleeping-platform, heated from underneath in winter, big enough for fourteen people. Little Dan was off on a picnic with the other children. She wouldn't be back until much later. We couldn't wait.

'Could I see a picture of her at least?'

The aunt hurried out, and back with a photograph. Little Dan, the most foreign-looking of all, had a fine, typical Chinese face. The only thing different about her, to my eyes, was that she had dark brown hair with a hint of red. It is a little unfair to make a judgement on the basis of a one-day visit and a photograph, but the only evidence of foreignness in Zhelai seemed to be a girl whose hair was not completely jet black.

Dubs's paper might simply have become an academic oddity but for the passionate interest of an Australian writer, David Harris. As a postgraduate in Armidale, New South Wales, he heard of Dubs from a linguistics professor who had been at Oxford in Dubs's time. The story seized him by the throat with such force that in 1988 he set out to find the 'lost city'. No one could have been worse prepared. He knew little of China, had no funds and was trying to prove that westerners formed an important element in Chinese history, not a claim likely to win official support. His naivety produced some excellent material for his book, *Black Horse Odyssey* – his account of the reaction among students to the Tiananmen massacres is particularly vivid – but he managed no more than two quick visits to 'Li Qian'. He saw the bits of wall, and the ruins of the fortress, and came away determined to return with good financial and archaeological support. But, stymied by bureaucracy, he never did.

Still, his conviction and his search made a great story, which broke cover in December 1989 when the *People's Daily* reported the Dubs–Harris hypothesis. Then local officials, among them Song Guorong, the editor of the book, took up the theme. If this could become better known, it would do wonders for local tourism, for there was really no other reason for Great Wall and Silk Road travellers to stop off at Yongchang. Up went the statues, and the fence around the old wall in Zhelai, and the Roman pavilion.

More publicity followed. Do an internet search for 'Romans China' and you will see what I mean. The story almost made it to the silver screen. North of Yinchuan, on the great loop of the Yellow River, a Ming Great Wall fortress has been turned into a film lot, the China West Film Studio, which has provided settings for some 80 movies. (We shall see it in close-up later.) One of them was a Chinese–British made-for-TV co-production called *Homeward Bound*, being the story of what happened to the Romans when they tried to get back to Italy (not the point of the legend, but a nice twist). Much work was done, much film shot. Then what happened? I have been unable to find out. Maybe the money ran out, maybe some new executive pulled the plug ... in any event, nothing more has been heard of the film.

Now let's see what all this amounts to. In brief: absolutely nothing. It's rubbish, from beginning to end.

Glen Dudbridge, Dubs's successor at Oxford, was scathing when I asked for his opinion. 'Over the years, I have received a long string of enquiries about Dubs and his Roman city in China,' he e-mailed. 'The story refuses to go away, even though Dubs's claims were methodically refuted by generation after generation of specialists during the past 50 years.'

In an unpublished paper, he summarizes the critical academic responses, both western and Chinese: 'untenable' ... 'impossible to accept' ... 'a historical romance' ... 'a bizarre flight of fancy' ... 'a work of fiction of moderate interest'. There are so many things that simply don't fit. A hundred and forty-five men, who would anyway have been getting close to retirement, would not have been much of an addition to China's Great Wall defences. They were too few to found a city. A 'double palisade' was not a uniquely Roman defence – the Xiongnu fort at Ivolga had four sets of palisades.

Look at the two fundamental claims: that Li Qian equals Rome; and that the soldiers noted at the attack on Zhi-zhi's capital formed a *testudo*.

Many scholars have pointed out that there is absolutely

no reason why Li Qian should equate with Alexandria, or why Alexandria should equate with Rome – especially as Alexandria was Greek, and not conquered by the Romans until 30 BC, six years *after* the defeat of Zhi-zhi. Anyway, Li Qian was the name of a county a century before both the attack on Zhi-zhi's capital and the battle of Carrhae. If that is so, it is possible that Li Qian has nothing whatever to do with Alexandria; it could be that the famous jugglers were Chinese after all. The conclusion was right there in one of the articles in the proof copy of the book Mr Song had given me: 'Therefore there is no connection between Li Qian and any Roman prisoners.'[4]

Dudbridge undertakes a highly technical examination of Dubs's suggestion that a 'fish-scale formation' was a Roman *testudo*, and finds it wanting. The translation is simply wrong, he says. Dubs misunderstood both the grammar and a technical term. What the Chinese means is: 'More than 100 foot soldiers were formed up in close order on either side of the gate, practising military [i.e. weapons] drill.'

'The plain fact is,' he concluded to me, 'that Dubs linked together three entirely unrelated matters – the battle of Carrhae (53 BC), the Chinese capture of a Central Asian stronghold in 36 BC, and the ancient county of Li Jian in western China (already there in 53 BC!).'

---

[4] The article is by Zhang Defang (张德芳), Director of the Gansu Provincial Archaeology Team. For Chinese-readers, other references coming to the same conclusion are Wang Shou Kuan / 往受宽, *Dunhuang Journal*, vol. 1, no. 37, 2001; Liu Guanghua / 刘 光华 and Xie Yujie / 谢玉杰 , *2nd North-West Minority College Journal* (Lanzhou), vol. 2, no. 39, 1999.

So there's no historical evidence – and no present-day evidence either. If there are really people in the area who 'look foreign', it could not be a result of Italian genes carrying their information down the centuries, for 80 generations. No traits particular to individuals endure that long, because any trait as general as overall appearance is the result of uncounted numbers of genes that mix randomly. Even abnormal traits due to some genetic aberration, like the drooping lower lip of the Habsburgs, begin to vanish after some 300 years. And yellow hair? Doesn't sound very Italian. On the other hand, this was once the western frontier of China, where local people came into contact with all sorts of non-Chinese peoples, whose genes could well have filtered down to the present – enough to produce a few families who look foreign to Chinese eyes.

There is no need to believe the plaque on the wall in Zhelai, which suggests an association with Rome. On the contrary, there are many bits of the Han Great Wall quite close by, as well as at least one beacon-tower, let alone the others that have been reduced to dust. Or were the Romans supposed to have been responsible for the beacon-tower(s) as well? I think it's fair to conclude that the plaque, like everything else about this story, is nothing more than wishful thinking.

Official reactions to interest from outsiders are wary. Harris's plans to establish an academic exchange programme faltered and died, and permission to film a documentary was refused; as he e-mailed me sadly, 'There is no international cooperative work being done on Lijian at present.' But good stories like this are too appealing to be destroyed by disapproval and disproof. My guess is that, at the grass-roots level in China, this chapter, and all those statements by killjoy experts who prefer truth to good stories, will have absolutely no impact at all. The statues, the plaque and the pavilion are too solid to be denied.

And anyway, the story has now escaped from its roots. Four hundred kilometres away, on the other side of the Ordos, in the Ming fortress that is now the China West Film Studio, is a display left over from the making of the *Homeward Bound* film. It is the house of the governor whose task it was to look after the Roman soldiers in their new home of Li Qian. It includes some wonderful and thoroughly authentic furniture. Who, seeing this, as many thousands do every year, would doubt that the story is true?

9

A GRASSLAND MYSTERY

CHINESE MAPS CLAIM THE SECOND 'WALL OF GENGHIS KHAN' in Mongolia's eastern grasslands as part of the Great Wall itself, suggesting a little-known section of stone ranging over the steppe. Flying east to the provincial capital of Choibalsan, I already knew better from a Mongolian friend, the archaeologist Ishdorj. 'I think maybe an earth wall, once,' he had said, 'but not now.' It was just a ridge, but a large one. Despite having driven along it for a day, he knew nothing more. 'I asked the people why they called it the Wall of Genghis Khan. They say, "Our fathers called it that."' I had had hopes that, with Goyo as guide, I could do better than that – find stones to suggest a purpose, or bits of pottery to give a clue to its age. Now, looking down over the unfenced, roadless grassland, doubts came crowding in. I feared a total waste of time and money, and no discoveries.

Below were some puzzling features: hillocks next to big holes, which were perhaps tombs? No, not tombs, as our driver, Batbolt, explained on the way in from the airport. They were Cold War emplacements for Russian tanks, 400 of them. Tanks sat in the holes, camouflaged, facing eastward, ready to repel the Chinese hordes who lay over the frontier less than 100 kilometres away.

'There were twenty thousand Russians here. The officers lived in those apartment blocks, with the soldiers in camps.'

Then in 1992, in the wake of the collapse of the Soviet Union, they went – in the space of two weeks, loading up the tanks, abandoning their apartments, furniture, factories, everything. Now the Chinese were coming in, looking for oil.

Batbolt, with the build and battered face of a boxer, was a good find. He knew the way north, and had heard about what I wanted to see. He called it Genghis Khan's wall, ridge, road – he used all three words indiscriminately, as others had when referring to the other Wall of Genghis Khan in the southern Gobi. Then he added another complexity. Our destination, he said, was a little place near the Wall called Genghis's Vall, pronounced to rhyme with *cull* and *dull*, not with *wall*, though what a *vall* was he couldn't say, except that it was not Mongolian. Weird: it sounded almost English, too close to 'wall' for coincidence. We would set off the next morning, after a night in a hotel that was definitely on the rise. It had toilet paper, running cold water, and hot water too, if you collected it in a thermos from Reception.

Choibalsan is an odd place, all vast avenues and widely spaced apartment blocks, with not a *ger* in sight. It is a monument to old-fashioned socialism, Mongolian-style, and to its dreadful, dreaded and admired namesake, Mongolia's Stalin figure. Marshal Khorloogin Choibalsan was well qualified for dictatorship by dysfunctionality. His father left before his birth in 1895. His mother, Khorloo (hence his name, 'Khorloo's'), was a poor, devout woman with a notoriously foul temper, with whom he had little to do. Having received a rudimentary education in a Buddhist temple, he ran away to the capital, where he fell in with the revolutionaries who secured Mongolia's Soviet-backed independence in 1921. After an erratic career in government he became a favourite of Stalin, and as interior minister in 1937–40 supervised purges that practically extinguished the Buddhist church (witness the ruined monasteries I had seen in the Gobi) and killed over 20,000 of Mongolia's political, intellectual and religious élite. As a reward, he became premier, foreign minister, interior minister and commander-in-chief, all at once. In his favour, he turned down the idea of Mongolia's joining the Soviet Union. He died in 1952, and was revered until the fall of Communism in 1990. Now that his brutalities have become well known, you would think he would be reviled. Not a bit of it, as I would shortly learn.

Something peculiar was going on with place names, as Batbolt explained while we sailed the inland sea of grass. Tracking a railway line that led 250 kilometres northward to join the Trans-Siberian across the border in Russia, we were approaching Choibalsan's birthplace, a village called Kherlen, after the river that runs a dozen kilometres to the east. Except it was no longer called Kherlen. In his honour, it was being changed to, of course, Choibalsan. But that would leave two towns of the same name, the village ahead and the provincial capital. This lunatic arrangement is in the process of being rectified. How? By renaming the capital Kherlen. The two places were in the middle of a name-swap. Except that the capital's airport will still be called Choibalsan. It took Goyo and me several attempts to sort this out, and I can't swear even now that I've got it completely right.

The marshal's birthplace is a charmless collection of single-storey shacks and drab communal buildings tossed randomly across a vast space, in the middle of which is a statue of our hero – a new one put up in 2005, commemorating his 110th birthday. He is portrayed emerging from white rock, as if thigh-deep in snow. The plaque explains why he is so revered still: 'May Mongolian independence last for ever!' They're proud of him, they really are. A local signalled me on to a horse in front of him, as if to confer his blessing, and insisted on taking my photograph.

Now it turned out that Choibalsan was Batbolt's home town. There were friends to see, milky tea to drink, dumplings to consume, in a room sparsely furnished with a few chairs, a sofa, a wood-burning stove, a table and a fridge that doubled as a dressing table. Batbolt settled into intense conversation with four women. Goyo filled me in. This was not idle chat, but politics. The conclave were all local members of Mongolia's most progressive party, Citizens' Will, the one run by Oyun, the sister of the murdered Zorig, whom I had bumped into in

Dalandzadgad airport not long before. Physicists say there are four forces in the universe: the weak force, the strong force, gravity and electro-magnetism. Well, Mongolia is a universe unto itself, and it has a fifth force: coincidence. Our expedition acquired its fourth member, a smartly dressed matron named Munkhbat, who was a local councillor and Oyun's representative in Choibalsan.

Beyond, past the mole-hill tips of an iron-mine, a baked mud track gave way to soft sand, carrying us fast over the undulating shin-high grass, pale as wheat. We had been driving for hours, and seen just one other car. Batbolt explained more about the railway. It carried two trains a week, which must make it one of the least used of active lines. Once, it had been busier, when troops shuttled back and forth along this, the eastern frontier of the Soviet bloc. For that reason, it had been given a fence to keep animals away, in case they got flattened by a passing train. Now the posts were lopsided, the wires slack; but there were no herds, perhaps because herders were few in these industrialized parts, or perhaps because it was a sensitive border area.

We arrived at last at what looked like a war zone beside the railway. The shells of several abandoned apartment blocks, all gaping empty rooms and shattered concrete, surrounded a long-abandoned playground. I saw a sleeping dog, a woman holding a wild-haired baby that screamed at my approach, and a child of about five on a little blue tricycle. They came not from the concrete ruins but from four new Siberian-style log cabins, which were home (as I soon discovered) to 20 people. This was our destination: the railway station known as Genghis's Vall.

From one of the shacks emerged a slim, middle-aged lady, surprisingly dignified in a light-green cashmere jersey, a floppy white hat against the brilliant sun, and a touch of make-up. She was the station manageress, and proud of it. We were welcome. We wanted to see Genghis's Wall? No problem. Someone would guide us. We could stay in the 'hotel', a single-room building that was entirely empty except for two iron beds.

I was intrigued by the set-up. The conversation went something like this:

'When is the next train due?'

'Tonight. It comes through some time after midnight.'

'People get on and off here?'

'Oh, yes.'

'How many tickets do you sell?'

'We do not sell tickets. People just get on and off.'

'What people?'

'Us.'

I began to understand. Once this had been a thriving Russian base, populated by several hundred people, all busy defending the frontier with China, which lay 50 kilometres to the east. They were about to get nice new apartments when they were pulled out. The only Russians around now were in the cemetery, the result of a nasty train crash not long before the pull-out. Now, in an odd piece of circular logic, the only purpose in the train stopping at all was to provide a service to the railway employees who lived here.

Sustained by deliveries of food and fuel twice a month, the community seemed to be fine. The fuel was enough to run a generator, which powered a few electric lights.

There was no car: a couple of motorcycles and the train itself was all the transport needed. The ruined apartments could be ignored; new and much more charming places – the Siberian-style shacks – could be built. And, as I learned later, people could make a little extra on the side.

Meanwhile, what of the 'wall'? Was there a 'wall' at all?

Of course there was a wall, insisted the manageress, Urzhing-khand by name. That was how the station got its name – Genghis-Vall. This inspired some deeper questioning, because the word *vall* (*Валл* in Cyrillic, which is what Mongolia uses) does not exist in Mongolian, but it does in Russian, though with one *l*, meaning, among other things, a bank, earth wall or rampart. So the station had a mis-spelled Russian name. Not for much longer, though. Now that the Russians had gone, said Urzhing, the name of the station was changing. She had recently put up the new name: Genghis's *Ridge*, using a perfectly good Mongolian word, *dalan*, one of the terms used by our Gobi-dwellers to describe the other 'Wall of Genghis Khan' in the south.

I got the point. It was a ridge we were going to see. But wait a moment: why *Genghis's*? Surely this had nothing to do with Genghis? Oh, but it did. This was all part of Genghis's homeland, before he founded Mongolia in 1206. It was near here that he and his childhood friend, Jamukha, fought a battle after they became rivals. A professor had come, and identified the site, and put up a sign. That we could see as well.

Six of us piled into Batbolt's UAZ, with one of the locals, Batsaikhan, pointing where he was to go, now this way, now that, like a pilot guiding a ship through shallows. A faint track past the cemetery gave way to a blank of waving grass, with only the sun to give a sense of direction. We swished eastward towards the Chinese border, grasses brushing the mudguards and tickling the sump.

I saw, as we crested a rise, that this was a haven for gazelle, 'white' gazelle as Mongolians call them (*Subcapra gutterosa*). Almost invisible in the grass, they were startled into action by the Jeep. Often, if they are close, their reactions are odd. They start to run parallel with the car, closing in all the time, then when they are quite close and just ahead, they cut across your bows, as if trying to commit suicide by being run over. In fact, it must be a life-preserving manoeuvre. If you happen to be a predator, you would have to turn, lose speed, and miss making a kill. You might, of course, be a predator with a rifle, but even close up, aiming while bouncing is not the way to kill a gazelle. There's a better, easier way, as I would learn that evening.

There was a mound ahead, a low billow in the ocean of long, coarse grass. We rose on to it, stopped, and unfolded ourselves. This was it: the Wall of Genghis Khan. There would have been no way to find it without a guide. It was as invisible beneath its grassy mantle as a pillow beneath a duvet. At first glance the rise we were on was one among many, all clad in hairy grasses over earth roughened by mice and marmot burrows. It was remarkably silent. In the grasslands to the south at this time of year, the plains are alive with the electric fizz of grasshoppers. And flies. Thank God there were no flies, I suppose because it was too dry. We were a metre or two above the surrounding steppe, on a rise that was – I paced it – between 9 and 10 metres across, much bigger than the Gobi 'wall'. Only if I positioned myself right could I see it heading to the horizon, a vein raised from the body of the plain defined only by subtle differences of pastel greens, browns and pale yellows.

Well, it certainly wasn't a wall, and never had been. Like the Gobi feature, this was far too regular to be the remains of a wall. Anyway, there were no beacon-towers, which seemed to be the defining features of a defensive wall. It looked to me like an enormous, abandoned, over-grown highway, neatly cambered like a Roman road to allow the rain to run off. But it took only a few seconds to see that this didn't stack up. Why build a road across flat grassland? And why camber it, when there was no surfacing, and any rain was going to sink in?

To see it properly, you would need a plane, and early morning or late evening sun to cast a shadow. Then it would stand out for what it is, a huge, tidal surge of earth, millions of tonnes of it, made into a ridge hundreds of kilometres long – 700 kilometres, according to the few estimates I have seen. A little back-of-the-envelope mathematics reveals that to produce this prodigious feature you would have needed to move 7 million tonnes of earth. In fact, for a culture used to organizing massive projects, this would not have been too challenging: 1,000 men shifting 4 tonnes a day each for five years could have managed it.

But that was just the beginning.

'John,' called Goyo. 'They want to show us the overnight place.'

The 'Overnight Place', 'Wall of Genghis Khan', eastern Mongolia

in plan . . .

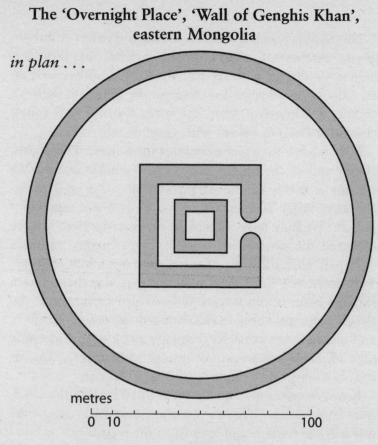

metres

0 10   100

. . . and in three-quarter view

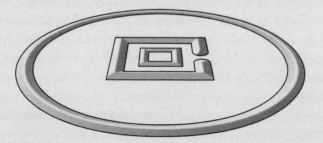

Batsaikhan pointed the way through patches of brown grass, patches of yellow grass, patches of shoulder-high grass shaggy with seeds, over a dried-up bog and up an escarpment to some low bumps. We were, I suppose, a couple of kilometres from the main feature, well raised clear of the marsh below, with good distant views.

It took a while to make sense of the bumps. There were circles and straight lines and shapes within shapes. We became a team, pacing and counting paces and cross-checking. After 20 minutes or so, we had put together a picture. We may have missed an entrance or two, but we captured the general sense of it: two squares within a circle, all made of banks of earth, with not a hint of stone. This could not have been a fortress; it was more like a camp, a place to put horses and camels (within the circle, which contains about 8,000 square metres of ground), and within that a place for baggage and a central sleeping area 13 metres square, small enough to be covered against rain in summer and the −40°C cold in winter.

It was not the only one. As we walked back to the UAZ, our guide said, 'There's another one like this, over towards the border, and a third to the west.'

A little discussion and some poring over maps on the bonnet of the car produced a hypothesis. These large 'overnight' areas seem to have been spaced at about 40- or 50-kilometre intervals, which is about the distance a camel caravan would have covered in a day, and also a reasonable gap to allow contingents of border guards to resupply each other. There was nothing to suggest defences, no beacon-towers to summon help from down the line. What is more, any caravan reaching these wild regions was two or three weeks from the sort of food Chinese traders needed. Did they carry all their food with them? It was a question which would soon answer itself.

Mysteries remained. Who had built it, for what purpose? Perhaps there would be more to see, but that would have to wait, because we were off to see what else was on offer, riding over untouched grassland towards the place that would link the road, or barrier, or wall, with Genghis.

The space around, empty of everything but the grass's subtle yellows and the dome of blue above, was filled with interest to those who lived here. Every square metre was an ecology. Someone pointed out a bird, and everyone laughed, because as Batbolt explained, 'this little bird farts like a horse, laughs like a man and whistles like a marmot'. We halted briefly to pick a sweet-smelling plant with a bulb as sugary as glucose that was 'good for the stomach'. I counted nine different species of grass, and then, to my surprise, spotted the rusted wreck of a car. Batbolt told a long story of smugglers who used to import foreign cars and drive them to the border, where Chinese partners picked them up (so now, as when 'Genghis's Wall' was built, this was an open road into China). It had something to do with avoiding Chinese taxes on foreign-made cars.

We came to a gentle slope leading up a low hill, featureless except for a post stuck in its flat top. It had been put there by a Genghis expert, Batsagur, who has made it his business to identify every conceivable spot associated with the nation's No. 1 hero. 'Chikhurgch, as mentioned in the Secret History', said the sign on the post, with no further explanation. It had a blue silk scarf tied around it as a sign of reverence. If there is no spot already identified by tradition, Batsagur finds one, even if there is no evidence except folklore for the connection, as was the case here. But it was worth it for the all-round view. There was nothing except pale brown grass and a few distant gazelles in any direction, except north, where the steppe drifted gently down to Mongolia's lowest point, Blue Lake, a huge shallow puddle with a muddy shore well trodden by animals.

Back at the station, sunset and the presence of Batbolt's UAZ inspired an idea: we should all go hunting gazelles. In the dark? Yes, it was much easier in the dark. Someone produced a battered old .22 rifle, and once again we were off over the infinite steppe, accompanied now by two motorbikes which wove about like fireflies in the velvet night.

This is how you hunt gazelles at night:

Your headlights cast a yellow pool, at the edge of which now and then shadows shift and eyes glow. At night, gazelles behave entirely differently. They do not skitter away, nor do they match the car's speed and cut across in front. They move at a steady jog, and soon stop, somewhere off in the dark, as if getting ready to doze the night away. It is easy to follow one, turning this way and that to keep it at the edge of the light, not too far, not too close. Headlights should be dipped. After a minute or two of this slow manœuvring, the gazelle stops and stares, apparently puzzled by the brightness that follows but does not threaten. Always, it stops side on and stares with a fixed gaze, politely waiting to be shot. You stop as well, about 30 metres from the gazelle. You undip your headlights. You can see the gazelle, the gazelle can see only the light. Your companion in the passenger seat opens the door, rests the rifle on the hinge, aims – all without haste, because the gazelle is stock still – and fires.

It is flattery to call this hunting. It is more like a slaughter, except that in this case the ancient .22 misfired with a little click about 50 per cent of the time. And with a basic V-shaped sight, it was easy to miss. But once in every half-dozen shots, the gazelle would jump as if stung, and jog off.

You follow. Another minute, and the wounded gazelle collapses. Probably it's not dead. You jump out, reach the gazelle, take its horns, wrench its head along its back, put your knee on its head, lean down hard and snap its neck. Then you haul the corpse, which weighs 35–40 kilos, into your Jeep and jam it under the legs of a visiting author. The next one, ditto, until his knees are by his ears. Other corpses fill the space behind the back seat. Lights dance towards you over the steppe – two motorbikes, laden. There is a meeting, and a dozen gazelle are dragged into the headlights.

Then comes some butchery, which you should know about just in case you find yourself short of food in eastern Mongolia. The squeamish should skip this paragraph. First, you cut off the lower legs. Then, if it's a male, you rub your hand along its penis, extract a few drops of urine, sniff it and wipe it over your face. Ah, you say, now I am refreshed. Then the stomach is cut open, the guts spilled by two of you taking the legs and flapping the animal like a blanket. Fat is cut away and kept separate. You tear up some grass and use this as a cloth to clean up, then reload the Jeep and head for home.

Next morning came the business of cooking. In the tin-walled enclosure of a shack made of railway sleepers, Batbolt gathered materials that would not have been first choice for a western chef: dried dung, a milk churn, some stones and a blow-torch. The dung went into a stove, and so did the stones; the blow-torch blasted the hair from the gazelles, which had been flung together overnight in a shed; many corpses were cut up and placed in the milk churn, alternating with red-hot stones. We waited. A dog with a foot missing limped from a shadow.

'What happened to his foot?' I asked.

'He stepped into a marmot trap.'

Half an hour later, the whole churn was a casserole of gazelle, cooking in the purest, most intense broth I had tasted since sampling marmot done in much the same way three years previously.

'These people could go into the meat business,' I said to Goyo.

'No. Hunting is illegal.'

'*What!?*'

'Yes. They can fine you eight hundred thousand tughriks.'

'That's ridiculous. Why?'

'Gazelles are protected. Marmots too.'

'But they could hunt gazelles every night for ten years and make no impression. There must be tens of thousands of them.' And the same goes for marmots, which are just as easy to shoot, just as tasty.

I think now I understand the reasons. One is that Mongolians have a traditional respect and reverence for nature. High places are often called 'holy' this or 'sacred' that. The forested flanks of the Bogd Uul (Holy Mountain) just outside Ulaanbaatar, protected since the eighteenth century, form the world's oldest national park. But respect has always gone hand in hand with a passion and a necessity for hunting. There's something else behind the contemporary enthusiasm for protecting places and species. Protection these days is tied up with publicity and national income. Mongolia has more national parks than anywhere else on earth – some 65,000 square kilometres, over three times the US figure, for a country one-sixth of the size with a hundredth of the population. One-third of Mongolia is protected, making Mongolia, in terms of parkland, the richest nation on earth. For this, money flows from the United Nations, to the tune of $750 million a year. So protection is good business for the government.

Bad news for hunters around the 'Wall of Genghis Khan', who would otherwise be able to earn their little community a nice bonus. Not *that* bad, though, because we had an official with us – Oyun's representative, Munkhbat – and she was having a terrific time along with the hunters. No one, apparently, took the regulations seriously, as long as the meat was consumed locally. Certainly Batbolt didn't give them a thought as he carried several slabs of meat, his reward for driving the previous night, to the UAZ.

Westward, the wall, or road, or border barrier, or all three, was easy to follow across the gentle grass, a knee-

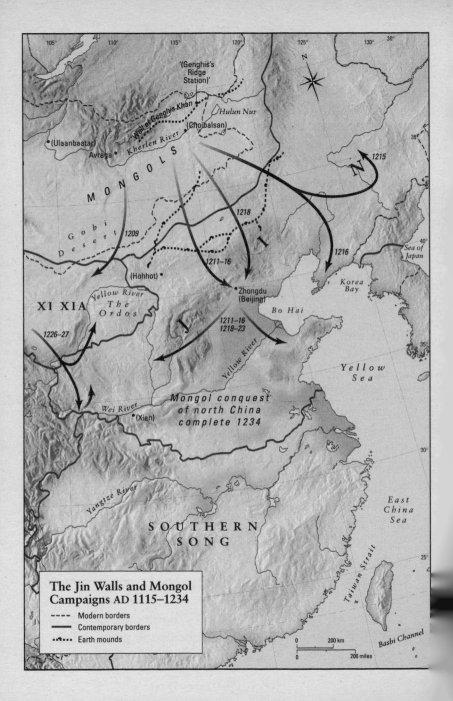

The Jin Walls and Mongol Campaigns AD 1115–1234

high mound 9–10 metres across, with slight dips either side from which the earth had been dug. In this direction, away from the Chinese border, steppe life normalized. We came to a well-head, where horses bickered over water spilling from a noisy pump. A herder with a pole-lasso directed a herd of sheep. Beyond, half a kilometre from the ridge, was a second, smaller campsite: two simple squares, a larger one of 56 metres per side, a smaller one half that size. Onward the ridge ran, rising and falling as the steppe began to roll like waves gathering to break against the Khenti mountains 150 kilometres ahead. That's where the ridge ends, in the original heartland of the Mongols, and not far from the birthplace of Genghis, whose rise to power is wrapped up with the origins and fate of the non-wall, the great ridge that bears his name.

II

STONE

10

THE COMING OF THE MONGOLS

THE MONGOLS WERE TO BECOME CHINA'S ENEMY NO. 1, THE archetype of the barbarians who threatened death and destruction from north of the Wall. It was they who galloped through the Wall in the thirteenth century, seized the whole country and set up their own alien regime, which lasted nearly 150 years. It was to ensure they never, ever came back that the old earth Wall became the new stone one, under the Ming dynasty in the fifteenth century. Today, what tourists hear and read about these invaders implies almost without exception that the fore-bears of modern Mongolia's 2 million inhabitants were little better than wild beasts who had been whipped back into their cage and penned, like so many Hannibal Lecters. Go to Mongolia today, see a people who could hardly be more peaceable – unified, democratic, outgoing, cosmopolitan, ecologically minded, undogmatic – and you have to wonder what happened to set them going.

What happened, mainly, was Genghis Khan. To non-Mongols, Genghis seemed to spring from the dark, like a nightmare come to life. But it was not quite like that. There was a context, and reasons, for his thrust southward into China.

The context was set by events in north China. Today, with Beijing as the capital, all China takes its cue from the north. But for four centuries at the beginning of the second millennium AD north China, with its 50 million people, was not ruled by Chinese at all, but by three lots of 'barbarians', the last of which were the Mongols. First had come the Khitans, a tribe that exploded into empire in 907. They called their empire Liao, after the river in their Manchurian homeland. In the mid-eleventh century Liao was twice the size of France and Germany, stretching from the Pacific across to the Yellow River and northward across the Gobi into the future heartland of the Mongols, then an insignificant little tribe who were no trouble to anyone but their immediate neighbours.

Off to the east in Manchuria were another tribe, the Jurchen (女真 / nǚzhēn), the ancestors of the Manchus. From a homeland along an obscure river named Golden in their language, they sprang into prominence in the early twelfth century, broke with their Khitan overlords, struck south and in a mere ten years (1115–25) booted out their former masters, Liao's Khitan owners, who fled westward and set up a new state in the depths of Central Asia – leaving as their legacy their name, which turned into both the Mongol for China, Khiatad, and 'Cathay', widely used in the Middle Ages as a synonym for China.

Though not Chinese themselves, north China's new Jurchen élite admired Chinese culture and gave their new creation a Chinese name, Jin (Golden), after the river of their homeland. The name came to refer to the state, the dynasty and the people. Both Liao and Jin moved away from their hunting, fishing, farming and herding roots to batten on an existing city-based culture. Having established themselves on this foundation, they copied and envied and fought with the rest of China, their great southern neighbour, Song; and Jin was successful enough to seize all north China from Song, setting up a new capital in Beijing and forcing Song to the status of a vassal. But this new empire would last only a century, until the coming of the Mongols.

Jin's brief existence coincided with a ferment of state-building in Inner Asia. To the west, beyond the Yellow River bend, was another kingdom, Xi Xia, set up by a Tibetan people, the Tanguts, in the eleventh century. Even further west were the remnants of the Khitans, who, after fleeing the Jurchens, had established a new state, Khara Khitai (the Black Khitans). With centralized administrations one could negotiate, which is what Jin did with Southern Song and with Xi Xia. But what about the unreliable and notoriously acquisitive nomads across Mongolia's eastern grasslands and north of the Gobi?

For the Mongols, who had arrived from places unknown some 500 years before, had had a sudden inkling of what might be achieved by unity. Around 1140, Genghis's great-grandfather Kabul had become the first chief to rule 'over all the Mongols'. To the south and east,

Jin, elbowing its way into full possession of its territory, saw Kabul as a new threat. The Jin emperor – Altan Khan, the Golden Khan, as the Mongols called him – invited Kabul to Beijing for talks. He came, drank too much and felt relaxed enough to lean over and tweak the emperor's beard. The court was appalled, for such a gesture revealed that Kabul did not feel the awe expected of a vassal. When he left, soldiers followed to capture him. He escaped, leaving Jin determined to deal with these dangerously insolent nomads when they had the chance.

The chance came a few years later when Kabul's cousin and heir, Ambakai, was travelling towards Manchuria, on his way to arrange a daughter's marriage into a sub-group of the Tatar tribe. Jin employed Tatars, along with several other tribes, as border guards on the unruly north-western frontier. No doubt there was a price on Ambakai's head. Some Tatars seized him, and dragged him off to the Jin emperor. Before he disappeared he managed to get a message home, recorded by *The Secret History* in verse, which it does for phrases that were probably sung by bards:

> Until the nails of your five fingers
> Are ground down;
> Until your ten fingers are worn away,
> Strive to revenge me!

Vengeance: the word echoes down the generations. In retribution for his cousin's presumption, Ambakai died in agony and humiliation, crucified on a frame the Chinese called a 'wooden donkey'. Ambakai's heir, Kutula, sought revenge thirteen times against the Tatars, and died in battle with them in 1164. Leaderless, the Mongol tribes collapsed into anarchy. As *The Secret History* puts it, again resorting to verse:

> The crusty earth was turning and turning,
> The entire nation was in turmoil.

But Jin was taking no chances. A solution to the problem lay before them, in the form of the Qin, Han and later defences that ran smack across the newly acquired Jin territory. They would build walls.

The motive was not entirely to do with the threat from the north. The part of Jin that abutted the Gobi – present-day Inner Mongolia – was becoming rich in farmland as settlers came to what was once a pastoral nomadic borderland. Twelfth-century taxation rolls show a settled population of a million people, who built numerous settlements, towns, even small cities.[1] This meant property as well as territory to protect; taxpayers to keep tabs on as well as subjects to rule. This was the Jin's new pale, beyond which lay barbarism.

To quote the Great Wall expert, Cheng Dalin: 'To protect themselves against the Mongols' southward advance, the Jin rulers in 1138 undertook to build walls along the border, a giant task that took 60 years.' The figures he quotes are astonishing: 4,000 kilometres of wall, all of rammed earth, doubled up (an outer wall up to

---

[1] This is based on Buell, 'The Role of the Sino-Mongolian Frontier Zone'.

6 metres wide, a main one 5–15 metres wide), and with two moats; 250 castles in one year alone (1181), each of which kept 300 men busy for a month; arrays of platforms, blockhouses and beacon-towers.

Most of this section of the Wall is strung across Inner Mongolia. At present the only sources are in Chinese, drawing on Jin records. Whether these records mirror what actually existed on the ground in Inner Mongolia is a moot point, which it would take a lifetime to establish. But there was also a further 'wall', stretching across the 700 kilometres between China's Manchurian grasslands and Mongolia's Khenti mountains – the ridge labelled on maps as 'The Wall of Genghis Khan', on which one goes night-hunting for gazelles. I don't believe this was ever a defensive wall, because to stop horses you need a sheer drop a couple of metres high. I don't believe in the moat. (Where would the water come from? How would it be kept in?) I don't believe there were ever any beacon-towers or platforms here. The 'wall' that I saw was an utterly regular ridge, a simple bank worn and washed and wind-blown, with no sign of any other defences. The only theory that makes sense, on the basis of a brief and superficial visit, is to see it as a border wall, guarded by Jin troops in encampments, a sort of red light warning the Mongols: thus far, and no further.

But almost as soon as these huge barriers were made, the Mongol threat receded into anarchic feuding. What with the feuding and the barriers and the border guards, surely there was nothing for the Jin to worry about on their north-west frontier? Yes, there was: they were not to know that a threat of an entirely different nature was growing, unseen by outsiders.

* * *

In 1162 (or thereabouts) Kabul's grandson, Yesugei, returned from a raid against the Tatars (yes, the Tatars again) with a captured Tatar chieftain named Temujin. Though much disputed, the name probably meant 'black-smith', from the Mongol for 'iron' (*tömör*), plus the active suffix *-chin*: 'iron-person'. Artisans, especially smiths, were important people in medieval Mongolia, and were worth more alive than dead. It was also common practice to name a child to commemorate a victory, or after a favoured material, like a jewel, or silver – or iron; so when Yesugei's wife gave birth to the son she was carrying when her husband returned from his raid, he was given the Tatar captive's name. Little Temujin, growing up surrounded by the mountains, rivers and grassland of the tribal heartland in northern Mongolia, would have known by heart the stories of Ambakai and Kutula. Vengeance against the Jin and Tatars would have been in his blood, a drive reinforced in the most painful way when his own father was poisoned by Tatars.

This was more than a tragedy. Without an adult male, his family were rejected by their clan, forcing his tough and resourceful mother to secure their survival by grubbing for roots on the banks of the Onon, one of the three rivers that run from the Mongols' mountainous heartland. In addition, Temujin, a prince by descent, was a potential leader, and thus a target for rival clans. He was captured by one clan, and just escaped death at the hands of another. On the second occasion, when he was about 20, he fled on to the flanks of Burkhan Khaldun, the sacred mountain of the Mongols, where for three days and nights he hid among the firs and willows that cover the lower slopes. When he was sure his attackers had gone, he came down from the mountain, and was overcome with gratitude.

> I climbed the Burkhan [Holy One]
> On a horse hobbled with the halter strap,
> Following deer tracks;
> A shelter of elm twigs
> I made my home.
> Thanks to Burkhan Khaldun
> I escaped with my life, a louse's life.

He faced the sun, hung his belt around his neck, beat his breast with his fist and, nine times kneeling towards the sun, he offered a libation and a prayer, swearing that he and his heirs would pray to the mountain every day. That, I think, was the beginning of a slowly dawning revelation. Wondering why he had been spared, Temujin found an answer. Heaven had marked him out for leadership, not simply of his tribe, not simply of all Mongolia's nomad tribes, but of the whole world.

This was the vision that from now on infused his life and inspired his heirs, who came to see their leader's vision as preordained from the time of the Mongols' mythical origins. *The Secret History*, written soon after his death, begins by intoning: 'The origins of Genghis Khan: At the beginning there was a blue-grey wolf, born with his destiny ordained by Heaven above.' The destiny becomes explicit as Temujin rises: 'Together Heaven and Earth have agreed . . . Temujin shall be the lord of the people.' 'The door was opened,' he says, 'and the reins were loosened for me by Eternal Heaven.' His childhood friend, Jamukha, calls him 'my sworn friend, whose destiny was ordained by heaven'. His heirs had no doubts. As one of his grandsons wrote to the pope in 1247: 'By the power of God all lands from the rising of the sun to its setting have been made subject to us.' All the Mongols had to do was get everyone else on earth to acknowledge that they were Mongol subjects. It is an extraordinary idea. But then, of course, no Mongol knew the true size of the world, and anyway success – defined first by mere survival, then by local conquest, then national unity, then international conquest – seemed to prove its truth.

It's worth taking a closer look at this bizarre notion. Genghis was not the only leader, the Mongols not the only people, who have believed in divine backing for world domination. Two of the major religions, Christianity and Islam, claim to be universal, and some of their adherents have also claimed that any act, however brutal, is justified if it works towards that end. This statement can be turned around to suggest a hypothesis: any leader or group aiming at world domination must do so in the name of religion. Every year, English people gather for a strange ritual known as the Last Night of the Proms (I say English, not British, because the sentiments they express do not easily equate with Scottishness, Irishness or Welshness). This gathering concludes a long series of concerts performed in London's Albert Hall, a temple to the arts. Part of the ritual involves the crowd singing a very politically incorrect paean to the British empire:

Land of Hope and Glory,
Mother of the Free,
How shall we extol thee,
Who are born of thee?
Wider still and wider
Shall thy bounds be set;
God, who made thee mighty,
Make thee mightier yet.

Of course, everyone today understands that this is merely a tribal ritual, empty of meaning, a piece of fun. But once it was serious. Millions of English people really believed that the empire was ordained and sustained by God; that the English were thus free to conquer whomever they liked; that if the final outcome was world dominion, well, that was God's idea, so who were the English to argue? They were a Chosen People, at a time when to be born English was to win first prize in the lottery of life (as one of the winners, arch-imperialist Cecil Rhodes, said). It is a commonplace of history: everyone claims God or Allah or Heaven to be on their side when they wish to win, and a winning streak seems to justify the claim. Chinese emperors were no exception: they ruled by the Mandate of Heaven, which approved its choice by sending good times and withdrew its mandate when revolution succeeded.

So Genghis's claim was no wilder than those of many rulers. But it was different in two respects. First, at the time he first made it, he was not a ruler. There must have been other non-royal people who have wished to rule the world, maybe some who have claimed God as a supporter; but you would have found them mumbling to themselves in slums and lunatic asylums. Second, loonies are not known for their self-critical abilities; and Genghis had these aplenty. His own acts and those of his heirs tell us that he firmly believed in his mission, but never ceased to wonder at the mystery of it. Why him? And what was the nature of the divinity that had chosen him? These were questions to which he sought answers in other religions, willing to see them all as perhaps offering different routes to a heaven he could not fathom. He did not kill because others believed differently. He killed when he thought it strategically necessary, when it was the only way to assert his supremacy.

First things first: the Mongols had to be reunited, local tribes conquered, revenge taken on the Tatars. This was a 20-year process that involved much politicking. In 1196, for instance, Temujin joined with his father's blood-brother, Toghrul, khan of the Kerait tribe, to crush the Tatars. At the time, Toghrul was an ally of Jin, which wanted the Tatars controlled. Toghrul and Genghis reported in person to the Jin court (thus acquiring first-hand knowledge of Beijing). Here Toghrul was honoured with the title 'Prince King', Wang (or Ong in another transliteration) Khan. Temujin, too, received a title, but such a minor one that its meaning is unclear. The title came from the court chancellor, who hinted that something better – 'Pacification Commissioner' – might come his way from the emperor some time. It never did, no doubt adding to Temujin's resentment at Jin, and to his determination not simply to conquer the Tatars, but to exterminate them.

The brutal climax came in about 1202, when Temujin, now master of most of Mongolia's tribes, led a coalition of tribes to destroy the Tatars. As often, *The Secret History* gives no details about the battle, which the Mongols won. It focuses on the extermination that followed: 'We shall measure the Tatars against the linch-pin of a cart,' he said, referring to the pin that holds a wheel on to an axle, this being a standard way to sort adults and older children from those of about five and younger. Then 'we shall kill them to the last one', by which was meant not everyone, but the male members of the leading clan. Foolishly, one of the Mongol generals chose to humiliate the prisoners by telling them what was in store for them. Knowing they had nothing to lose, the captives 'raised a barricade', behind which they staged a last stand that cost many Mongol lives. Even in renewed defeat, the Tatars fought on, individually, with knives concealed in their sleeves. It made no difference. The Tatar leaders died, the women and children were enslaved, and the clans scattered, never to rise again. Revenge was complete.

And Temujin went on to unite the rest of Mongolia, found a nation and in 1206 have himself declared khan, with the new title of Chingis,[2] or Genghis as it still is in non-academic English.

Now he was ready for the next step. He needed to move

[2] That's how it is in Mongolian, sometimes transliterated 'Chinggis' to represent the name as it is in old Mongol script. 'Genghis' is the less correct English spelling, which is just about OK in French, from which the English took it, but encourages the totally incorrect habit among English-speakers of pronouncing the G hard, as in *gross*.

fast, for two reasons. One was to do with leadership. When you have created a new nation and a new model army, you cannot leave them unoccupied: *use them or lose them*. But to use them would take them away from their economic base, their pastures and their herds. Hence the second reason: they would need rewarding, in the form of booty. Where to look? One obvious target lay south-east across the Gobi and Mongolia's rolling eastern grasslands: Jin.

Genghis already had two sufficient, if base, reasons to attack Jin: to take revenge, and to seize loot. Now he had two more. The first was that Jin was in crisis. The emperor had died, and a court clique had given the throne not to his brother, as tradition demanded, but to the compliant seventh son of a former emperor and one of his concubines. It so happened that this prince, Wei, had once tried to extract tribute from Genghis, who gave him short shrift. When he succeeded, Genghis is supposed to have spat in disdain. Could the new emperor be 'a person of such weakness'? he said. 'Why should I kowtow to him?' His succession coincided with the collapse of Jin rule on the frontier. One border group, the Ongut, had already allied themselves with Genghis, who had married off one of his daughters to an Ongut prince. Now another frontier group, the Juyin, rose in rebellion. They had been recruited as soldiers in a campaign against Song, and had never seen any payment; they saw the Jin wall as a device to cut them off from their northern relatives. 'The Jin sent troops to pacify them,' says one source. 'The Juyin people scattered and went over to the Mongols.' The result was that the frontier was up for grabs. If Genghis could move in, he would have a good foundation for an advance southward on the Jin heartland and Beijing. The Jin frontier, marked by the ridge I had visited, had been overrun in his campaign against the Tatars. By 1207, the year after his coronation, everything was in place for an assault on the Jin.

But the border would be only a first step. The taking of Beijing and the destruction of Jin would be no easy task. The Mongols were mounted archers, with no experience of besieging cities. And Jin, having ceased fighting with its other neighbours, could well turn to them for aid. Better to remove the possible aid first, namely the Tangut state of Xi Xia.

The Tanguts were sophisticated people. For over a century they had ruled an empire that ran westward from their capital, present-day Yinchuan, along the narrow strip of grassland we now know as the Gansu Corridor and which has cropped up time and again already in this story. This key segment of the Silk Route that linked China and the West through Central Asia gave the Tanguts access to trade and infused them with Buddhist traditions of art and literature. The Tanguts had devised their own Chinese-style script and printed vast numbers of books, many thousands of which were bought in 1907 in Dunhuang by the Hungarian–British archaeologist Sir Aurel Stein; many more thousands were carted off by the Russian Petr Kozlov from Xi Xia's northern outpost, Khara Khoto, a couple of years later. In 1209 Xi Xia had half a dozen cities and an army of some 300,000. But it was also vulnerable. Most of it was desert. Its towns were widely scattered. It was a nation ruled by scholars and bureaucrats. And the Mongols had close links with the Tanguts. Compared to Jin, Xi Xia was a soft target.

The invasion came in 1209, with Genghis leading his army south across the Gobi, down the desert that flanked the Helan mountains, through a low pass and thus on to the broad sloping plain that led to the Yellow River and the Tangut capital. The Tangut king sent a desperate plea to Jin, whose leader failed to see the emerging threat and sent a short-sighted answer: 'It is to our advantage when our enemies attack one another. Wherein lies the danger to us?' Then as now, Yinchuan was fed from fields watered by canals tapping the Yellow River's silty waters. Genghis's army lacked the siege machinery that other armies had – the huge siege bows, the battering rams, perhaps even the first explosive devices – so he broke the canals and flooded the area. Unfortunately, this included his own camp, forcing a rapid evacuation, but still left Yinchuan isolated. To break the stalemate, both sides gave ground. The Tangut king handed over a princess and rich gifts; Genghis, convinced he had a new vassal, withdrew to focus on Jin.

That assault came two years later, in spring 1211. It was then, surely, when the old Jin frontier was overrun, that the steppeland 'Wall of Genghis Khan' was left to the wind and rain, to the gazelles and marmots. The armies gathered in the Mongol heartland, the plains and valleys that tumbled out of the Khenti mountains, and headed south across the Gobi. Imagine several hundred camel-drawn carts and something like 100,000 horsemen, each leading three or four remounts, stretched out in several columns in order not to make too much impact on the Gobi's scattered springs, moving at walking pace for a couple of weeks. *The Secret History*, notoriously skimpy on military matters, leaps the 600 kilometres of gravelly expanses and sparse pastures in one bound: 'Genghis Khan set out against the [Jurchen] people. He took Vujiu,' i.e. Fuzhou, a place on the borders of Inner Mongolia north of present-day Zhangjiakou – formerly known by its Mongol name Kalgan, from the Mongolian for 'gateway', because it guards the bottom of the pass that drops from the Mongolian plateau. Today, your car swings down this escarpment in a few minutes with the help of many S-bends. In Genghis's day this route meant taking the pass called the Badger's Mouth (Huan-erh-tsui / 獾兒嘴). This was no blitzkrieg. Having seized the border, Genghis remained in camp up on the plateau all summer, watching, waiting, pillaging.

Somewhere along the way we lost several bits of the Great Wall. What happened to the Jin's forward lines of defences, the gazelle-rich ones that run into the Mongol homeland? And the more extensive wall built across Inner Mongolia, the one that was supposed to keep farmers in and nomads out? And the Qin and Han walls, which ran through the mountains north of Beijing? They would have been well known to Genghis in his youth. He and his family lived and fought over this area when the Jin were at the height of their power in the late twelfth century. A border wall of any kind would have stated a claim of ownership over prime Mongol grasslands, a claim that the founder of the new nation would have been eager to remove as he expanded south and east. When push came to shove, these markers proved totally useless. Genghis's Ongut 'brother' saw his army safely through the Jin fortifications, and the border zone was in his hands. No other mention of any walls in any source, Mongol or Chinese. When it came to the crunch, they might just as well not have existed.

Genghis was still acting more like a robber baron than a conqueror and empire-builder. There was a great victory when that autumn the Mongols broke the Jin defences at the Badger's Mouth, leaving the countryside scattered with bodies, the bones still visible ten years later. Two other victories followed, opening the way to Beijing. He drove on down over the valley that separates the Mongolian plateau from the mountains guarding Beijing, then sent his close friend Jebe ahead along the narrow, winding valley from today's Badaling, where tourists by the million walk on the (much later) Great Wall, down the 18 kilometres to Juyungguan, just over 50 kilometres from Beijing. At this point the approach was barred by a gate. Jebe ordered the manœuvre familiar to anyone who knew the tactics of mounted archers, which the Jin apparently did not. He turned and fled. '"Let us pursue them!" yelled the foolish soldiers. And they went in pursuit until the valleys and mountains were completely covered with them.' Once well out in the open, the Mongols turned and cut down their disorganized opponents. Meanwhile Genghis himself led another force to clear the remaining defenders, killing Jin troops until they lay all along the defile 'like heaps of rotten logs'. Jebe returned, took the Juyong fortress and forced open the doors.

Beijing was before them. But so too was winter. The Jin capital was in panic: all men capable of bearing arms banned from leaving, the emperor only just restrained from hasty flight. But confronted by Beijing's defences – 15 kilometres of 12-metre walls, 13 gates, 3 lines of moats, 900 guard-towers, 4 external forts connected to the main city by underground passageways, all defended by vast siege bows that could fire 3-metre arrows half a kilometre, rock-throwing catapults, fire-arrows, and fire-balls filled with petroleum – Genghis saw that he was not yet ready to seize cities and occupy territory. He sent contingents east and west, raiding as far as the Pacific coast, then, in February 1212, with bitter weather threatening to trap him, pulled back through the northern passes to the borderlands, as if to ponder what his next step should be to turn himself from booty-hunter to empire-builder.

This allowed Jin a brief respite, time enough to re-occupy the pass through the mountains north of the capital. But that achieved little. The Mongols stayed where they were through the summer of 1212, beginning operations when their horses were fat with grass in the autumn. In Jin, chaos reigned. In Manchuria, Khitans, former rulers of north China who had been taken over by Jin, revolted and swore allegiance to Genghis. Back in Beijing, Zhizhong, the general who had lost so disastrously at Badger's Mouth Pass, staged a coup, killed the emperor and installed a compliant prince through whom he could rule. But that November, one of Zhizhong's generals, Gaoqi, having lost a battle with the Mongols and knowing his own head would be forfeit as a result, galloped from the scene of the disaster, sought out Zhizhong, killed him, cut off his head and ran with it into the emperor's quarters. Perhaps pleased by the death of the murderous regent or else scared witless by the fearful sight, the emperor put Gaoqi in charge.

Meanwhile, the loot gathered by the Mongols in the 1211–12 campaigns was running out. Genghis began collecting more, keeping a small force around Beijing and dividing the rest into three armies which, over the winter of 1213–14, he sent off to run riot across all north China between the Pacific and the Yellow River, an area about the size of Germany containing a dozen cities of over 100,000 inhabitants. To take them, the Mongols devised a nasty technique. Prisoners were taken in the surrounding countryside and driven up to the city walls to erect siege engines and take the full force of any retaliation. Often there was none, because those inside would recognize relatives in the crowd of prisoners, and refuse to fight. In any event, resistance would be followed by massacre. As city followed city in surrender, the Mongols snowballed their way back and forth across Jin, growing in siege machinery, expertise and wealth.

And still Genghis did not stay at the gates of Beijing, but returned that winter to his base at the foot of the mountains some 50 kilometres north-west of Beijing, hoping for a breakthrough in the siege. It was perhaps at this time that he sent off a delegation to Song in an attempt to make an alliance; not surprisingly, his diplomats were arrested by the Jin before they reached the border, a slight that would come in handy later (they were presumably released, because the ambassador, Jubqan, was killed on a similar mission in 1231). Several attacks on Beijing failed. All around was a desert from which had been stripped all potential ammunition, like stones and tiles, and all food and fodder. It must have been a tough and depressing winter for the Mongols, relieved only by information that the Jin were discussing peace proposals. Genghis sent a message: 'The whole of Shandong and Hebei are now in my possession, while you retain only [Beijing]; God has made you so weak that, should I further molest you, I know not what Heaven would say; I am willing to withdraw my army, but what provision will you make to still the demands of my officers?'

The message sparked a debate among the Jin leaders. One said the Mongols were exhausted, and would crumble under a decisive attack. Another pointed out that the Jin troops were from all over, and without their families; win or lose, 'they will fly like birds and animals . . . and who will then guard the capital?' Better to sue for peace, and (in the words of *The Secret History*) 'after their withdrawal, we shall there and then take up another different counsel'.

The emperor agreed. By the peace agreement of April 1214, the Jin handed over a princess with a retinue of 500 boys and girls, 3,000 horses, 10,000 *liang* of gold (150 kilos, some $3 million in present-day prices) and 10,000 bolts or rolls of silk (which, when stretched out, amounted to either 90 or 270 kilometres, depending on whose conversion you trust). It sounds to me like too little gold and too much silk, suggesting that the '10,000' was not a real figure but, as so often, shorthand for 'a large amount'. *The Secret History* is both vaguer and more realistic: the Jin 'sent gold, silver, satin and goods – as much, in their judgement, as their strength and that of their horses could carry'. Believing he now had a compliant vassal, Genghis promised to withdraw – but keeping the vital pass of Juyung in Mongol hands, leaving him free to advance again whenever he chose.

As soon as the Mongols were out of the way, the emperor looked to his future. The view was grim: Jin was now a rump state, with Mongols pressing in from the north-west, Xi Xia in the west, rebel groups in Manchuria and Song in the south. His conclusion was that he and his retinue had better get out, fast, and re-establish themselves in Kaifeng, almost 600 kilometres to the south across the Yellow River. This underlined the change the Jurchen had undergone since their emergence from Manchuria a century before. They had become Chinese. Now they were abandoning their original homeland and all the border areas for the heart of China.

The exit from Beijing in June 1214 was an immense operation, involving 3,000 camels and unnumbered horses and oxen hauling 30,000 wagons full of documents, possessions and people. Moving at about 10 kilometres a day, it would take almost two months to reach its destination, and would surely have become known to Genghis sooner or later. In the event it was sooner. Fifty kilometres outside Beijing, the emperor suspected the loyalty of 2,000 Khitans, thinking, probably rightly, that they resented moving so far from their Manchurian home. When a rumour of his suspicion reached the men, his fear fulfilled itself instantly. The Khitans rose, killed their commander and galloped back to Beijing, where they stole more horses and offered themselves to Genghis.

Hearing what had happened, the khan was enraged, according to a Chinese source. 'The Jin Emperor mistrusts my word! He has used the peace to deceive me!' He had to move fast, for, as a Khitan officer who had joined him said, the Jin emperor would soon be able to mount a counter-offensive. Still, there had been nothing in the peace terms stating that the emperor should remain in Beijing. Genghis recalled his ambassadors to Song; but they remained under arrest in Jin. This became his excuse to go back to war.

So even before the Jin emperor arrived in Kaifeng in mid-August, the Mongol army was back at the walls of Beijing. This time there would be no peace talks. Beijing would be taken, not by outright assault but by siege. Winter was coming; if they could stick it out, time was on their side, for there would be no relief sent from Kaifeng until spring. As usual, *The Secret History* is vague or just plain wrong on what actually happened. It offers no account of the siege, dropping only one detail that hints at its horrors that winter: 'As the remnants of his [the emperor's] troops were dying of starvation, they ate human flesh between them.' Other sources say that, come the spring, two relief columns from Kaifeng tried to break through, with over 40,000 men and 1,000 wagonloads of food. Both were annihilated before crossing the Yongdeng river, 40 kilometres south of the city. Nearby towns fell one by one, releasing ever more troops for the main siege. Clearly it was only a matter of time. In April, Genghis was confident enough to leave his forces to it and head up on to the Mongolian plateau to meet the spring, to the place his grandson Kublai would later choose for his summer palace, which would eventually be named Shang-du (Upper Capital) or, as English-speakers call it, Xanadu.

Inside Beijing, the civilian and military commanders argued about what to do: surrender, fight on, throw open the gates and die heroically in a hopeless assault? They could not agree. The civilian chancellor, Wanyen Fuxing, committed suicide. The military commander, Moran Jinzhong, his nerve broken, sneaked out, breaking a promise to take a number of princesses with him. On the last day of May, leaderless, the remaining officers finally opened the gates in surrender.

Without Genghis's restraining influence, the Mongol troops ran wild. Palaces burned, thousands were slaughtered. Again, Mongol and Chinese sources do not record details. A hint of what happened, although it was already the stuff of folklore rather than record, came the following year from a Muslim, an ambassador from the expanding empire of Khwarezm (what is now most of Iran, Uzbekistan, Turkmenistan and Afghanistan). The shah, who would soon become Genghis's enemy and victim, was at this moment in the lead as an empire-builder, and had his eye on China, for trade and possibly conquest. The fall of Beijing was a blow to his ambitions; so, contemplating what to do next, he sent one of his aides, Baha ad-Din Razi, on a fact-finding mission. Apparently the envoys met Genghis and saw Beijing, where, to quote Barthold,

signs of terrible devastation were everywhere visible; the bones of the slaughtered formed whole mountains; the soil was greasy with human fat; and the rotting of the bodies brought on an illness from which some of Baha ad-Din's companions died. At the gate of [Beijing] lay a vast heap of bones, and the envoys were told that on the capture of the town 60,000 girls threw themselves from the walls to avoid falling into the hands of the Mongols.

Now, all this is second-hand many times over: an English translation of a Russian original, published in 1900 and based on a translation of the Persian historian Juzjani. Juzjani had lived through the Mongol invasion of his lands, but he was still only reporting what he had been told, and already some of that is fanciful. How big is a 'mountain' of bones? How much ground was still greasy? And 60,000 suicidal girls? I think not. But the very idea is evidence of the emotional impact of the event.

There was one detail *The Secret History* did record, a matter crucial to Genghis's leadership. It was to do with the handling of the booty. Once news came of the city's surrender, Genghis sent off three of his aides to make an inventory of Jin treasures.

A word about one of the aides, Shigi, a Tatar who had been picked up as a child and taken in by Genghis's mother. He was 20 years younger than Genghis, and when his mother died he joined Genghis's family as a sort of stepson. Different sources call him both brother and son; in effect, he was both. He must have been exceptionally bright as well as close to Genghis, because Genghis put him in charge of his up-and-coming bureaucracy, which was run using the Mongols' first script, taken over from another of their new conquests, the Uighurs of today's western China. After Genghis's death, Shigi would have been a natural choice to edit together the inside story of Genghis's rise, the epic we know as *The Secret History*. He may have been less than rigorous in historical matters – after all, the only sources would have been verbal – but he knew all about administration and law, so what happened now was close to his heart.

Entering Beijing, Shigi and his two colleagues were met by the Jin governor, offering gifts of 'gold-embroidered and patterned satins'. Wait a minute, said Shigi. These were not exactly gifts. Before, everything in the city belonged to the Jin emperor. Now, by long-established precedent, everything belonged to the new ruler, Genghis. This was theft disguised as generosity. Shigi's colleagues were happy to accept, but Shigi took a puritan view. 'How can you give us the goods and satins of Genghis Khan, stealing them and bringing them here behind his back?' he asked. He made the same point to Genghis himself, who commended him for his honesty and his understanding of the 'great norm', the fundamental principles governing the relationship between a lord and his subjects. The principle here was that all war booty belonged to the khan, who had the sole right to distribute it to his followers.

What does all this mean? It means that Genghis was maturing fast, developing from tribal chief and robber baron into conqueror and now long-term ruler, determined to use the tools of government: writing, records, taxes, bureaucracy, the rule of law.

Quickly, Mongolia swallowed all the northern swathe of Jin. In ten years, Genghis had burst the bonds of his homeland to take over an estate that reached from Mongolia's far west to the Pacific, from Lake Baikal down to the borders of the rump Jin empire, a wavy line that ran north-east from the southern fringes of the Ordos to the coast about 200 kilometres south-east from Beijing: an area of some 4 million square kilometres, almost half the size of the USA. It incorporated the forested and mountainous expanses of southern Siberia and Manchuria, Genghis's own flowing grasslands, the gravelly wastes of the Gobi, the eastern sections of the vital east–west trade route that would later be known as the Silk Road, and now a foundation for wealth undreamed-of: China's north, with its thick, rich soils, its 20 million peasants, hundreds of towns and a dozen major cities. No leader since Alexander had conquered so much territory. The two of them took much the same time to seize the same amount; but Genghis was only just starting.

From China, his attention was taken by the murder of a trade delegation to the brash new kingdom of Khwarezm, at the far western end of Central Asia. His armies fell upon the Islamic world in a cataclysm that killed perhaps a quarter of its population, wrecked a dozen cities and doubled his empire. He himself pursued his enemies deep into Afghanistan, perhaps even descending through the Khyber Pass into the plains of north India. He then turned back to fulfil his original purpose, the seizure of the rest of Jin. In the meantime, Genghis having taken his eye off the ball to deal with Khwarezm, his very first major conquest, the Tangut empire of Xi Xia, had reclaimed independence. Having dealt with them, he was realigning his forces in north China for a final assault on the Jin capital, Kaifeng, when he was taken ill. He was rushed to a hidden valley in the Liupan mountains, in the south of present-day Ningxia province. Now a national park, the valley was noted for its medicinal plants – and still is, as I know from a trip there in 2002.[3] It is a glorious combination of steep mountains, forests and once open areas that locals still call by names that seem to have been passed down the centuries: the Medical Treatment Place, the Meeting Place, the Command Centre – and the Sitting Place of Genghis Khan, where senior officers could review troops set out below. Here, after perhaps a week in the late summer of 1227, Genghis succumbed to his illness.

Imagine him reviewing his achievements and plans, knowing himself to be on the brink of death. His empire, now the largest the world had ever seen, reached from the Pacific coast across to the Caspian, 6,000 kilometres from end to end. Xi Xia was just about to be brought formally back into the fold. Then, carrying out a plan he had already devised, his heirs would finish off Jin. And the future? The rest of the Middle East, of course, for Baghdad and other great Islamic cities were unfinished business. Then beyond. From one exploit by some of his most brilliant generals – a 7,500-kilometre gallop into southern Russia and back – he had heard of other grasslands across the Ukraine and beyond. Grass was fuel to an army of horse-borne archers. Why, if they chose their route right, his horsemen would have fuel enough to carry them to the Great Plain in Hungary, a twin (it must have seemed) to Mongolia; and from Hungary it would surely be possible to seize all Europe, which – so travellers and now his own people told him – was another treasure-house, with cities that might rival Beijing and Samarkand. Then, of course, there was the rest of China, ruled by the Song

[3] For details of the trip, see my *Genghis Khan*.

dynasty, which no outsider had ever conquered: that would be the jewel in his crown. And then, with Heaven's backing, his heirs would set his imperial bounds wider still and wider, to include peoples and places hardly heard of: Vietnam, Burma, Japan, all South-East Asia, India. With no knowledge of Africa and the Americas, let alone Australia, it must have seemed that the whole known world must eventually become Mongol.

At one point, it all seemed possible. That point was 1280, when Genghis's family ruled half of Eurasia: much of Russia, much of the Middle East, all Central Asia, all China. That one family should govern a fifth of the earth's inhabited land area is one of history's more startling facts. But that 'seemed' in the first sentence of this paragraph points to a hidden reality – that world, or even Eurasian, dominance was a pipe-dream. It was Genghis's grandson, Kublai, the khan of Xanadu, the khan turned into both fact and legend for Europe by Marco Polo, who discovered the limits to Mongol growth. It was he who had brought the rest of China and Tibet into the empire. But as early as 1260 the Mongols had been defeated by the Egyptians, mainly because, in their high summer incursion into Syria and Palestine, they had galloped off the edge of the pasture-lands that sustained them; in brief, they had run out of fuel. And almost from the beginnings of empire, the family, though always remembering that they owed their existence to Genghis, paid only nominal homage to their family's CEO, Kublai. In the west, they went native, which meant Islamic, and fought their own corners, which meant fighting each other, and him. He himself discovered that even the world's most powerful man had limits, imposed by the very Heaven which had inspired his vision of world rule. In the summer of 1281 Kublai's armada of 5,000 ships, despatched to invade Japan, was destroyed by a typhoon. Other invasions, of Burma, Vietnam and Java, also foundered.

If you drew a graph of the Mongol empire, you would see it zooming upwards for a century (1180–1280), then faltering; then, after Kublai's death in 1294, heading downward again for another seven decades as distant Mongol regimes tumbled, until in 1368 the unpopular Mongols in China, ruling as the Yuan Dynasty, turned soft by power and wealth, were kicked out by their successors, the Ming. They returned to their grassy homeland, embittered and resentful at their ejection, and eager to regain what they had lost.

Only then did the Wall, useless, redundant and forgotten for 134 years, regain its status, as a defence and as a symbol of Chinese determination that the Mongols should never, ever, return.

11

DISASTER AT TUMU

IF YOU DRIVE THROUGH THE WALL AT BADALING, PAST THE
tourist buses and the T-shirt salesmen, you see before you
the lowlands of north China – probably veiled in a haze of
diesel fumes, so you will have to imagine the view –
rolling north-west to the clear blue skies of the Inner
Mongolian plateau. The motorway bridges a reservoir,
and thrusts straight on to Zhangjiakou, which used to be
called Kalgan, the *khalkha* (gateway) to Mongolia.[1] On
one occasion, directed by Cheng, the son of the wall
expert Cheng Dalin, our car turned off the motorway on
to the old road. There was something Cheng wanted me
to see. We pulled up on the road's broad edge, where

---

[1] The word exists in two versions. *Khalkha* is the major ethnic sub-
group in Mongolia, and a river; *khaalga* is 'a gateway'.

trailer-trucks hove to like galleons for repairs, and tea, and dumplings. It was autumn, with a gritty wind that snatched at jackets and eyes as we got out of the car. Across the road was a ditch, and across the ditch a village of single-storey brick houses. Cheng led the way down a lane, past enclosed courtyards and stacks of dead sunflowers and piles of leaves stripped from corn-husks. On our left, the houses gave way to an earth wall, all to my baffled eyes utterly without interest. We came to a gap in the wall, and my perspective changed. The gap was big enough for a double-decker bus, with holes in the surrounding packed earth that must once have held stonework. It must have been quite a gate.

'Tumu Fortress,' said Cheng. 'I need to see too, for my thesis on medieval towns.'

Beyond the 7 metres of rammed earth – you could still pick out the vague horizontal stripes of the planks separating the layers – were more houses, more piles of leaves, more trees that had sprouted in unkempt corners; but the grey shoulders of earth walls looming over distant roofs showed this was indeed a fortress, the inside of which had long ago filled up with houses, lanes and courtyards.

'This is an important place. Here Mongolians beat a great Ming army. Very important especially for me, because before not many towns had walls' – they had no need of walls, of course, when the Mongols ruled all China – 'and after Tumu they built walls.' We had wandered back through the cavernous entrance, and round a corner to, of all things, a little open-air theatre which faced the town's administrative offices, and a small temple. 'This temple was built in memory of the officers who fell here. Oh, locked. Sorry.' But we had been seen. A woman appeared, along with four of her shy colleagues, one of whom had a key. While they whispered and giggled about the foreigner, the one-room temple whispered through dust and shadows about disaster. On the wall was a roll-call of 68 officers and officials who had died here in the summer of 1449. A plaque recalled a foolish emperor in the power of an emasculated official, and the loss of 500,000 soldiers; of the building of this, the Ancestral Temple of Loyalty, of the loss of memorial tablets, of fire and decay and rebuilding. *Half a million* troops killed? Was that true? Even if only one-tenth that number had been lost, this was a first-order, top-drawer catastrophe. Cheng told me the outlines of the story, which I filled out later: how the emperor and his senior adviser – his Svengali, his Rasputin, his Rumsfeld – hatched a crazy scheme to crush the Mongols, and how their blinkered arrogance led to a catastrophe that produced the Wall as we know it today.

Having thrown out the Mongols in 1368, their successors, the Ming, were faced with a question: what was their China to be? Theoretically, since they had replaced the Mongols, they might lay claim to the whole empire as established by Kublai Khan. But even in his lifetime much of it – Central Asia, Persia, southern Russia – fell away into independence. Even the remaining core of China, Tibet, Manchuria and Mongolia would be unrealistic, because the defeated Mongols had reclaimed their own homeland. So the Ming made do with Kublai's Chinese estates, minus Mongolia – 'a shrunken form of the Mongol empire', in the words of the Japanese scholar Hidehiro Okada.

That forced the Ming to wrestle once again with an ancient problem: how best to deal with the northern barbarians? They might have relied on the Wall, except that for a century and a half under the Mongols no one had bothered with it, because it had all been inside the Mongol Empire. Its bits and pieces had become relics, eroded and hacked into insignificance. But so what? The new dynasty's military was strong. The Mongols had left behind 500,000 households; all their men were in the army, and the Ming increased the total to 1.2 million. To emphasize their victory, Ming forces reached Karakorum twice (1370 and 1380); other victories in 1387–8 secured Manchuria and eastern Mongolia.

These successes in consolidating the new regime were largely down to the man who fought for and won the Ming throne, Zhu Di, son of the dynasty's founder. It was he who, as a prince, masterminded the reconquest of Yunnan, shifted the capital back to Beijing, and began rebuilding Kublai Khan's palace into the Forbidden City as it is today.

A word about Zhu Di, who very nearly made China into a world empire that would have been the envy of Genghis Khan – and who, rather oddly, was rumoured to have the blood of the Mongol conqueror flowing through his veins. It was all talk, but it affected events on both sides of the Wall. This was what people said: that when Zhu Di's father defeated the Mongols and founded the Ming, he married the wife of the last Mongol ruler; and she, unbeknown to the new emperor, was pregnant at the time. His son, Zhu Di, was therefore a Mongol. This story gives a peculiar twist to Zhu Di's reconquest of Yunnan in 1382, when he had adult Mongols killed by the hundred and the male children castrated. Among the surviving castrati was a Muslim boy – many Muslims having settled in Yunnan under the Mongols – who was taken into Zhu Di's household. Eunuchs, usually non-Chinese, and usually social rejects, were employed in the Chinese court, as they were in courts across the ancient world, as sex-spies to ensure the imperial succession was untainted by scandal. This gave them privileged access to the inner workings of the court, an opportunity that those with ambition relished, for it offered political influence without the constraints endured by officials. Soon they would have their own ministry, with directorates that controlled court ceremonies, punishments and the flow of documents to the emperor, giving them enough power to cause the occasional disaster, such as the one we shall soon witness. In this case, the court and the nation were as lucky as the boy. Renamed Zheng He, the survivor grew up to be an imposing and intelligent commander, becoming Zhu Di's top aide as the emperor embarked on a series of massive new projects that would proclaim China as the world's greatest power. These included rebuilding the imperial heart of Beijing as the Forbidden City – with 9,000 rooms (over 8,000 of which still survive) – restoring the Great Wall and establishing forward bases some 150 kilometres beyond it, widening the Grand Canal, and finally creating a fleet that would, if not conquer the world by force of arms, at least record it and master it with trade.

He commissioned 1,681 new ships, among them 250 gigantic nine-masted 'treasure ships' 145 metres long and 54 metres across. (Europe's biggest ship, Henry V's *Grace Dieu*, built in 1418, was a quarter the length and one-tenth the weight. Even the longest western sailing ships, built in the early 1900s, were 20 metres shorter.) The man entrusted to oversee and lead this new navy was none other than the Turkic Mongol eunuch Zheng He.

Meanwhile, the other side of the Great Wall, the Mongols also clung to the idea that they were still the 'real' rulers of China, calling themselves the Northern Yuan, buttressing their claim with the Chinese title and the myth that the Ming were 'really' Mongols. To their advantage, Mongolia was now emerging as a proper Mongol homeland: before the rise of Genghis in the twelfth century there had been several other Turkic groups claiming it; since Genghis, it had been all part of the Mongol/Yuan empire; only after 1368 did it start becoming the Mongolia we know today.

But in the late fourteenth and early fifteenth centuries, the Mongols were their own worst enemies. Westerners (Oirats) rivalled easterners (Khalkhas), squabbling and feuding as their ancestors had before the rise of Genghis. Commerce declined, craftsmen forgot their trades, the people scattered and returned to nomadism. If either side seemed to gain in influence, the Ming sent help to the underdog. For China, peace depended on these inter-tribal rivalries, and on three docile buffer-zone tribes on the Manchurian border known as the Three Guards. It was not enough. A leader named Arughtai refused to pay the usual tribute and won over the Three Guards.[2] In an attempt to assert his authority, Zhu Di unleashed four campaigns in 1410–23, each one involving some 250,000 men, none to any great effect.

In 1421, only two months after Zheng He's last and greatest fleet of exploration had departed, the whole vast imperial enterprise came to a sudden halt. Lightning set fire to the new Forbidden City and burned down much of it. The emperor was distraught. 'In his anguish he repaired to the temple, saying "The God of Heaven is angry with me and therefore has burnt my palace."'[3] A public request for help in understanding what he had done wrong produced a flood of opinions, mostly focusing on his grandiose projects, including Zheng He and his fleet. As if in support of the criticisms, disasters multiplied. The emperor suffered strokes, impotence, sex scandals at court and rebellions. In 1424 he embarked on one last campaign to crush Arughtai, the biggest of all – a million men, 340,000 horses and mules – only to discover that his opponent had once again vanished over the steppe. It was too much. Zhu Di, a 64-year-old broken by failure, died on campaign.

Why had he failed? Some would say because he had wasted the nation's wealth on foreign adventures and vast

[2] Arughtai was not a Mongol but an 'Asud', i.e. an Ossetian, from the Caucasus. Today, Ossetia straddles the Georgian–Russian border. After the Mongols invaded the Caucasus in 1223 they brought back a contingent of Ossetians, some of whom became guards under Kublai. They bred, forming a community of 30,000. In 1368 they accompanied their Mongol overlords back to Mongolia. There is still a clan of Asud in eastern Inner Mongolia.

[3] Hafiz Abru, *A Persian Embassy in China, 1421*, trans. K. M. Maitra (Lahore, 1934), quoted in Menzies, *1421*.

schemes. After his funeral, his son and heir reversed all his large-scale projects. In line with Confucian policies, poverty would be relieved, foreign adventures – including campaigns across the Gobi – banned, spending on the navy cancelled. The great ships returned to the junkyard, Zheng He to a pension, his records to the equivalent of the shredder. To reinforce the country's renewed isolation, a coastal strip 1,000 kilometres long and 50 deep was cleared, its inhabitants moved inland. The colonies planted by Zheng He in Africa, the Americas and Australia languished and died. China, which might have seized the world as European nations were soon to seize it, turned inward again, back to its proper business: defence against the barbarians beyond the Great Wall, not with forward campaigns, but with the regarrisoned Wall itself.

So what does the northern frontier look like to you, in Beijing, in 1440? Not too bad. The frontier was secured by vassal Mongol tribes. The expensive and exposed outer defence points beyond the Wall had been pulled back, and the Wall itself largely rebuilt. Beijing was safe behind two lines of the Great Wall, one running across the mountains either side of the Juyung Pass, the other through today's Zhangjiakou, backed by armies based in two walled cities, Datong and Xuanhua. The emperor, Yingzong,[4] was a boy

---

[4] This was his temple name, granted posthumously. Other emperors are known by their personal names or reign names. But this one ruled twice, with different reign names. By convention, historians refer to him as the Zhengtong or Tianshun Emperor (his reign names) or call him by his temple name, Yīngzōng (英宗 / Hero-Ancestor), for the sake of simplicity.

of twelve, but he was well supervised by his wise and strong-minded grandmother, the Grand Dowager Empress Zhang. A major concern of hers was to limit the influence of the eunuchs, particularly their boss, Wang Zhen, whose ambitions were the very opposite of Zheng He's: self-serving, malign, overweening.

Two years later, all this began to unravel. The key event was the death of the Grand Dowager Empress, which gave Wang Zhen, one of China's most notorious villains, the freedom he wanted. He controlled the eunuch bureaucracy, the secret service, and soon the mind of Yingzong, now a foolish fifteen-year-old. It was he who made the road on which the emperor would march to disaster.

The young emperor had been raised to admire soldiers, and in 1449, aged 21, he decided it was time to prove himself in action. There was only one region from which invasion threatened: the Great Wall frontier, beyond which lay what could be a unified power, the Mongols.

It so happened that a force for Mongol unity had recently emerged. His name was Esen,[5] and he had inherited control of the western Mongol groups, the Oirat. In the 1440s he took over what are today Uzbekistan and the other Central Asian -stans, then the Chinese–Mongol borderland groups along the Gobi to Manchuria. In his rise to power he had killed Arughtai, the chieftain responsible for humiliating Yingzong's father

[5] Esen: pronounced Yisun, it means 'nine', a number of 'special symbolic significance for the Turco-Mongolian peoples' (de Rachewiltz, *Secret History*).

to death. It looked as if he might one day become another Genghis and lead the Mongols to reclaim China. One way he increased his popularity at home was to exploit the 'tribute system' by which China dealt with the 'barbarians'. The system, designed to buttress China's superiority complex, served several unstated functions, which we can understand by the liberal use of inverted commas. The idea was that, since barbarians were inferior, Chinese emperors could deal with them only in so far as they showed evidence of being good subjects. Trade with inferiors was beneath Chinese dignity. So if barbarian leaders brought 'tribute', like horses and furs, Chinese emperors would shower them with 'gifts', like silk, iron goods and (later) tea. The reality behind the euphemistic exchange of barbarian 'tribute' and imperial 'gifts' was trade (trade with barbarians! Unthinkable abasement!) but also payment to keep the peace, always with the (unstated) threat of blackmail – that if the emperor's gifts were not good enough, the barbarian leaders might go on the war-path. Esen, gathering followers, exploited the system by sending ever bigger 'tribute missions', who would arrive in Beijing expecting to be housed, entertained and rewarded for their 'submission' with 'gifts'. In 1448, 2,000 arrived, with the mission head claiming there were 3,000. This was nothing but extortion.

Wang Zhen, the eunuch who whispered in the emperor's ear, was not a man to advise diplomacy. He took a cut of every deal; he had his own secret service, with its own military-style enforcers, the Embroidered Uniform Guard; he rewarded toadies, and punished critics. Finally, with Esen's power and demands alike increasing, he decided to force a crisis and then capitalize on the emperor's passion for military glory. When that latest oversize mission arrived in 1448, Wang Zhen cut the expected 'gifts' by 80 per cent. A request for a Chinese princess – a latter-day Zhaojun – was rejected.

Within months of the disgruntled embassy's departure, reports came from the Great Wall of raids and skirmishes and scouting parties, suggesting that Esen was planning a major attack. This was the chance Wang Zhen was looking for. Let us, he said, campaign across the Wall, with the emperor in command and himself as generalissimo. He, Wang Zhen, would command the generals to do his bidding; he would lead an army of 500,000 in a march to Datong and beyond the Wall that would destroy the nomad armies once and for all; then, in triumph, he would parade through his home town, Yuzhou (today's Yu Xian), south-east of Datong, where he would present the emperor to all his relatives, an outward and visible sign of his power and glory.

Wang Zhen was no general, and this was lunacy.[6] Officials banded together to tell him so. The defences are adequate, they said in a memo to the emperor. This is the height of summer; the heat is intolerable, there is little water and fodder. The emperor's absence will paralyse government. 'Armies are instruments of violence; warfare is a dangerous business . . . [yet] the Son of Heaven, though the most exalted of men, would now go personally

[6] The whole debacle is analysed in detail by Frank Mote in 'The T'u-mu Incident of 1449'.

into those dangers. We officials, though the most stupid of men, say that this must not occur.' Yingzong, parroting Wang Zhen's words, refused to listen: 'The bandits offend against heaven . . . We have no choice but to lead a great army in person to exterminate them.'

What he did not know was that Esen had sent four columns, two to attack the garrison towns of Datong and Xuanhua, and two more to divert attention (one to Chengde, 250 kilometres eastward; another into Gansu, about 800 kilometres to the west). None of them had any problem crossing the Great Wall, which still had many gaps in it. What was Esen's aim? Almost certainly to secure his leadership of the Mongols by wringing better trading concessions from China.

Now the action picks up pace. On 4 August 1449, with two days' warning – two days to mobilize half a million troops! – the emperor departs, swaying northward in the imperial palanquin, his army trailing behind. A secretary tries to talk sense into him, throwing himself in front of the entourage: 'Your majesty may make light of your imperial person, but what of the dynasty, what of the state?' Wang Zhen curses the man, and he is ignored. Moving at 20 kilometres a day, the immense procession – for Wang Zhen alone has about 1,000 carts for himself and his entourage – heads north-west, through the mountain pass that runs through today's Badaling. It's hot, but also raining. The sodden troops are miserable and near mutiny. No one can speak to the emperor except Wang Zhen, whom officials must always approach on their knees. The head of the Directorate of Astronomy says the signs are bad. 'If it is to be so, then fate has ordained it so,' says Wang Zhen. At Xuanhua, six days and 130 kilometres from Beijing, two distinguished old officials plead for the campaign to be called off; Wang Zhen makes them kneel for a whole day in punishment. Still it rains. No one can remember such rain in August. Some officials mutter about assassinating Wang Zhen – 'It would require only the strength of one armed man to seize Wang Zhen and smash his skull' – but they cannot quite summon the will to do it. Meanwhile the Mongols watch and wait for their chance.

The thirteenth of August was a bad day, and not just because of the continuous rain. At Yanggao, 30 kilometres north-east of Datong, Esen had beaten an army sent from the city against him the previous week. On the sixteenth they see the sodden battlefield, still strewn with thousands of unburied Chinese corpses, and 'the chill of terror grips all hearts'. At Datong three days later, the commander who had escaped death by hiding in long grass tells Wang Zhen, 'Give it up! If you go on, you will simply fall into Esen's trap.'

And now, at last, Wang Zhen begins to have second thoughts. The rain; the adverse heavenly signs; the field of dead bodies; and now violent storms – perhaps the omens really are bad. 'He decides to declare the mission victoriously accomplished and return to the capital,' not as planned via Yuzhou, because he is afraid the restive troops will lay waste his estates, but by retracing his tracks. As the expedition sets camp the following evening, 'a black cloud descends precisely over it and hangs so low it seems to press down on people's heads, though beyond the camp on all sides clear sky can be seen'. Rain falls through the night, accompanied by lightning, 'inducing fear and disorder'.

After another nine days of this, the emperor, his eunuch and their entourages are back where they were over three weeks previously, 30 kilometres from the inner wall at Badaling, camping short of a little town called Tumu. Behind them straggle half a million men, spreading westward up the valley of the Yang river, which cuts between hills past an old postal relay station where, under the Mongols, horses had been kept for messengers galloping back and forth between Beijing and Kublai's summer palace at Xanadu. Further west still is the rearguard, two days' march and 50 kilometres away in Xuanhua. Exactly what happened is unknown, because the records vanished; but early on 30 August messengers gallop into the imperial camp with the news that the rearguard, having just left Xuanhua, had been attacked. With what result? Wang Zhen decides that the imperial party should wait and see. The evening brings more bad news. Wujin, the son of one of the rearguard commanders, gallops in. The rearguard had been ambushed in a narrow defile. 'The enemy forces occupy mountain tops; arrows and stones fill the air like rain. The government troops have virtually all been killed or wounded.' The two generals, including Wujin's father, lie dead on the field of battle.

At once, a large force of cavalry – maybe 30,000, maybe 50,000, sources being as usual vague – is sent back to fight the Mongols and rescue survivors. It is commanded by a venerable old general, Chu Yung, who owes his position to his father, a high official under the early Ming a good 60 years before – a typically inept choice by the campaign's self-appointed civilian leaders. Chu Yung was 'full of respect towards scholars and officials', and 'appeared to be quite heroic, but both his courage and his tactical sense were deficient' – as any military man would know, because he had been blamed for bungling a campaign against the Mongols only five years before. To pile idiocy on idiocy, the man who should have been in charge – Xueshou, a Mongol who had served the Chinese with distinction – is made second-in-command. Chu Yung leads his force straight into an ambush, and is killed along with his men. Xueshou is also killed, but dies heroically, his arrows spent, his bowstring broken, wielding his bow like a club until he falls to Mongol swords. His attackers then find out who he is. 'He is one of us,' they say. 'No wonder he was so strong and brave.'

The next day, as the emperor reaches Tumu, officials urge him to keep moving through the inner wall and the Juyung Pass, deploying a rearguard against Esen's approaching army. But now the imperial wagons are ahead of the 1,000 carts full of Wang Zhen's possessions. He wants to wait for them. When the war minister remonstrates, Wang Zhen curses him: 'You fool of a bookworm! What do you know about military affairs? Say another word and you will be beheaded on the spot!' He is dragged away by guards, and left weeping in his tent.

Now the rain has stopped, and the imperial party is short of water. There's a river nearby, but the Mongols have caught up, and a flanking party blocks access to the river. By late afternoon, the Chinese and their horses are not only parched; they are surrounded. That night, guards report that 'numbers of the enemy on all sides swell beyond all expectations'.

Next morning, 1 September, the sun rises in a clear sky. The Mongols hold back, and send in a letter offering peace talks. The emperor sends a reply, stating his terms, but at the same time Wang Zhen orders an advance. The imperial palanquin struggles forward in the midst of jostling guards. The Mongols attack, and cut off the imperial party from the army. 'Throw down your arms and armour, and be spared!' comes the cry from the Mongols. The Chinese soldiers panic, strip off and run, only to be cut down. In the emperor's group, the emperor, in his armour, climbs from his palanquin and sits on the ground, while his guards fall under the hail of arrows. A Mongol soldier breaks through and, unaware of the emperor's identity, is on the point of killing him to seize his armour when a Mongol officer stops him.

'Are you Prince Esen?' asks the emperor, without revealing his identity. No, replies the officer. His brother? Any of his other brothers? The emperor names them in turn, at which the officer suspects that this is someone important, and leads him away. He is kept for two days nearby, and is allowed to send a messenger to Beijing to announce his capture and order gifts. Meanwhile, all the emperor's senior staff have been killed, including Wang Zhen, perhaps murdered by his own enraged officers. A quarter of a million men lie dead; the rest have scattered.

*   *   *

Esen is astounded to discover that the emperor is his prisoner and has him sent back to his camp at Xuanhua, where a debate ensues about what to do with him. 'He is the enemy of our Mongol khans,' says one old officer. 'Kill him.' One of Esen's brothers slaps the old man. 'The Emperor of China is no ordinary mortal. Look how he sat there unharmed through the thick of battle,' he says. 'We have all been the recipients of China's beneficence. If we keep the emperor unharmed and return him, we will earn undying gratitude and fame.' Esen agrees.

What now? The emperor is well treated, being given a few survivors as servants. The Mongols feast, entertain him, offer him a Mongol wife (who is politely declined), and discuss what use they can best make of him. Jewels arrive, sent in panic from the Forbidden City. Obviously, as Mote says, Esen had not engaged in this major military enterprise 'just for a few mule-loads of baubles' – he needed to be acknowledged by his own side as the new Great Khan; but from the Chinese, he wanted no more than a steady flow of trade and gifts.

Instead, fate had presented him with an astonishing prize. The way to the capital lay open. As an enthusiastic captive eunuch told him, he could use the emperor as a bargaining chip to force all border garrisons to open their gates, and seize the capital itself. All north China lay at his feet. The half-rebuilt Wall would become irrelevant even before it was finished. Even Genghis had not been granted so much so quickly – and Esen's sudden good fortune nonplussed him. He was not set up for conquest, let alone regime change and administration. He dithered, withdrew to make new plans, and advanced on Beijing only after six weeks' delay.

That allowed the Ming capital time to pull itself together. Out went the incompetent eunuchs, in came new brooms. A new minister of war, Yu Qian, backed a new candidate for emperor. The old one was now the 'Grand Senior Emperor', and suddenly redundant. Yu Qian castigated as cowards those who advised surrender, reorganized the defences, restocked the granaries, restored confidence. By the time Esen arrived in mid-October, he was too late. When he offered his captive, he received an uncompromising reply: It is the dynasty and the nation that matter; 'the ruler is unimportant'. In brief: no deal. Militarily he could not dent Beijing, and he was not prepared to mount a ten-month siege, as Genghis had. After five days he turned back, contenting himself with a little useless plundering, like a petulant teenager slamming doors on his way out.

From Mongolia, he tried one more ploy. A captive eunuch, Xining, suggested a grandiose invasion plan that foresaw Mongols living in China rushing to join Esen, an advance with the former emperor to Nanjing, the installation of a puppet regime, and more in this vein. To show he meant business, Esen sent Xining as an ambassador to Beijing, where he was promptly executed. Genghis would have attacked at once; Esen collapsed along with his pretensions, resumed tribute payments, quietly sent the ex-emperor back to Beijing with no demands attached, and focused on extending his power at home. In 1453 he declared himself Great Khan of the Great Yuan, claiming the mantle of Kublai and Genghis. His followers did not follow. One of them assassinated him the next year, and the Mongols went back to raiding and futile feuding.

In Beijing, the Tumu debacle, which made all eunuchs pariahs, inspired an incident of high drama that turned into something extremely vicious. Officials knelt before the emperor-to-be, Prince Cheng, and demanded that Wang Zhen be punished posthumously, that his family be eradicated and his property seized. When the prince ummed and aahed, the officials said they wanted certainty, and would not move until they got it. So they stayed kneeling – and stayed, and stayed. The tension rose until the commander of the secret service's military wing, Ma Shun, declared the officials to be out of order, and called for them to get out. At this one of the officials lost control, leaped to his feet, grabbed Ma Shun by the hair, yelled: 'Are you then also one of the traitors?', wrestled him to the ground and bit him. That broke the courtly shell of decorum. Everyone leaped on Ma Shun. Some tore his boots off and beat him with them; others scooped his eyes out; and within minutes he was a bloody corpse. Then the mob turned on two of the eunuchs' secret police-men and beat them to death as well. The prince tried to slip away, but the war minister (and de facto leader of the government), Yu Qian, grabbed him by the clothing and told him it would be fatal not to resolve matters, which he could do by declaring that Ma Shun deserved death and that Wang Zhen's family would be punished.

So he did, and calm returned. For a while it seemed that the anti-eunuch party had won. Not quite. Eight years later the 'caretaker emperor' fell ill, without an heir. Officials who had been humiliated by their craven behaviour during the Tumu Incident seized the moment. The ex-emperor Yingzong, who had been living in

ANOTHER NON-WALL,
IN NORTH-EASTERN MONGOLIA

This 700-kilometre feature, also wrongly called the 'Wall of Genghis Khan', is probably a frontier mound thrown up by the Jin dynasty in the twelfth century. It runs right into the heartland of Mongolia, but was obviously not designed to block Mongol horsemen. It was punctuated every 50 kilometres or so with protected camp-sites for traders and/or frontier guards (see p. 181). You can get to it from a desolate ex-Soviet base, now a station newly named Genghis's Ridge on a branch line of the Trans-Siberian Railway (inset, with the chicly dressed station-mistress, Urzhing-khand).

Three views of Jiayu's western tower, restored to its original three tiers: from beneath the eastern gate (above); a camel's-eye view from the desert (above right); and spotlit by the rising sun against the Qilian mountains (below).

Left: *This brick – so they say – was left over when the fortress was built, by the architect, to protect himself and the fortress. The bricks at the end of the shelf are also loose, to booby-trap thieves. For the details of this unlikely tale, read p. 273.*

Ming: 14th – 17th centuries
A BARRIER IN THE FAR WEST

When the Ming (1368–1644) finally decided to seal the way west, they did so in the late 15th century at Jiayuguan (Jiayu Pass). To do this they built a wall across a 15-kilometre tongue of land between the barren Black mountains and a ravine carrying meltwater from the snow-capped Qilian mountains. In the middle rose the great fort itself, once a regimental HQ and a thriving base for trade. Today, the nearby town has sucked the life out of it, leaving it for tourists.

To the south, Jiayu's 'left arm' ends at the First Beacon Tower, which looms above a sheer drop to the Daolai river (above), while its 'right arm' runs up into the dark rocks of the Black mountains (below).

Ming: 14th – 17th centuries
GUARDING THE WESTERN FLANK OF THE ORDOS

In China's mid-west, Yinchuan dominates the flood plain of the Yellow River as it swings into the great loop that embraces the Ordos. Northward is a tongue of fertile land that needed protection; westward, the towering peaks of the Helan mountains are pierced by a single pass, the Sanguan, through which Genghis had once swept. The Ming blocked both approaches, with two fortresses (now a film studio) and an earth wall that zooms from plain to mountain.

The China West Film Studio, advertising itself below, has provided sets for some 80 films, many of which are retained as a combination of heritage site and fairground. Visitors can take horse rides (above) or explore a 'medieval' village (left).

Above: *To the west of Yinchuan and the Yellow River, the earth Wall swings northward across barren lowlands to the Sanguan Pass into Inner Mongolia.*

Below: *Hardly more than a crumbling mix of rock-flakes, it then climbs up into the Helan mountains. You can see the new main road through the pass at right.*

Ming: 14th – 17th centuries
ACROSS THE ORDOS

There is not much left of the Ming Wall running east–west along the southern fringes of the arid Ordos. Beacon towers still rear up here and there, as do bits of gap-toothed wall. One fortress has been restored. Towns with the suffix *-bian* (border) recall their long-ago strategic importance. But today the border is hundreds of kilometres away, and has been at peace for centuries. People ignore the Wall and focus on their work, their fields, their crops.

Beacon towers like these (right and below), each once home to a dozen men, stand forlornly in the semi-desert, at the mercy of the elements.

Above: *On a side-road off the new expressway linking Yulin and Yinchuan, the wall has been eroded into tombstone remnants.*

Right: *Just north of Yulin rears the newly restored Ming fortress of Zhenbeitai (Suppress-the-North Platform).*

Left and below: *Frontier folk? No longer. Living on the southern fringe of the arid Ordos, the townspeople of Anbian (Oppress the Border) thrive on fruit and vegetables from fields irrigated from newly dug wells.*

Ming: 14th – 17th centuries
NORTH AND SOUTH OF DATONG

The Wall doubles as it passes Datong. To the north is a derelict fortress, Deshengbu, that has now been colonized by villagers who have mined the old walls for bricks to build their houses. To the south, a road guarded by beacon towers leads through hills to Yanmenguan (Wild Goose Pass). Once the main arch, topped by a (rebuilt) temple, was the heart of a vast military complex. Now it stands silent, except for a few summer visitors who climb its steep approach tracks.

Deshengbu's main gate (above), once faced with bricks, now leads to a village street where locals gather to chat (left).

A clear day (below) reveals Yanmenguan to be a well-restored gate-and-temple complex.

retirement in a small palace, was reinstalled; and five days later the heroic war minister who had saved the dynasty, Yu Qian, was charged with treason and executed (which, as Mote writes, was 'one of the great cases of injustice in Ming history').

Tumu brought the problem of the northern frontier into sharp focus. From now on, there would be no forward bases the other side of the Wall, and no campaigns into Mongolia. The Great Wall would be the frontier. No question, therefore, that the Wall had to be well maintained and strongly garrisoned. But without defences beyond the Wall, occasional breakthrough raids by Mongols had to be expected. That meant that the communities on the Chinese side would become armed camps. Cities and towns were walled, as they had been in ancient times. One seventeenth-century analyst, Ku Yenwu, who walked the whole area, listed over 1,000 fortified places in northern Shanxi (one province westward of Beijing) alone – an area whose Great Wall border is only 200 kilometres long. He also listed 100 road barriers 'erected to inspect persons of variant speech or of variant dress'.

You can see what happened if you visit the old relay station 20 kilometres west of Tumu. The Ming turned it into a massive square fortress, with 12-metre walls, 600 metres per side. This staggering piece of architecture is not on any tourist trail, but it should be, not only for its own sake, but also because of its wonderful setting, in the lee of a pile of crumpled ridges called Clucking Chicken Mountain; hence the fortress's name, Clucking Chicken

Station (Ji Ming Yi / 鸡鸣驿). I climbed its main gate, where I was picked up by a cheery local wearing a knitted cap. The fortress's huge interior has long since been colonized and made into a village, into which he led me. The place was a time capsule of courtyards and houses left over from a century ago. A little house that was once a hostel for officials on their way to Beijing still had its Ming furniture and heated sleeping platform. Up a tiny alleyway was the house used by the Empress Dowager Cixi (Tz'u-Hsi) when she fled Beijing in the Boxer Rebellion of 1900. With German troops on her trail, she had slept here, in a doll's-house room with paper instead of glass in its window. In a ruined eighteenth-century temple, locals were busy turning grey bricks and timbers into the upturned eaves and painting frescoes on rough-cast plaster made of earth and straw, one man using a hammer and a nail to tap intricate patterns in stone. One day, tourists will come here to admire huddled houses contrasting with massy walls inspired by the fear that the Mongols would return.

Suddenly, every town had walls again, as they had when China first emerged from chaos in the third century BC – except this time they were arming themselves not against each other, but against the common enemy, the outsiders. The whole strip of land within the Great Wall became an armed camp, a very Long City living with the ever-present danger of invasion. Or *perceived* threat; because in fact after Tumu nothing much happened for a century.

But Tumu was enough, with effects that defined attitudes over the following two centuries. Prejudice against Mongols became an item of faith in Ming China.

The idea of understanding and accommodating Mongol ways was disdained. Chinese statesmen became fixated by the 'problem' of the northern frontier, justifying the massive expenditure, reinforcing the prejudice, exacerbating a problem that might have been solved by a more broad-minded approach.

12

TO THE ORDOS, AND BEYOND

TUMU CHANGED EVERYTHING. THE IDEA THAT THE MING might eventually take over Mongolia was now revealed as a pipe-dream; the harsh reality was the threat of exactly the opposite, only too nearly realized: the dynasty had almost fallen to a lesser Genghis. Something had to be done that would secure permanent peace. The Ming had several choices. They could revive a forward policy, sending in troops to retake and hold steppe areas; they could engage the Mongols in all the old ways of diplomacy – trade, ambassadorial exchanges, intermarriage; or they could pull back and rebuild the Wall. In the end it was the third option they went for.

It didn't have to be that way. The Mongols were not enough of a threat to justify such a venture, and never a threat to the dynasty and the nation as a whole. As Esen had revealed, even the khan of a unified Mongolia at the walls of Beijing did not have the will or resources to reclaim China. What the Mongols wanted was trade, a chance to offer their horses and furs in exchange for iron, cereals and textiles. To meet them halfway would have been fair; it would have acknowledged a truth, that the two cultures were intertwined, with many Mongols living in China and vice versa. But this kind of accommodation did not fit with the dominant Chinese view of themselves, or at least the official and courtly view of themselves, as expressed by the pro-Wall faction. To them, as to their ancestors, China was the centre of the universe, and had to exude effortless superiority. One did not deal with barbarians. One accepted tribute, one was generous in return, one gave gifts; but one did not engage in diplomacy as if between equals. So, in official eyes, Mongols remained desperate creatures who sought any means to dump unwanted goods on the Middle Kingdom in order to acquire imperial favours, which would be used to finance attacks. Naturally, this being the dominant view at the all-powerful centre, those on the border, many of whom knew better, were careful not to let facts undermine the official fiction. No, the Mongols had to be kept at a distance; and the only way to do this was to build a Wall so long and strong that no nomad horse would ever appear south of it without permission.

For a century, roughly 1450–1550, to wall or not to wall was a matter of great controversy. Walling would be very expensive, and there was almost always a more enlightened, pragmatic, non-traditional faction who argued for an open-door policy. Sometimes their views held sway. Attitudes swung back and forth, careers and lives with them. Now a pro-Waller would find himself out of fashion, and would be executed, becoming a patriotic martyr. Now an anti-Waller would find himself included in official accounts as one of the 'treacherous ministers'. The Wall-builders – predominantly southern literati who had no experience of life on the frontier – prevailed, with results that millions of tourists see every year. The decision to build was not really a decision. It was always the policy of last resort, as one might accept the need to take a long-established but unpleasant medicine, with lots of nasty side-effects, to combat a chronic disease.

A first step was taken in 1455, when rebuilding around Beijing got under way at the Juyung Pass. It would go on, with new building giving way to repairs, for another 189 years. When the last bits of this vast edifice clunked into place around 1600, its Nine Defence Areas ran from the Pacific westward. It switchbacked over the mountains that are Beijing's natural bastions, guarding the 100 or so passes through which alien forces might pour; headed south-west over the hills that border Inner Mongolia; jumped the Yellow River into the badlands of the Ordos, where it took a mighty S-bend back over the Yellow River and along the Helan Mountains; headed on westward along the bottom fringes of the Gobi Desert; and ended at the great fort of Jiayuguan, gateway to the Western Regions, Central Asia and all points west. Because of its twists, doublings, even occasional triplings, there is no telling its length, only that as crows fly it spanned 2,400 kilometres. It made a simple statement: to the north – them, and barbarism; to the south – us, and civilization.

History offers many examples of arms races. They happen when an idea of how to do things drives out alternative ideas. That was what lay behind the race of trench-building that locked armies into the Western Front in 1914, and behind the piling up of nuclear-armed rockets in the Cold War. It also happened in fifteenth-century China, when its leaders settled on wall-building as the only answer to the problem posed by the northern frontier. This became the conventional wisdom, and it hardened mental arteries for 200 years.

Yet the disease was mostly caused by the medicine itself. Faced with the official Chinese prejudice unquestioningly nurtured by a convention-bound bureaucracy serving an emperor as remote as a queen bee, it was hardly surprising that the Mongols – never the threat they were cracked up to be, always excluded, always reviled – remained resentful and aggressive, for ever justifying the prejudice. This vicious circle, writes Mote, 'was the greatest failure of Ming statesmanship'. How ironic that from this failure should spring the Great Wall, 'the very symbol of Chinese historical greatness'.

Attention focused first on the Ordos. For half a century this anomalous tongue of land had been virtually empty; but after the Tumu Incident and again after Esen's death in 1453, nomadic families swarmed back in, reclaiming areas from which many of them had been evicted 50 years earlier and bringing with them objects and *gers* sacred to the memory of Genghis Khan, with which they established the 'mausoleum' that remains south of Dongsheng today. Inevitably, the men formed raiding parties, threatening the settled lands to the south. If no action were taken, the threat would go from bad to worse. At court, the old dispute reopened: campaign or wall?

There could be no doubt now that security could not depend on forward garrisons or campaigns to crush the Mongols. The only other possible response was to build a wall, or at least a line of forts and signal towers. But – for every argument has its buts – building demanded security; and that demanded a campaign to clear the areas; and now that the Mongols had resettled the Ordos, such a campaign would require tens of thousands of troops, and the Ming army did not have the manpower. But *without* a campaign, things would just get worse, as a series of raids in 1471–2 showed. When a Tumu veteran proposed a major campaign, the emperor unwillingly approved a force of 80,000, only to have commanders say that because of the cold and the distance they needed at least twice that many troops, and another 200,000 baggage handlers. Back and forth flew the messages, emphasizing unwelcome truths: the Mongols were strong and fighting on their home ground; Ming armies could hardly get there, and if they did would be lured to their death in deserts and steppes. No campaign was undertaken.

There was, as always, a pro-Wall faction. One member was Yu Zijun, a senior official (Right Vice-Censor-in-Chief) in Xian, the First Emperor's capital, and a city traditionally vulnerable to raiders from the Ordos, since the border was a mere 300 kilometres away. At court, walls meant trouble. They were expensive, which meant taxing the population; and they needed armies of labourers, who resented being taken from their homes. Anyway, anyone could see what happened to earth walls – they wore away, so were not permanent. In 1472, in the wake of the Mongol raids, Yu pressed his case – arguing in the first instance not so much for a wall as for a ditch. If 50,000 people were exempted from taxes and put to work in spring and summer, before the Mongols' horses had become strong with new grass, they could create a barrier of some kind, the sort of thing the English call a ha-ha. The emperor was impressed.

By luck, a chance to build came in 1473, when a scholar-general named Wang Yue, commander of the region just south of the Ordos, heard that a group of Mongols had set off for a raid from a place called Red Salt Lake, about 60 kilometres into the Ordos. They had left their families behind. Wang Yue took a small force of cavalry – 4,600 men – and headed north, surprised the helpless group, killed several hundred (mainly women and children), burned the tents and took thousands of animals. When the Mongol force heard the news, they returned and galloped straight into an ambush. These brutal actions worked: the survivors fled northward, leaving the Ordos's southern border free for wall-builders.

Wang himself built a section, which ran from the Yellow River opposite Yinchuan almost 200 kilometres south-east, blocking off the part of the Ordos he had secured. Yu, the instigator of the new wall policy, supervised a second, much longer, section underpinning the rest of the Ordos, running north-east to meet the other side of the Yellow River loop at Baode. This was wall-building on a scale to rival the First Emperor's: 40,000 men securing

850 kilometres with 800 forts, beacon-towers and sentry posts. It passed its first major test in 1482, when Mongol raiders were trapped between two sections of wall. It would be much strengthened over the next two centuries. By the mid-sixteenth century it was a formidable barrier, doubled in many parts, with a penumbra of beacon-towers and fortresses by the hundred, dividing the Mu Us (Mongol for 'Bad Water') desert[1] from military farms that could produce some 4,000 tonnes of grain a year.

It is still there – the first sections of the Great Wall we know today.

The Ming wall across the southern Ordos is clear on the map, running all the way south-west from the Yellow River near Baode, holding the Ordos as if in a scoop. I wanted to track as much of it as I could. In Beijing, my adviser, the Wall expert Cheng Dalin, said it was possible, but I had to take care to 'follow the old road'. It sounded easy. In fact, a few days of Wall-hunting in the Ordos merely showed how hard it is to find the Wall in China these days. You need an off-road vehicle, and backpacks, and weeks to spare.

Approaching the Ordos from the north-east, the road to the Yellow River falls through hills of rich earth, where fields drop in broad, graceful terraces. Lower down, in a ravine that cuts to bedrock, people build by burrowing into hillsides, making houses that are also caves. The air thickens, trucks and three-wheeled putt-putts begin to clog the narrow, pitted road. At Baode, where the road

[1] In Chinese, Máo Wū Sù / 毛乌素 .

leads down to a bridge, we ran into a new great wall, made of trucks: hundreds of them, hauling coal from the Ordos to feed China's hungry industries. At the moment they were going nowhere, because, as we discovered while winding past them, two of them had jammed at a narrow junction. The line stretched for kilometres on both sides of the river. I started counting the trucks, and gave up at 500. It would take days to clear. But jams like this will soon be things of the past. A few miles on, in the steep-sided ravines that flank the Ordos, a fine new road swung like a helter-skelter beneath a railway. Coal trucks and coal trains rumbled east loaded with grimy riches no previous dynasty could have guessed at, and soon there will be no more narrow bridges and muddy junctions.

And where amid the mess of industry was the Wall? Off to our left somewhere, high up, along ridges – impossible to say where, because the new road was not on the map. Nor, after a while, was it on the ground either: it ended, in a mass of dust, potholes and swaying trucks. We used the car as a blind man uses a stick, probing lanes for a way to the high ground. We sought guidance, turned back, found the right side-road, and at last headed upwards.

On a ridge ahead were two towers, beacon-towers, which are often the Wall's outer sentries. Once manned by small teams to provide advance warning of approaching marauders, they survive in their hundreds, blurring the Wall's path, holding out the promise of its presence. There was another ahead at the top of a steep-sided ravine. I scrambled for 60 metres over soft peat, with a covering of grass that offered foot- and hand-holds, reaching long-abandoned terraced fields. Across long grass thick with yellow-and-white butterflies and whirring grasshoppers stood the beacon-tower, a 6- or 7-metre cube of rammed earth. Once faced with stones, which now lay in a ridge all around it, it looked like a tooth jutting up from decaying gums. There were the remains of a square enclosure, an outer wall of crumbling earth, 30 metres along each side. It was obvious what its purpose had been, for northward was a terrific view for 10 or 15 kilometres back along the approach road. Several other such towers ranged outwards on neighbouring ridges.

But of the Wall there was not a glimpse, because it's not there. As I learned later from Waldron's book, in this 60-kilometre section 'many forts and towers remain, but no continuous wall'. The solid red line on my map was a lie: here, the Wall has been eroded into insignificance by farming, road-building and 500 years of wind and rain.

Perhaps if we could find the 'old road', which ran across the semi-desert between Shenmu and Yulin, we would have better luck.

We left Shenmu fast, on a nice new road, framed by scrub-and-sand hills.

'Now let's remember,' I said to my guide, Peter, a diffident, studious and weasel-thin young man of 22, though he could have passed for 18. He had glasses, and a crew-cut that made him look like a startled lavatory brush. 'We have to go by the old road.'

'The old road, yes.' He repeated my words to the driver, a solidly built old hand with the roundest face I had ever seen. He was a Chinese man in the moon, and almost as impassive.

The map was clear. We had to keep the railway line on our right, start off heading due south, and make for a village called Goujiabou. A minute later, we dived under the railway line, which was now on our *left*, and we were going *south-west*, at the speed of sound.

'Hang on, Peter. This is not the old road.'

'I don't know.'

'I do. It's new. And it's going in the wrong direction.'

Words were muttered. The driver took one hand off the wheel and produced a battered old map, extremely large in scale, on which roads wandered immense distances, like ant-trails. Look, he said. *There* was Shenmu, *there* was Yulin, *there* was the road between them. What was it I couldn't understand? It was like being addressed by a football with features. He had driven this way many times. There was no other road, this was the one we wanted.

But it couldn't be. I checked the compass, and the map. No denying it: we were on the wrong side of the Wall and the railway. I could see the track, a few kilometres away, over the semi-desert.

'Let's ask,' I said to Peter, rather too quietly. Nothing happened.

'Peter.'

'Yes?'

'We have to ask.'

Peter plucked up courage and almost spoke.

'Peter. There. *There!*'

By the side of the road, an ironmonger was doing something vicious to a window frame, with a teenager assisting him. We pulled over in a cloud of dust. As Peter prepared his question, a bus went by. The teenager turned out to be exactly the force we needed.

'Goujiabou? Take the next left! *Follow that bus!*'

So we did. Almost 30 kilometres later we bounced through the village, the road having turned to dry mud, crossed a fine stone bridge and found an old sign: 'Yulin 60 kms'. This was it: the old road at last. It was very old; also very rutted and very dry. Our car was built for nice new highways. We bumped along the woodland track at walking pace, sump and exhaust taking the tops off hillocks of mud with unnerving thuds. There were no houses, no fields, no cars or tractors, no farm workers to offer help if we broke down.

'Wait.'

'What?'

'Just wait, OK?'

I checked my watch, and the sun. It was hopeless. The old road needed a 4×4, not a limo. If we made it, with or without an exhaust, it would be in darkness, and I wouldn't see any of the Wall at all, let alone explore it. I had risked the car, set us back a couple of hours and wasted fuel, all for nothing.

Beyond Yulin, we took off along 100 kilometres of fine, newly opened and totally empty motorway, proclaiming itself in English, with a Manhattan typeface, the Yujing (i.e. *Yulin–Jing*bian) Expressway. Two beacon-towers marked the entrance, so the Wall was somewhere near. It flickered into sight a few times, shielded by dunes, fences and the motorway barrier. Only once could we escape to see it. A sign pointed to a famous battle-ground of the

Revolution: 'Heng Shang Insurgency Site'. It did *not* point to the Wall, which we crossed a minute or two down the road, because there was nothing much to point to. It was a pathetic remnant of its former self, a ragged line of little pinnacles, the tallest no more than 3 metres high. It must have held up the bulldozers for about ten seconds. Wind, rain and now road-builders had smashed its face in, and all that was left was a line of rotting teeth. A donkey cart, a motorbike and a truck passed. No one gave it a glance. Why should they? It was no more imposing than a child's sandcastle.

I felt as if I had found a hero made feeble by age. I thought: what sacrilege. A monument of such significance deserves better than this. Then I thought: how could it possibly be preserved, except by piling up again the earth from which it was made? What exactly would be preserved, except the desert's own mud? There comes a point when you have to bow to the flow of time, especially here, where there was no one to see it.

All the way across the bottom of the Ordos to Yinchuan there were similar experiences. The Wall was there all right, roughened and cut by age, on its way back into the earth from which it sprang, but most of the time, no sooner did I see it than it was gone, a blur the other side of expressway fencing. The names of towns recall the former importance of this ribbon of land: Jingbian (Warn the Border), Anbian (Oppress the Border), Dingbian (Settle the Border). Here the Bad Water Desert pushed southward from the Ordos's barren heart, there well-watered fields yellow with corn spread northward, but always we shadowed the Wall: sometimes ruined as a broken saw, sometimes a grassy bank, occasionally still proud, solid and sheer. At Anbian, where a motorway exit sliced through it, the gap was neatly lined with stone. It ran on through a refinery, it picked up either side of roads, it carried telegraph poles, it had been used as a mine for soil, and at one point (as a plaque proclaimed) a Ming regiment had dug out a line of caves to make barracks.

Nearing the far side of the Yellow River's great bend, the Wall bent away from the road, with only a lone, blank-faced beacon-tower as evidence that it was still there, somewhere off in the scrub and gravel. Road and Wall came close again at the river itself, a great grey-brown swirl of silt half a kilometre wide. Here the Wall runs through badlands known as the Yellow Plateau, all eroded gullies and bare earth with the occasional tussock of grass. Where it tracks the banks of a Yellow River tributary, it is so unlike a wall you could mistake it for the bank itself. It was a wreck, its eroded and wind-blasted hillocks turning it into a misused, gap-toothed saw. In 500 years, half of it had already returned to the grey earth from which it had been dug, much of which had been carried away as a tiny addition to the Yellow River's silty waters.

Before completing the Ordos wall, perhaps even before starting it, armchair strategists in Beijing would have spotted a problem. As the wall swings around the bottom of the Ordos and approaches the Yellow River, the land becomes more fertile. Across the river around Yinchuan, it is even richer, well watered by Yinchuan's ancient canal system (back roads around Yinchuan are practically impassable in autumn for all the crops drying on the road-ways). Fertility spreads northward, along the Yellow River itself, forming a tongue of agricultural land sticking up between two vast deserts, the Ordos's Mu Us (Bad Water) to the east and the Tenger to the west. Ecologically, this slab of watered land, 100 kilometres long and only 60 wide at its base, belongs to the south, as the Ordos and the Tenger do to the north: today this little thumb is part of Ningxia province. A quick glance at the map puts you inside the mind of our Ming strategists: would not Mongols on the war-path want to snip off this thumb and give themselves a good rich base straddling the Yellow River from which to supply southbound armies? Of course they would. They had done it before, and could do it again. The next step was to stop them, with defences that ran north–south, parallel with the Yellow River and with the great natural wall, the Helan mountains.

If you are in business, there are good reasons for going to Yinchuan, the capital of the province of Ningxia. It's huge, and growing. But if you are touring, there are good reasons to leave. Don't bother going to the Yellow River, which swirls past, vast, sludgy and uncharming, a few kilometres to the east. Look west. There, looming above the haze of petrol and desert dust and industrial fumes, are the Helan mountains, dark bastions against barbarian hordes from the western deserts and the Silk Road. As bastions, they were not quite good enough, as Genghis's assaults in 1209 and 1227 showed. So the Ming blocked the Helan's main pass with their Wall and built a great castle to keep it supplied and garrisoned. These are good reasons to head out of town.

First the castle, which carries the fitting name
Zhenbeibao, 'Pacify-the-North Fortress'. Your way lies
westward towards the Helan along an immense highway,
lined with new apartment blocks. For 25 kilometres the
Helan acquire bulk and majesty until, almost at their base,
the road turns 90° right. The mountains fall away to semi-
desert and canal-fed fields, and there, opposite a line of
some very ordinary shops, is a sight that is not ordinary at
all – eroded earth walls defended by cannons, fluttering
flags, horses and soldiers . . .

. . . and crowded with tourists; for the Ming castle has
been reincarnated. And not just the Ming castle, as you
see when you turn into the site. In 1739, after two
centuries of service, the old castle was shattered by an
earthquake, and its owners, the Qing Dynasty Manchus,
built a new one next door. Now the whole complex – the
old castle, its earth walls beaten down by wind, rain and
feet; the 8-metre walls and brick gate of the new castle;
the semi-desert parking lot – has been turned into the
China West Film Studio. As an entrance sign tells you in
six languages: 'Chinese movies march towards the world
from here.' That's true. Of the 79 films made here since
the early 1990s, several have been acclaimed internationally. But the opposite is also true: that the world
now marches towards the studio, to see the scores of film
sets that have been preserved on their own lots. The
combination of fairground and open-air museum is
Yinchuan's favourite day-out destination, drawing
300,000 visitors every year.

Since north China made its houses of earth bricks,
nothing much survives to show how ordinary people lived

centuries ago; but here you can walk through a medieval village, convincing enough if you don't look too closely at the stuffed doves, ducks and donkeys. You can swamp your jeans and open-neck shirt in an antique robe to pose for photographs, or become a prisoner tied in the traditional portable shoulder-stocks known as a cangue. In an ancient kitchen, bellows lie ready to blast a stove into life. A millstone, siege machines and battering rams stand in unreal proximity, while crowds smile and snap.

Across the way, in the Qing castle, the high walls hide a small town, with mock-up shops full of fake hams and fruits. Up on a balcony, actors stage a scene – a girl prepares to throw a ball, claiming she will marry the man who catches it, but the ball is on a string and she jerks it away from hands that reach up from the laughing crowd. And up a side-street, in a corner of the castle, is a cloistered courtyard centred on a garden and a Roman fountain. Along one side are rooms forming a mansion, complete with stage furniture, jewellery, weapons and food, all used in the film *Homeward Bound*, about the Romans who, it is said – wrongly, as we know – founded a community along the Great Wall in 36 BC.

I was disconcerted by the overlapping layers of information and misinformation. I was in a genuine castle, which had been coopted to display mocked-up but authentic artefacts to make spurious films, but was making most of its money from tourism, and I had just been admiring the authentic set of a film that had vanished, and might not exist at all, about a myth disguising itself as history. How, I wondered, had something so real and grim as these two castles become a patchwork of history, pseudo-history and non-history?

In 1961 all this lay in ruins: the earthquake-battered Ming castle wind-blown and rain-washed into desolation; the Qing castle abandoned in 1958 by soldiers who had dug themselves a campsite in its courtyard and then left it to a few impoverished villagers who had sought the shelter of its walls. But by chance one of China's most famous authors was living nearby. Zhiang Xianliang, scholar, poet, best-selling novelist, long-term thorn in the side of officialdom, became famous in the late 1950s with a poem about imprisonment. Over the next 20 years, he was in and out of labour camps several times. Rehabilitated in 1972 and recently much honoured, he turned to novels to portray the realities of official oppression, prison camps and their impact on human, in particular sexual, relations. In 1961 he found himself briefly released from a labour camp near Yinchuan. 'One day,' he wrote in a little pamphlet about the studio, 'I was going to market to exchange some products – some brought vegetables and fruit, others brought cows and milk to barter – when I came across these two old castles, and saw them as symbols of our national spirit. In 1980, I returned, and wrote them into a novel, *Mimosa*.'

This was how the Qing castle is reimagined through the eyes of Zhiang's hero:

This so-called market town, a stockaded village built by some cattle owner in the old days, stood on stony sandy ground at the foot of the mountain, surrounded by weeds. Its earthen wall enclosed about a dozen cottages, fewer even than our village. The gate in the wall had been removed, so that the entrance looked like a gaping jaw . . . since today was market day, it was swarming with people and reminded me of a small Arabian bazaar in a Hollywood film.

Later Zhiang returned with the film director Zheng Junzhao, who thought the place would be a good setting for his film *One and Eight* (1984). Since Zheng soon became one of China's new wave, the so-called 'Fifth Generation' of film directors who brought Chinese films international recognition, other directors followed his lead, notably *One and Eight*'s cinematographer, the future director Zhang Yimou. The film everyone mentions at the studio is Zhang Yimou's *Red Sorghum*, some scenes of which were shot here. When he was making the film, he swore that if it was not a success he would never make another film. It went on to win the Golden Bear at the Berlin Film Festival in 1988, becoming the first mainland Chinese film to win a major international film competition. So he had a soft spot for this place. In 1992 Zhang heard that those who ran the castles were keen to make some money out of them. At his suggestion, the decision was made to turn the castles into a 'film city' – the only example I came across of a Great Wall installation becoming home to big business.[2]

West of Yinchuan, dotted across a gently sloping plain that falls away from the Helan mountains, are nine very

[2] To be joined, perhaps, by the museum at Yangguan, if it ever becomes profitable.

odd-looking objects: 30-metre-high cones of rough earth, 2 or 3 kilometres apart. From the road that leads into the mountains, it looks as if the outwash from the Helan has buried rockets, leaving the nose-cones poking above the surface. Closer up they are even odder, because they are as rough as termites' nests and pock-marked with holes, which, when I first saw them, I thought were made by birds. A huge collection of tiles beside one of the tombs explained the holes: they once held the ends of beams, which supported tiled roofs. The solid earth cores, towering over the subterranean burial chambers, were once gleaming, porcelain-clad, Chinese-style pagodas: a fitting tribute to the rulers of the rich and sophisticated Buddhist empire which had existed for two centuries before Genghis Khan brought death and destruction to Xi Xia in his two campaigns of 1209 and 1227. It may have been in 1209, when his troops flooded Yinchuan into surrender by breaking the canals, that the tombs were shattered; but more likely it was after the final campaign of 1227, when his armies came the long way round, the other side of the Yellow River, for it was only then that he aimed for destruction rather than submission. Now Yinchuan's main tourist attraction, they were in much the same condition in the late fifteenth century, when the Ming must have looked upon the rain-worn remnants as additional proof of what might lie in store if ever the Mongols were allowed to break through again.

The Ming answer lies a few kilometres further west, where the Helan mountains dip from their 3,500-metre heights to make a narrow but gently sloping pass, the Sanguan. This was where Genghis first broke through in

1209, luring Tangut forces out into the Alashan desert, turning to tear the pursuers apart, then taking the fortress that defended the Sanguan. The Ming knew that a fortress alone would not be sufficient. Mongol horses would simply scramble past it through the mountains. Nothing less than a wall would do. It came, eventually, in the late 1520s, and was finished in 1531.

I was with my Mongol friend Jorigt on a late summer's day, heading past the tombs and on up the long, gentle slope that led through the mountains into Inner Mongolia. The first time I had come here, five years previously, the road had been old and pitted, and the area in the hands of the military. The hillsides had borne huge white numbers, from zero to seven. 'Targets for bombers,' said the driver, adding nervously as I focused my camera: 'If they see you taking pictures, they will arrest us all.' Now the pot-holed road had become a fine highway of black asphalt, smooth as new paint, the hillside numbers were fading into tussocks of grass and grey-brown scree, and camera-bearing tourists would, I'm sure, be welcome.

The Wall came in from our left, firm and straight over gently undulating ground, until it met the road at a cubic pillar bearing big square Latin initials: we were leaving 'NX' (Ningxia) and entering 'NM' (Nei Mongol/Inner Mongolia). Except we weren't, because, on this sparkling and windless afternoon, I wanted to climb the Wall right along the border, upwards into the Helan, and see what exactly the Ming had built.

It isn't much of a wall, actually. They hadn't bothered to cut and dress slabs of rock, as the Qin (or their predecessors) had done north of Hohhot. Here it was just the stuff of the lower slopes – earth and rock-flakes – scraped into the semblance of a wall, 1 or 2 metres high. But that didn't matter, because the wall topped a slope so steep it was virtually a cliff.

'You couldn't bring horses up here, could you, Jorigt?'

'One horse, yes. Maybe a few. Many horses, no.'

We climbed on upwards. Jorigt, I remembered, didn't like heights. We'd been on Xumi Shan, Treasure Mountain, a sixth-century Buddhist retreat about 200 kilometres to the south. The mountain is a cliff of 100 caves reached by vertiginous steps cut from the rock. It is a good place to contemplate infinity; not so good if you are used to two-dimensional grasslands. There came a moment when he let me go on alone. Now, on this mountain, the wall wound on upwards on top of its cliff towards a ridge. It looked high enough for a good view; after that we would turn back.

At the ridge I stopped, panting, to stare down. Back east, guide-books compare the Wall to a dragon. I can't see it myself. But here, the image worked, if you imagine the dragon dead and desiccated in the heat, its spine – that's the Wall – exposed, its ribs the falling ridges of grey grass-pimpled rock. We sat together on the dragon's head to recover our breath. Way below, the road was nothing more than a black ribbon. A three-wheeled tractor, turned into a child's toy by distance, was the only sign of life, its putt-putt rising up into the hills the only sound. Over the road, the Wall, graven on the landscape by its own shadow from the afternoon sun, stretched away over rolling ground towards the Yellow River, lost over the horizon.

Honour was not yet satisfied. Above, the Helan beckoned, ravines and ridges as chaotic as crumpled paper rising to another, grander spine. I'd never make it up there, not in an afternoon, a day, perhaps a week. But a few hundred metres further up the Wall took a sudden twist and turned into what looked like the base of a fortress.

'Come on, Jorigt. Let's get there. No further, I promise. Are you OK?'

We were not walking a cliff-edge. With the low Wall as our guard-rail, we were on a faint trail made by occasional walkers, hunters perhaps on their way to wilder parts in search of bear.

'Some people get sick,' said Jorigt, firmly. 'I am not that person.'

But then we came to the place where the Wall turned, bridging a ravine, turning itself into a cliff of stone. I pressed on, round the shoulder of a pinnacle that acted as a pillar. Jorigt, I noticed, did not follow. I edged along a shelf to a little plateau which was both mountain and wall, not a fortress at all, but a good lookout point. Westward, the Wall tumbled and wove down, but the road was almost invisible now and across the valley the Wall faded into haze. I turned, with my back to the sun, and looked eastward towards Yinchuan, and saw nothing but light grey ridge upon lighter grey ridge, fading into the distance, with not a road, or a house, or any sign of habitation. And above, no doubt, the Wall continued for – how much further? Waldron says 40 kilometres; Cheng Dalin refers to a 'ditch' of that length; others say the Wall runs the length of the Helan, 200 kilometres.

What a wonderful hike it would be to find out the truth.
'John Man!' came a faint and distant voice. Hundreds
of feet below, my own shadow fell on a tussock-speckled
slope. It occurred to me that if I twisted an ankle, let alone
fell, I would be something of a problem for Jorigt, and so,
setting curiosity aside, began a careful return.

13

GUARDING THE WAY WEST

THE GREAT WALL WAS AN ALL-OR-NOTHING PROJECT. AGAINST nomads who could cover 150 kilometres a day, there was no point in half a wall. Blocking the Ordos meant blocking everywhere else as well. In the east, mountains and passes would take decades of analysis and work, but in the west, where the narrow Gansu Corridor funnelled travellers and armies through a narrow space, the problem boiled down to a single, and more easily answered, question: where to end the Wall. Every dynasty with ambitions to control the Western Regions had been spoiled for choice, ever since Zhang Qian had come this way in 138 BC, but no one had yet got it right. The Xiongnu had tried to control the corridor from their Black Water fortress near Zhangye, which was too far into China; the Han went for Yumenguan, which was too far west into the desert; only in the fifteenth century did the Ming come up with the Goldilocks solution, neither too far nor too near. Jiayuguan is just right.

The town itself is the end of the Great Wall, or 'the first city of China', depending on which way you are going; so I imagined, as the train pulled in, that I would find a little, end-of-the-road sort of a place. Michael, my fresh-faced and know-it-all guide, was keen to enlighten me. Yes, for 500 years there had been nothing here but the fort. But in the 1970s iron was found in the Qilian mountains, and a smelting works arose, and a tumbledown fort turned into a town, which is not end-of-the-road at all. China's longest highway – Route 312 from Shanghai, 2,500 kilometres away – runs right through it, and 150,000 people live here, one-fifth of whom are iron-workers.

Drive five minutes out of town and you see why this is a good place to build. It helps that the snow-capped Qilian mountains block the southern horizon, but that's true all along the Gansu Corridor, which owes its greenery to the run-off from the mountains. The real attraction of Jiayuguan is that it plugs the corridor at its narrowest point.

You can see the result well from the Wall's northern extension, which runs into hills, the Hei Shan (Black Mountains); better still if you go early, when a low sun picks out the contours. This section, named the Hanging Wall, had just been restored by a local businessman, who had taken it over from the local government. 'It used to cost eight yuan three years ago,' grumbled Michael. 'Now it's twenty-one. Well, I suppose he has to make a profit.' Not from us, though. We were there so early that there was no one to take my money. The sun spotlit a smart new gate that straddled a small river, from which the Hanging Wall, a narrow, raised walkway of clean stone, chased its shadow upwards to vanish over barren ridges of dark rock.

But I was after an overview of the whole valley in the other direction. High up on a side-ridge was a beacon-tower. That would do nicely. At the far corner of a small fortified enclosure, a branch of the Wall led up to a rough path. Ankle-twisting rubble and uneven steps took me to a shaky chain-and-wood ladder hanging from the tower. Tourism may have its disadvantages, but not here. The path was for the foolhardy, of which on this bright autumn day I was the only one; but at least it turned a rock-climb into a scramble. From the top, I could see beyond the craggy lower slopes of the Black Mountains right across the Gansu Corridor, with the Wall streaking across the plain to join the fortress itself. Then, beyond a haze rising above a distant river, there stood the Qilian mountains, their line of snow-capped peaks some 40 kilometres from where I perched on what Michael called 'the right arm of Jiayuguan'.

What I could not see was the left arm, which ran across the flat land the other side of the fort. This turned out to be a section of wall only 7 kilometres long, running straight and true across semi-desert, paralleled by the furrows of a moat that had once carried water right across to the Black Mountains. The wall ended in a weather-worn lump of rammed earth known as the No. 1 Beacon Tower, the Wall's first and most westerly outpost.

You see at once why it has to be No. 1: it stands on,

indeed seems to grow out of, a cliff that drops 80 metres sheer into the icy and silty-grey waters of the Daolai River – the source of the mist I had seen from the Black Mountains.[1] No nomad warrior could ever have bypassed this (although now tourists can, on a one-way trip, as I would soon learn). The canyon is so sharply cut, the walls so sheer and the waters so powerful, especially in spring, it is a wonder the river has not undermined the rock-face and gobbled up the tower. It may yet do so: the tower's southern face has already sheered off to become an extension of the cliff.

That the cliff and tower survive is fortunate for local entrepreneurs, who have burrowed down from the surface and dug out an underground chamber with a startling view of the ravine below, including, rather oddly, a 'Mongol' military base of round white tents. I thought at first this was a terrific way of adapting an archaeological site, because beneath a glass floor was a palaeolithic tomb, proof (said a notice) that Jiayuguan's history reaches back over 3,000 years. For a moment I was intrigued: what luck that a stone-age hunter's tomb had survived so deep down, so close to a cliff! In fact, the tomb is a copy of one in the town. I felt vaguely cheated by this piece of pseudo-authenticity, and moved towards an exit.

No ordinary exit, as it turned out. Set in a hole in the cliff, wheels and cables made an upside-down ski-lift offering a quick ride down to the bank opposite. Obviously it was safe, but I had never parachuted or

---

[1] Some sources say it is the Baode, which is an alternative name.

bungee-jumped. As hands adjusted straps around thighs and waist, the sight of the drop and the swirling grey river below pumped me full of adrenaline and apprehension. A push and I was away, the wheel above singing on the cable, the wind pulling at hair and clothing. In half a minute I fell several hundred metres, flying over river, clay shores, a low cliff and gravelly scrub, before slowing and landing at a run on gravel. Then, with heartbeat back to normal, there was a walk through the Mongol camp, which turned out to be a film set of mock-*gers* made of concrete, and up a suspension bridge to the cliff-top, and so back to No. 1 Beacon Tower, the inert inspiration for these incongruous activities.

The body from which these two arms reach is, of course, Jiayuguan itself, which had acquired its first small-scale military outpost in 1372, only four years after the expulsion of the Mongols. The main fort arose a century later. A weather-worn sign above its east gate makes a claim that in most translations reads 'the strongest pass under heaven'. That's stretching a point, because its double walls form a compact place compared with others. Its military heart, the square inner courtyard where its 1,000 soldiers would muster, is 160 metres per side, which is exceeded by a dozen other forts along the Wall. In fact, the Chinese says only that the pass is 'strong' / 雄 , with no superlative. The claim points to one of Jiayuguan's defining traits: like a talented but insecure person, it encourages exaggeration; not lying exactly, but enhancing the truth with tall stories.

So you have to put the 'strongest pass' claim in the

context of the early sixteenth century, when there was not much behind the departing traveller except the Wall and its strongholds, and even less in front. In this void, Jiayuguan was imposing indeed, with its 1,000 soldiers and its outer courtyard crammed with traders coming and going to the Western Regions and with locals hawking wares to travellers. Today, the eastern gateway, the ramp up to the courtyard, and the courtyard itself are empty of life, its few buildings stark in the burning light. But go back in time, and you walk into a throng of camels and stalls. You can hardly see the temple to Guan Di, god of war, patron of numerous trades, spirit of a real-life hero who was China's Robin Hood. You have to fight through the throng to find the little theatre, with its frescoes – the Eight Common People who suffer in this life but find spiritual release hereafter, the hypocritical Buddhist monk who acts the saint by day and the lecher by night, and his poor pregnant victim. Against one wall, you find a small crowd of women and children, the families of soldiers about to go on campaign, some of whom are using stones to knock on the wall, because, they believe, the knock of stone on stone sounds like 'Good luck! Good luck!' Or, if you prefer another legend, the sound recalls the tale of a nesting swallow who killed himself by flying into the wall, and people think that the clinking stones sound like the call of the swallow's widowed mate. Today, there are those who know the stories and like to produce the 'Good luck!' and swallow-chirp sounds, ignoring a notice: 'Please do not knock on the wall!'

'Do you see that brick?' asked Michael. We were wandering round the battlements of the inner castle, with the Qilian sparkling to the south, the Black Mountains closing in the north like a dark frown. 'Look at the shelf above the gateway . . . now look along to the middle? You see?'

Yes, a solitary brick lay on a shelf. So what?

'There is a story. I will tell you.'

The architect of the pass was to be a certain Yi Kaizhan. It so happened that Yi's boss was a corrupt official, Lu Fu, who had his eyes on the fee. So the official told Yi to calculate exactly how many bricks he needed, down to the nearest brick. One brick out either way would mean his death. Yi was very confident, and signed the contract. But when the pass was finished, there was one brick over. Happily, Lu Fu planned to have Yi killed and to seize his money. But before the scaffolding came down Yi engraved the brick with his name 'Yi's brick', which is a pun, for '*yi*' also means 'one'. He placed it high up on its shelf above the gate, and made it known that this was no ordinary brick, but a Heaven-sent magic brick, on which the gate's future depended. 'If anyone, friend or enemy, takes it,' he said, 'the pass will fall. Just to make doubly sure, I have loosened the two bricks at either end of the shelf. Anyone trying to remove it will surely fall and die.' Thus was Jiayuguan's future secured with Yi's single 'stabilizing-the-castle' brick. Lu admitted defeat, and the brick is there to this day, a symbol of the architect's expertise and a guarantee of the fort's survival.

Well, it's a nice story, carefully buttressed by guides, guide-books and on-the-spot evidence. Cheng Dalin, my Great Wall expert, makes the same claim: 'the single brick left over after the completion of the fortress', says the caption to his picture. I could even see through my zoom lens that the shelf's end-brick is without cement, carefully balanced as if to booby-trap an enemy. But it won't wash. I'm sorry to be a spoilsport, but Cheng's picture and mine do not show the same brick. Someone sees to it that a brick is on show, carefully cleaned and/or replaced now and then, and that the bricks at either end have their gaps kept clear of sand, to preserve the illusion of the booby-trap.

OK, it's a story. But that's no reason to reject the idea behind it. Social anthropologists claim that such stories point to deeper truths, in this case about the brilliance of the architecture, which has as much to do with stone and earth as brick. Take the foundations, which have a story of their own. For foundations and for flooring the gateways the builders needed stone, slabs 1–2 metres long weighing some 300 kilos each. The closest such stone is in the Black Mountains, 15 kilometres away. But the quarry was high, the way down tortuous, winter coming on and the schedule tight. How to transport them? An old quarryman came up with an idea: dribble water on to the slope at night, let it freeze, make an ice-road, and slide the stones down to the ox carts. In another version, the ice-road leads all the way to the castle, and people drag them.

There's another story about the bricks themselves: that they were made from a source of clay in the Black Mountains – or, in another version, were made 60 kilometres to the west – and then, as Michael told it, 'the local people found that a sheep could carry two bricks, so they used sheep to carry all the bricks to the fort'. It is a pretty image but, again, unlikely. Back in Beijing I wondered aloud about the story to Cheng Dalin, whose reaction was fast and scathing. 'I tried it. The sheep would not move.'

If there is truth lurking behind these tales of native ingenuity, it lies buried rather deeper than you might think, because the fort's first walls were of earth, but with some vital treatments and additions that must have been the products of much experimentation, perhaps inspired by the fact that the new Ordos wall was already eroding fast. The first step was to spread the earth on flat stones and allow the sun to scorch all seeds to death, to prevent the wall from turning into a vertical garden. The barren earth was then mixed with hemp fibres, to bind it; then with lime and rice starch, which harden into a sort of cement. The slurry was tipped and pounded between boards, which, as the mud dried, were raised to make the next layer, until the outer walls reached 3.8 metres and the inner ones 7.3 metres. The result was tested by an archer firing an arrow at it: if the arrow bounced off, the wall was good; if it stuck in, that section failed the test and had to be redone. On these earth walls came the brick battlements, raising the inner walls to 9 metres. It is a tribute to the expertise behind the original design that earth should support bricks, and go on doing so until today.

Above the three gates – the double one facing west, the single one in the east – rose three three-storey towers, with the typical curved tiles and upturned eaves sheltering meeting-rooms and offices. (One of them, the most westerly one, burned down at some unrecorded time, but has recently been rebuilt, along with other work that has restored the fort to its former architectural glory, if not its busy life.)

The towers, with their vulnerable wooden pillars and refined eaves and wide windows, tell us something about the castle and its times. Remember that building started here in the second half of the fifteenth century; there are various dates, but all are after the 1449 disaster at Tumu that inspired the Ming to start their wall-building programme. But by the time it was ready, almost a century later, there were hints of change in the air, reflected in Jiayuguan's architecture. Although the fort bars the way to barbarians, although it has *inner* inner courtyards to trap them if they break in, it is also designed to entice and lull them. The name of the second west gate is Rouyuan (*róu yuǎn* / 柔远), Gentle-Far, i.e. 'be gentle to those who live far away'. By the 1530s, then, there were some in authority who saw that there were more creative ways to deal with the tribes of the Western Regions than outright hostility. Given what was about to happen further east, this generous notion would not be given much of a chance for some time to come.

14

THE CENTRE GROUND

WITH THE ORDOS AND THE WEST SECURED AGAINST THEM, Mongol raiders had no choice but to look eastward again, aiming at Datong and Beijing and at the mountains between Beijing and the sea. And the Ming responded, repairing old earth walls, building new ones, turning earth into stone, locking prejudice in place with its greatest visible symbol. Let's see how these themes worked out in the Wall's central section, from the Yellow River to the passes leading to Beijing.

Like many prejudices, anti-Mongolism did not spring from nowhere. After all, the Mongols had once ruled all China, and no one could be sure it would not happen again, as events in Mongolia in the early sixteenth century suggested.

In 1479, about the time the Ming wall across the Ordos

was finished, the khan of the eastern Mongols, those who claimed Genghis as a direct ancestor, died. There was no heir, the only possible male successor being a distant relative, a six-year-old boy whose mother had placed him incognito with ordinary herders to ensure his survival. It was the khan's widow, Mandukhai, who took over as regent. All Mongolians know what happened next, or think they do (hard facts being thin on the ground), because it has become the stuff of folklore. The story runs like this: A man appears at court with a boy just the right age, whom he has kidnapped from a herder and who – he claims – is the lost heir. Mandukhai, aged about 32, marries the boy and has him crowned as Dayan Khan. With little Dayan as her talisman, she unites all the Mongols, and saves Mongolia from domination by the villainous Chinese. This is the tale as told in songs, story-books, dance, an opera, and the Mongolian film *Queen Mandukhai the Wise* (1988) which is often repeated on Mongolian TV.

At this point, folklore gives way to history. Amazingly, the union worked rather well. As soon as Dayan hit puberty, Mandukhai began producing children – eight of them, a daughter and seven sons, including twins, in as many years. In 1500, when Dayan was about 27 and Mandukhai over 50, the two led an army into the Ordos, setting up their headquarters at the place where newly resettled Mongols had established the cult of their hero, Genghis.[1] From here, they launched a huge raid across the

---

[1] Edsen Khoroo, the Lord's Enclosure, is still there today. South of Dongsheng in the eastern Ordos, it is known as the Mausoleum of Genghis Khan. For an account of it, see my *Genghis Khan*, ch. 15.

Wall, only to be driven out again the following year, back to the Mongol heartland. Over the next six years, Dayan launched several more raids. After Mandukhai's death in about 1510 he became sole leader, imposing unity that lasted for a century. In 1513–17 he was powerful enough to build two forts almost up against the Wall, mounting two full-scale invasions involving 70,000 cavalry before his death in about 1517.

It's true that these raids were in part inspired by Ming intransigence, but it's also true that Mongolian unity led to invasions, even if they were never going to threaten the existence of the Chinese dynasty.

It was under this pressure – constant raids, with the everlasting threat of a Genghis-style invasion – that the Wall began to take its present form. The Ming were slow to grab the nettle. Up until the 1540s, the Wall from the Yellow River eastward to the passes north of Beijing was hardly a wall at all, more like a sieve: all decaying sections and scattered forts, many of them manned only in the autumn, when Mongolian horses were strong from summer grass and attacks were most likely. Over the years, the defences were strengthened haphazardly, a section here, a pass there. Mutineers (1524 and 1533) killed overseers and delayed progress. In two centuries (1368–1569), the Ming managed to build only 72 forts in the Datong area, all of earth, one every two or three years.

The man who put some vigour into the enterprise was a dynamic commander named Weng Wanda, who had built a reputation on the Vietnam frontier in 1537–40. He knew how expensive and ineffective campaigning across the Gobi would be, and advocated a combination of diplomacy and serious wall-building. In 1547, when he was 49, he put his ideas down on paper in detailed proposals addressing the Yellow River–Beijing section. Here there were few steep mountains to act as barriers, but ranges of hills and rivers that were easy to penetrate. Over these 350 as-the-crow-flies kilometres, he said, the current fortifications – already 70–80 per cent finished – needed to be joined up in two lines of defence, manned by permanent garrisons. Over the next 30 years the whole system was completed: 850 kilometres, some of it doubled, tripled or, in a few small stretches, quadrupled. One 73-kilometre section east of Datong had seven forts and 154 beacon-towers; another 212-kilometre section had 1,000 beacon-towers – evidence of the importance of signalling in defence.

If you visit Datong, it will probably be to see the fifth-century Buddhist caves that honeycomb a sandstone cliff at Yungao, to the west of the city. You will no doubt be amazed, in equal and opposite ways, by the Buddhas that loom with beatific smiles and dangling ears from the living rock, and by the treacle-flow of interweaving cars, tricycle-trailers, trucks and people through which you must go to get there, not to mention the mess put out by a city that is built on one of north China's biggest coal-mines. You will wonder, no doubt, whether you will ever see anything charming anywhere in north China. Yes, you will, if you recall that Datong was once vital to the defence of both central China and Beijing itself, that the Great Wall around here doubles, triples, quadruples, like a bit of DNA coming apart at the seams, and that

Datong lies between the two main lines, safely away from both. Take my advice: to find charm, seek fresh air, hunt the Wall.

Go north, through rolling farmland, where the thick red earth is gashed by rain-cut ravines. In this direction the approaches were easy for horsemen, and the Ming built three parallel lines of earthworks, some 45 kilometres apart, each with its beacon-towers, which are scattered over the whole region by the hundred, like little islands breaking through from a subterranean archipelago.

Twenty kilometres out of town, a road leads off to the right. The lane ends at what looks like a bomb-site. It is in fact a wall, eroded into spines and fins. A stone lion sits by the roadside, not on guard, but discarded. There's an arch of brick in the battered earth wall, the sort of thing that should lead into a medieval town. Go through, and you will find not a town but a village, its unpaved street lined with single-storey mud-brick houses. The scene would have a timeless quality except for a scattering of electricity poles and a motorbike. Old people stand around. A kid pedals past with sunflowers spread wide on his carrier. As you walk on you will see, beyond the houses, other walls which make a huge square. Only then will you understand, as I did. We – that is, Jorigt and I – had just entered a Great Wall fortress that has been entirely colonized by a village, rather like Tumu, but twice the size, with enough space left over for good-sized fields. Fortress and village are called Deshengbu, and it struck me as a very good thing that the one had become the other, because otherwise the whole place would be one vast, decaying waste of space.

We walked through the village, along little grass banks that separated fields of potatoes, corn and barley, and climbed the fort wall where it had fallen away. The great square of light brown earth was now more the work of nature than of man, smooth where a slab had fallen, elsewhere rough with brackens and grasses. There was a watch-tower set into the wall, with rough steps cut into it. I scrambled up and looked around. This was an immense structure, 400–500 metres per side, a base for many thousands of troops, big enough to grow food inside, safe from trampling hooves in case of an attack. From up there, looking over the surrounding fields, I counted six beacon-towers, so those based here would have had good warning of any impending assault.

Back in the village, three middle-aged women in waistcoats, trousers and elastic-sided shoes had gathered on a street corner, and were happy to chat with a strange-looking foreigner about their home town. They were sitting on some substantial stone blocks, curlicued and patterned as decorative supports for long-lost pillars. The blocks posed the very question that had been at the back of my mind. What had happened to the fort? How come the village had grown up inside?

'I've been here since nineteen sixty-one,' said the chattiest of the women. 'At that time, the wall was quite OK. But in the last fifty years, all the brick parts were taken for building houses. Every year there was more damage. Look at the gate behind you. There used to be another two like that, east and west, with wooden pagodas on them. Now there's just this one left.'

The gateway looked as if it had been used as a quarry,

and the surrounding earth was cracking. I could see what had happened to some of the stones; they supported the corner of the earth-walled house beside me. 'You mean, no one comes to tell you about preserving the wall?'

The idea sent them into gales of laughter. 'No one.'

'So this is like a gift from the Ming emperor to you!'

'You are right.'

This was hardly a model village, with its simple little earth houses and new walls built on stones stripped from the old walls, and concrete electricity poles plonked down randomly, but there was something secure about it, enclosed by the surrounding walls. 'You know,' I said, 'I think I would feel very safe here.'

Yes, they agreed, but there was a problem. It was increasingly old people who liked living here. Young people left. The whole place was in need of a resurrection – the village, the castle, everything. But for what? Did they have many visitors? Oh, yes, many. 'Every week people come, sometimes three, sometimes four. Perhaps you would be able to give something for repairs?'

But obviously there was not going to be a resurrection. The fort was too big, and too ruined, and the visitors too few. It would take huge sums to restore the place. And how could this be done? Only by knocking down the village, expelling the ageing residents, reclaiming the bricks and carved stones and the odd imperial lion, and putting the whole thing back together. And then what would it be? A sterile piece of heritage architecture for non-existent tourists. Better, surely, that it sustains real life, even if that means the dissipation of a great edifice. Reader, you should see it as it is, before it vanishes.

*   *   *

To read of Yanmenguan, Wild Goose (*yàn* / 雁) Gate Pass, is to expect another Badaling. It is, writes Cheng Dalin as if selling the place, a famous fortified pass nestled amid towering, rugged mountains. A nearby peak of over 2,000 metres is said to deflect migrating geese through the pass, hence its name. It is the main pass in the 400-kilometre inner wall that runs in a giant S-shape through north Shanxi. It was always a prime route through the Heng and Wutai mountains, which 150 kilometres beyond gave way to the rich plains of central China. Here the Han had stopped the Xiongnu, the Song had stopped the Khitans, 130 battles had been fought in 1,000 years, etc., etc. Finally, in the late fourteenth century, the Ming had turned it into a three-gated fortress. It seemed to have everything: setting, history, dramatic architecture. I was expecting great things of Yanmen.

Jorigt and I, driving south from Datong on a featureless expressway, almost gave up before we started. It was a drab day, with bursts of rain from a leaden sky. But when we turned off following a sign to Yanmen, our spirits lifted marginally. We wound uphill into a village apparently besieged by walls and beacon-towers that had once hemmed in travellers and marauders like night-club bouncers shouldering an unwelcome guest. Now the ruins overlooked coal-trucks as they heaved upwards into the mountains, preferring a free walking-pace climb to the toll-paying highway across the plain below. I climbed for a better understanding, and found none. The whole valley was a maze of walls and terraces and fields rising into hills veiled by mist. A dozen low towers suggested there had been a grand design, a fortress with barracks and outposts ranging out from it, but all sense of its structure had been lost under the gentle assaults of the weather and farming. Courtyards had become fields, walls their borders.

We drove on, turning along a battered road that followed a dry river-bed, then climbing through damp forest. With the plain and the trucks behind us, we found ourselves in a wild area of ravines and boulders and autumnal trees, with only the occasional terraced field to show that people sometimes came here. Then the road came to an end at a guard-house, where in high season cars and buses dumped visitors.

A simple flat bridge, barred to traffic, led over a stream to a narrow, decaying road. The decay had once had a purpose behind it, because right alongside was a rather fine hump-backed bridge with three arches, all paved and ready for a new road. But no new road had come. The bridge had been left unconnected, stranded, and had become instead a drying-floor, covered now with a shaggy mat of corn-stalks. A poster proclaimed Yanmen's glories: five sub-fortresses grouped around the central fortress, a 50-square-kilometre complex that once housed 9,000 troops. It looked as though we were in for a treat, if we could just summon enough energy to put this depressing approach behind us.

We walked on upwards, through slowly swirling mist and silence, and came to a village of fine old dry-stone walls. I thought it was abandoned until, through a court-yard gate, I saw two bedraggled camels with sadly drooping humps. Somewhere a donkey brayed, and a dog barked. The road opened out, and a poster-wall loomed through the mist. Beyond was a small house that turned out to be a guide-hut, with, to my astonishment, a guide, Miss She Yifeng.

Yes, she confirmed, this is the province's most important Great Wall pass. Was it far? An hour's walk, I thought she said, as she led the way steeply upwards, over a broad road of slate that faded ahead into deepening fog. An arch loomed up, and then another, the second one topped by the eaves of what I took to be a temple. Beyond the arch were a slender pillar, two stone lions on low pedestals, a platform overgrown with fir trees, a temple. It looked charming, and no doubt offered stunning views on clear days, but since this was a small area and we supposedly had an hour to go, I assumed it was merely an outer guard-post.

'Shall we go on?'

'Well, of course.' It was self-evident. There was no point coming this far and not seeing the main pass.

A winding mud road led downhill, through a wilderness of low trees. It turned out to be an ancient way, because set in a roadside cliff was a plaque: a builder named Fu had come here to repair the road in the late fourteenth century at the beginning of the Ming dynasty. A new concrete building emerged from the gloom. A toilet – a 'five-star toilet', no less, according to Miss She, for all the tourists who came along here: 200 a day, in high season. This was some build-up for what I now expected to be a high point of my research. The road rambled down into a ravine, and crossed it precariously. 'The Japanese bombed the old bridge,' said Miss She. 'Now it has been replaced.' Above us was the new bridge, in forlorn isolation, waiting to be connected to the road.

And suddenly there was a village, which could obviously be reached by car only from some other direction. 'You mean we could have *driven* here?' I said. 'We could have driven to Yanmenguan?'

Miss She looked at me, baffled. 'To the village, yes. But only tractors can come along here. People must walk.'

'But how far from here to Yanmenguan?'

'What do you think?' She glanced back the way we had come. 'Perhaps two kilometres.'

The embarrassing truth filtered into my foggy brain. 'You mean . . . That was Yanmenguan, back there?'

'Of course.'

'So why are we walking down here?'

'You said you wanted to,' said Jorigt, with a laugh.

Confusion fled, replaced instantly by disappointment. Expecting something as impressive as the Wall near Beijing, confused by the fog, I had come right through Yanmenguan without realizing what I was looking at.

We made our way back up the muddy path to the fog-bound arch with its damp lions. I explored a little along the Wall either side, but could see nothing of the mountainous, forested surroundings. Even in fog, though, there seemed to be something odd about the place. The shrine on the top of the gate seemed rather too delicate for a military structure. There were big poles lying about, apparently ready for some renovation project. No, said Miss She, they had already served their purpose. 'They were sent by a businessman in Taiwan. He wanted to restore the temple to General Yang,' Yang being a Song general famous for fighting against the barbarians. This place, remember, had been a pass for centuries before the Ming developed it.

'But what were barbarians doing attacking up here? Surely it would have been easier to attack down on the plain?'

'No. Down there, we could see them coming, and the wall was strong.' (It was indeed, as I saw later from the train at Yangfangkou, where beacon-towers blossom.) 'If they could break through here, the way is open down to the plains.'

Later, when I saw Cheng Dalin's pictures of the pass, I understood. Only a few years ago, it was a total wreck, its walls picked at by locals wanting bricks, only one lion and no temple. It is not, as I first thought, decaying. It is in the midst of a slow-motion restoration. Some time, the roads will connect to the bridges, the accesses will be paved. It will always be difficult to get to, but for those who make the journey it will offer a reminder of what once stood here: the final barrier to the rich plains of central China.

But still the defences were not good enough; partly because the Mongols simply flowed to the places where they could get through, and partly because they had just been reunified by a new leader, Dayan Khan's grandson, Altan.

In 1524 Altan, aged sixteen, inherited control of the region north of the Yellow River's Great Bend and began leading raids over the Great Wall, growing in intensity by the year even as Weng Wanda's wall-building programme got into its stride. In March 1549 Altan had an arrow shot into Weng's camp with a message attached, stating that unless trade were resumed – this being the only way ordinary Mongols could turn their excess livestock into Chinese silks and the like – he would attack Beijing in the autumn. And so he did, in an assault frustrated by Weng's new walls blocking the way through the mountains at Badaling. But this was only a minor setback. Next year, Altan gathered 100,000 troops and took them on a great sweep north-east to the still poorly defended passes around Gubeikou, and settled in a few kilometres east of the capital. Bands of nomads rattled the gates of Beijing, while from above generals watched grimly as the country-side went up in flames. This, though, was as far as it went. Altan could pillage, but he could not have seized Beijing, nor did he want to; like Esen, he had no intention of becoming another Genghis. His aim was to pressure the Ming into opening the border to trade.

Passions in Beijing rose as factions fought. If only trade and diplomacy had been allowed to flourish, Altan would never have invaded! If only there had been pre-emptive strikes and walls built sooner! Trade now! 'No' to trade, 'yes' to intervention! No one thought to involve Altan, until in October 1550 a Chinese official, who had been captured and now released by the Mongols, arrived at court with a letter from the khan. The court played for time. Troops were called up, and Altan's letter was returned with the appalling excuse that it was in Chinese, not Mongol, and therefore could not be authenticated. But Altan wrote again, in Mongol, finally getting himself heard. A few trade fairs were allowed to open – to a storm of objections from hard-line pro-Wallers. The Mongols wanted millet and beans, argued one, but everyone knew they didn't eat them (actually they did, and do), so they must be planning to use them to feed Chinese runaways. And anyway, remember tradition: don't talk to barbarians!

One hard-liner, Yang Jisheng, castigated as disloyal those who would even consider peace with these barbarian 'dogs and sheep'. For men like Yang, as Waldron puts it, tolerance of 'barbarians' was a violation of morality. This was a bold move – or a foolish one, depending on your point of view – because one of those he accused was the prime minister, Yan Song. Yang quickly found himself in prison, where he languished for three years in misery. He is said to have used the fragments of a broken bowl to cut rotting flesh from infected wounds. He was finally executed, leaving behind a famous verse supposedly composed on the way to his execution:

> The noble spirit returns to the great void,
> The loyal heart remains eternal.

Yang is remembered today because he died for his views (there's a temple in his honour in Beijing); yet he won in the end, because the border markets were reduced to two, and Wall-building continued at a frantic pace.

The years from 1549 to 1620 marked the high point of Wall-building, all along the mountains that commanded the northern approaches to Beijing. Beijing itself received new walls in 1553. Reports speak of Datong's signal towers being repaired (1553), and of that city's new defences, which fell in 1558, being repaired the next year with a forest of new beacon-towers. Pressures multiplied: the walls of Xuanfu needed repairing – 190,000 men working for three years. Datong's walls took five years to build, for half a million ounces of silver ($6.5 million). In 1576 two officials looked at a segment of 400 kilometres, most of this stretch around Datong. Not even a single horse should be able to get through, they said, estimating that 40,000 men would take up to thirteen years to do the work. The cost would be a mere 23 ounces of silver per 10 feet of wall and 6.5 ounces ($84) for each tower: surely a huge underestimate, but even so they were asking for 3.3 million ounces ($42 million) for the whole 400 kilometres.

Altan was understandably put out by all this. In 1553 he sent six envoys with some horses and a request to reopen the markets. All six were arrested; four died, and the other two spent the next 20 years in prison. From then on, for the next 18 years, the Mongols attacked somewhere along the Wall every year.

Altan had been approached by one of China's many secret societies, dissident groups that practised a mix of Buddhism and magic, with end-of-the-world overtones. This one, the White Lotus group, promoted strict diets and mixed-sex rituals. It was one of many underground sects with links to rebels known as Red Turbans, who for a century under the Yuan Dynasty had fomented rebellion against the Mongols. Now trying to do the same against the Ming, the White Lotus rebels saw Altan as their saviour. Some 16,000 joined him, boosting the Chinese population of his homeland and, since they were farmers,

settling to turn a little outpost into a new city, named
Hohhot (Blue City) in Mongol. (It had several Chinese
names, today's being a Chinese version of the Mongol:
Hūhéhàotè / 呼和浩特.)

There are two interesting things about Altan, both of
them of significance for Mongol–Chinese relations, and
thus for Great Wall politics. The first involves his involve-
ment with Buddhism, a connection with all sorts of
political ramifications. Altan's ancestor Kublai Khan had
become a Buddhist, largely because he had brought Tibet
into his empire and needed a religion with an ideology of
universal rule with which to unite Mongolia, China and
Tibet. Altan was not going to rule China, but his Chinese
subjects were predominantly Buddhist. It would help his
ambitions to become khan of all the Mongols if he could
lay claim to Kublai's mantle. So he too turned to
Buddhism. In 1578 he linked up with a top Tibetan lama,
and the two made a pact. The Tibetan declared Altan the
reincarnation of Kublai, while Altan conferred a new title
on the lama: Dalai, meaning 'ocean' in Mongolian, the
ocean being synonymous with grandeur and supremacy,
in this case religious supremacy. This is one of the very
few examples of a Mongolian word acquiring international currency.

(As an aside, Buddhism, which spread rapidly among
the Mongols, is credited with ending several gruesome rituals. Until then, for example, it had been accepted
practice to kill wives and slaves to accompany a leader
into the afterlife; now all blood sacrifices were forbidden.
In one particularly nasty practice, sufferers from gout
could supposedly cure themselves by placing their feet

within the opened body of a slave or a prisoner. Altan, troubled by gout, was persuaded not to indulge in this barbaric practice and instead to accept Buddhist remedies, which apparently cured him.)

Altan's second contribution to Mongol–Chinese politics started with an unpromising obsession with one of his granddaughters, a beautiful girl called Noyanchu, seventeen to his sixty. From this passion sprang many things. She was engaged to someone else, who was, naturally, angered at losing her. So Altan tried to restore peace by handing over another granddaughter as a replacement. This one was also engaged, to Altan's foster-son (a grandson in some versions), Daiching-Ejei, who took violent umbrage at the khan's cavalier treatment and defected to the Ming.

You might think this would lead to war, either within Altan's family, or between Altan and his arch-enemies the Ming, or both. What happened was exactly the opposite, though it was a close call. The officer who received the angry young man was an experienced commander of the Datong garrison, Wang Chonggu. Wang was a remarkable leader, who had already started to open a new chapter in Chinese–Mongol relations. He knew the border, led his troops from the front, and encouraged Mongol defections (unlike other leaders who killed those trying to submit to boost their body-count and claim the reward for heads taken in battle). Employing both Mongols and Chinese to gather intelligence, he understood much better than his superiors in Beijing that for the Mongols pillage was a last resort, and that what they really wanted was trade. So he welcomed the defector, treated him like a royal guest and sent a message to Altan suggesting negotiations about a peaceful settlement: the khan could be made a prince, and receive aid. Altan, who had indeed assembled an army, paused. An attack would inevitably lead to his foster-son's death and yet more of the cycle of pillage and reprisal. Yes, perhaps he would talk. Still sceptical, he rode towards the city gates of Datong, and there to meet him was his foster-son, 'attired in a red robe embroidered with dragon designs, girdled with a golden belt and wearing a cap of marten fur'.

This was a breakthrough. Fortunately, it occurred when policy was in the hands of a strong and highly competent grand secretary, Zhang Juzheng, mentor to the emperor Lonqing, and a staunch opponent of the idealistic, nationalistic, pro-Wall literati. At a stroke – several strokes, of brushes, at the foot of a treaty in June 1571 – peace broke out. Altan and his followers swore never to go to war with China again. Gates were opened, markets established, aid flowed – something over 5,000 kilos of silver a year, about $2.5 million at current rates: about one-tenth of what the regime had previously been spending on defence. Military expenditure plummeted by two-thirds. Production rates in the military farms along the Wall soared. Over 20 years (1571–90), no military action was necessary anywhere in the whole central section of the Wall. In Mote's words, it could all have happened a century earlier, if the Ming rulers had been less set in their ways. 'Statesmanship could well have spared the expense and sacrifice of building its fabled Great Wall!'

And the symbol of peace became none other than Altan's granddaughter and wife, the young, beautiful and shrewd Noyanchu. One account describes her as 'versed in military strategy, very resourceful, highly righteous, wiser than others, and too generous and courageous to stop at anything'. For the next ten years, as her husband sank into old age, she kept his people in line, thwarted raids, escorted trade missions across the Wall, and led diplomatic delegations to Datong and other Great Wall outposts. On his death in 1582, she became in effect queen of Altan's realm, sealing her influence by marrying her husband's grandson. At one point, when Mongolian troops went on a rampage after a Ming officer killed a Mongol, she returned kidnapped Chinese and restored peace. The Ming honoured her as Lady Sanniangzi, and after her death in 1607 a temple was built in her memory, in Meidaizhao, a few miles east of her home in Hohhot. It is still there today.

War and peace: after the treaty with Altan, the northern frontier teetered between the two. The peace dividend allowed a spate of building, as the Ming raced to prove a truth later captured by the poet Robert Frost: good fences make good neighbours. In just three years, 1572–4, 43 new forts went up in the Datong area, all with brick exteriors – a 50-fold acceleration in work, with results of much higher quality. You can see the consequences of the conflict between the warlike and the peaceful at the far eastern end of this section of the Wall, in the valley through which Genghis had come, and through which, as rulers of China, the Mongols commuted back and forth between Beijing and Xanadu. This was therefore one of the first places to be blocked by the Ming. When it was founded in 1429 the town was called Kalgan, from the Mongolian for 'gate' (*khaalga*) – it was the gateway in the Great Wall between China and the Mongolian plateau. Later it acquired its present-day name of Zhangjiakou, a bit of a mouthful for English-speakers, until you understand that it was named after a Ming general who made his home here; it is the 'Zhang Family Gate'. Through Kalgan (as foreigners continued to call it) ran the main trade route to Mongolia and Siberia.

The old main road runs due north along the Qingshui (Clear Water) river to the old North Gate. By 1573 – the date is impressed into its bricks – this gate stood between marauders from the north (*possible* marauders, I should say, because this was only two years after the peace treaty with Altan) and potential victims to the south. Nowhere is there a better place to see Ming strategy fulfilled. The gate itself is the epitome of gates, a body-builder of a gate daring barbarians to do their worst. Seven-metre doors faced with iron and studded with bolts in tight-set parallel lines stand open, still ready apparently to seal the arch.

You climb the gate's steps and then on, up the Wall, which is restored, not with the huge cemented blocks that you see nearer Beijing, but with stones laid in a fine example of dry-stone walling. The stones – which must surely be the original ones, for no one would commission so many thousands to be squared off like this – angle inwards as the Wall rises up to a height of 2 or 3 metres. On the gate below there are good old-fashioned battlements, but there are none higher up where steep slopes protect the Wall from attack. Eight hundred steps up, concrete paths wind through saplings to a pavilion with upturned eaves, and a startling view that brings geopolitics alive at a glance.

Below me, the town is a distant murmur. The Wall drops out of sight as if plunging over a cliff. On my left is the north, and the valley leading up into what was once Mongolia. The river runs at a right-angle across my line of view. The gap it flows through, just beside the gate, is only half a kilometre wide, and the Wall picks up again opposite, zooming upwards to vanish over a distant crest. Quite obviously, no Mongol force would get through here – both Esen and Altan skirted it – unless the defenders so wished.

Eventually they did so wish, when peace broke out, and Kalgan came into its own, becoming one of the greatest of the border entrepôts. So it remained, for over 300 years. A century ago it had 7,000 commercial enterprises, ox wagons by the hundred and camels by the hundred thousand. In 1909 it boomed again when China's first railway arrived from Beijing, bringing tea by the tonne, which in autumn was picked up by the hundreds of camel-caravans heading north to Mongolia and Siberia. You can still get a sense of what it was like if you seek out the old part of town, a maze of ancient lanes not easy to see from the car-clogged main streets. 'The ordinary houses have an unusual appearance,' reported the 1911 *Encyclopaedia Britannica*, 'from the fact that they are mostly roofed with earth and become covered with green-sward.'

You don't see much green-sward in the town these days, nor many camels either. It's hard to believe that this heaving mass of post-war apartment blocks and traffic fumes was once one of the most romantic places in the world:

the end of China, the beginning of Mongolia. Listen to the American explorer Roy Chapman Andrews, the driving force behind several expeditions into the Gobi to find the dinosaur fossils that still have pride of place in New York's Museum of Natural History. He came through Kalgan in the spring of 1922, and recalls in one of his memoirs, *Under a Lucky Star*, riding in a convoy that took not the direct route northward through the North Gate but a less direct one that runs parallel to the Wall, climbing the escarpment in a series of S-bends (it still does). His memory was of

> our motor cars, piled high with baggage, covered with brown tarpaulins, winding up the steep Wanshien [Wanquan] Pass leading to the great plateau. Wonderful panoramas unfolded at every turn as we wound higher and higher. We looked back over a shadow-flecked bad-land basin, a chaos of ravines and gullies, to the purple mountains of the Shansi border. [Or, as he put it in another account: 'A chaotic mass with gaping wounds and gullies, painted in rainbow colors, crossing and cutting one another at fantastic angles as far as the eye can see: a stupendous relief map of desolate land.'] Above us loomed a rampart of basalt cliffs, crowned with the Great Wall of China, stretching its serpentine length along the broken rim of the plateau. Roaring like the prehistoric monsters we had come to seek, our cars gained the top of the last steep slope and passed through the narrow gateway in the Wall. Before us lay Mongolia, a land of painted deserts dancing in mirage; of limitless grassy plains and nameless snow-capped peaks; of untracked forests and roaring

streams. Mongolia, land of mystery, of paradox and promise! ... Never could there be a more satisfying entrance to a new country.[2]

It's interesting: less than a century ago, the old geopolitical realities still held in Andrews' mind. As far as he was concerned, Mongolia and the Mongols began at Kalgan. But they didn't, not any more. The threat from the Mongols had long since vanished, along with the Mongols themselves – a theme we shall investigate in detail in the final chapter.

[2] Andrews was a great organizer and leader, but as a writer, frankly, he became a bit of a hack. The description in *Under a Lucky Star*, published in 1943, reproduces almost word for word a version that first appeared in *On the Trail of Ancient Man* (1926). The other extract I quote is from his more restrained, and very good, account of the expedition, in the first of the eight-volume *New Conquest of Central Asia* (American Museum of Natural History, New York, 1932).

15

CLIMBING AROUND
BEIJING

IN WAR AND PEACE ALIKE, THE MING WENT ON BUILDING
their Wall. But this was, remember, a building programme
fraught with dissension over the costs. Up until 1568 there
were still many gaps, and virtually no beacon-towers.

That deficiency was rectified by one of China's heroes,
Qi Jiguang, prime architect of the Wall in its most recent
and grandest manifestation, the Wall that everyone knows
around Beijing. Let me tell you first about Qi Jiguang,
then about his creation, starting with the most famous bit,
Badaling, and moving eastward to parts that are more
remote, harder to get to, harder to climb. If I were
choosing music for this chapter, I would start grand and
sedate (for broad-shouldered Badaling) and end on
something *fortissimo* and *vivace*, because that's what
happened to my pulse on the teetering heights of Simatai.

My choice would be dedicated to the master, Qi Jiguang.

Qi Jiguang is famous many times over, as the Wall's architect-in-chief, of course, but also for his austerity, sense of duty, writings, archery skills and leadership. A story is told of him when he was thirteen. His elderly father found him showing off in a pair of nice silk shoes, a gift from his mother's father, and scolded him: A love of nice shoes leads to a love of nice clothes and delicious food, and then what? Love of luxury, that's what, which leads on to corruption and failure. Another time, artisans came to install four carved doors in the family home. Only four doors? Surely such a family should have twelve, said the artisans to Qi. When Qi raised the matter with his father, the old man scolded him again: 'If you pursue and indulge vanity, you won't be able to achieve great things.' His true purpose should be to serve the nation and the people. Set aside extravagance, vanity, self-indulgence and the quest for status; develop loyalty and integrity with study and the practice of martial arts. Qi took it all on board, adopting as his model the greatest all-rounder of the early sixteenth century, Wang Yangming, scholar, official, poet, general and philosopher.

A word about Wang Yangming, because he is the *éminence grise* of the Great Wall, the ghost in the vast machine that turned out this austere masterpiece. As a general he was adept at dealing with unruly minorities, and as a philosopher he set the agenda for decades to come (one scholar has proposed calling the following 200 years 'the age of Wang Yangming'). We haven't the time, nor have I the knowledge, to explain Wang's influence here.[1] It is rooted in centuries of debates about Confucianism, Buddhism and Daoism as guides to life, government and thought, and derives from a vision that came to him in 1508, at the age of 56, when he heard the words 'Search within your own mind'. This became for him a sort of Cartesian 'Cogito ergo sum', a realization that knowledge and action are inextricably bound. Action stems from knowledge; knowledge is only completed in action. This is the basis of morality. Look inside you, he said, and you find you have an innate knowledge of good and evil. Then comes action: 'the investigation of things is to do good and remove evil'. In brief – and this is the radical conclusion – morality stems from the individual, not the state. This realization led him to produce a new edition of Confucius's famous text *Great Learning*. That he should dare do such a thing sparked huge controversy, and also attracted many followers, some of them un-conventional in the extreme.

Wang died just after Qi's birth, and Qi grew up feeling the impact of his teachings. Like Wang, Qi became an exponent of martial arts, in particular boxing (on which he wrote a book which is regarded as one of the foun-dations of t'ai chi) and archery. While still in his twenties, this austere, moralistic and tough young man was given a leading role in overcoming what had become a serious threat on the coast: Japanese 'pirates'. The problem had come about because the Ming had banned maritime trade (as they banned trade with the Mongols), with the result that would-be traders turned smugglers, who, when

[1] Mote does it, and I have tried to follow him.

confronted, resorted to violence. Qi, applying strong leadership, firm discipline, and a mastery of joint land–sea strategy, helped solve the problem, and in 1568, at the age of 40, found himself given the task of upgrading the northern frontier from Beijing to the sea.

It was a role he relished, because eighteen years earlier he had been in Beijing and seen Altan's Mongols running wild in the surrounding countryside. One reason why they had been able to do this was clearly the inadequacy of the defences. The wall was built of rubble, dotted with stone platforms – not forts or towers – on which soldiers, with no protection from the winter snows or summer suns, were simply walking targets for arrows. The wall tended to wash away in storms, and the top was so rough that soldiers could not easily move along it. As Qi wrote in a memo to the emperor, he intended to seal this whole sector, all 2,000 *li* (1,000 kilometres) of it, though what he was measuring exactly is anyone's guess. China could not afford any gaps, he wrote. 'If there is one weak point, and then 100 strong points, the whole is weak. In recent years it [the Wall] has been annually repaired and annually destroyed. This is futile and unprofitable.'

So it was mainly thanks to the brilliant and dutiful Qi that this section of the Wall from Beijing to the sea took its present form. Qi saw that his task was to face the Wall with bricks and stone, and also turn the top into a road, so that men and horses could rush to threatened spots. His plans were thought out in detail. Ideally, forts would be close enough for archers to bridge the gap between them – say, 200 metres in vulnerable areas. These forts – 3,000 in all – would stand on stone blocks 10–15 metres above the Wall itself. They would be three to four storeys high, each big enough to accommodate up to 50 men, together with their stocks of grain and weapons. Construction brigades would complete 70 forts each every year. Every fort would be crenellated, as would the Wall itself, to allow troops to keep watch and return fire while protected. The ground floor would be reserved for cannon. There would be garrisons in the rear, in HQs in full view of the forts, ready to be summoned by signal-fires. The whole thing would be ready in three years.

That was his blueprint when building started in 1569. Naturally he didn't get all he wanted from central government. The number of forts was cut from 3,000 to 1,200, of which 1,017 were built, and construction took ten years, with much of the urgency draining away following the treaty with Altan in 1571. No one, though, drew from the peace the rather obvious conclusion that the Wall was not necessary. Why not simply save the cash and work on keeping the peace?

No, conventional wisdom has its own momentum. The peace was seen as a window of opportunity to prepare for war. For instance, Qi pointed out that the whole garrison, some 160,000 men based at Santunying, about halfway between Beijing and the sea, had been trained only on the parade ground. There had never been an exercise preparing them for real warfare. So in late 1572 Qi staged one for the benefit of observers from the war ministry in Beijing. Cavalry appeared over distant hills north of the new Wall, beacon-towers blazed, troops ran and galloped between forts. Within hours, the whole section was alerted. Still, the 'invaders' broke through, and reinforcements of foot soldiers, cavalry and war chariots rushed to the spot. By nightfall, no conclusion had been reached. Finally, with secretaries recording every move, the 'barbarians' tried to retreat through the Wall, only to be blocked by defenders. The few who made it back were duly 'slaughtered'. The men from the ministry left suitably impressed.

In 1580 Qi was still in war-harness, having invented a new version of a land-mine known as a 'rock-bomb'. Rock-bombs were simply rocks drilled hollow to hold gunpowder and buried with a fuse sticking out, which was set alight when the enemy approached. Qi's invention was an automatic fuse-igniter. It consisted of a flint, an iron wheel and a lever. When a man or a horse stepped on the lever, it turned the wheel, struck a spark from the flint and lit the fuse. Whether it worked or not, we do not know.

Throughout all this time, he was also writing. There was his boxing book. Then his account of quelling the Japanese pirates. From his experiences of the 1572 manœuvres he wrote his *Records of Military Training*, which became a standard reference work for military leaders. And there were shorter works of poetry and prose, which he compiled into the *Collection of Zhizhi Hall*, named after his office in his Santunying HQ.

In the early 1580s he fell ill, spitting blood, presumably the onset of TB, exacerbated by overwork and a back-stabbing campaign by bureaucrats in Beijing, who wanted him indicted for overspending. In the spring of 1585 he stepped down. When he left office, as Cheng Dalin puts it, 'all business ground to a halt as people turned out to say farewell, many of them clinging to his sedan chair and weeping'.

* * *

Work on the Wall continued steadily for the next 60 years, until the end of the dynasty. What it became was pretty much what Qi wanted it to be, and also what we see today. You've seen the pictures, the 8 metres of masonry and brickwork running from west of Beijing to the sea. It is a lesson in geostrategy, for it clings to the topmost ridges, wherever they lead, forcing invaders to undertake the most difficult ascents before they even reach the Wall. No high points nearby overlook the Wall; no trees were left to offer protection on the approaches. Slopes were turned into precipices, lakes and mountains into bastions.

It is also an architectural masterpiece, created with three fundamental units: the stone slab, dressed stone, and the Great Wall 'brick', measuring 36 × 19 × 9 centimetres, which was made locally in kilns. First, the builders dug two parallel furrows, which they lined with stone. Then came two brick walls, the gap between which was filled with earth and rubble, rammed down hard and bricked over. No gradient was too steep, until it became vertical. Slopes turned to terraces, then long steps, and then stairs, and finally, in some places, hip-high mini-cliffs. On the outside of the wall run battlements, usually of a standard height, 1.6 metres. Stairways at regular intervals lead down and out of the back. Drains from the walkway carry rainwater through the battlements, where stone pipes jut out to carry the overflow far from the stonework. So much for the standard walls. In some places, where it was hard to make bricks, slate or stones were used.

But there are bricks by the million (something like 36

million to build the battlements alone), and many of the stone slabs weigh over 500 kilos. Some weigh a tonne. Locals speak of goats carrying two bricks each, a theory that Cheng Dalin dismisses: 'Experiments have shown that it is absolutely impossible for a 30-kilogram goat to go uphill bearing a load of 25 kilograms, which is about the weight of two wall bricks.' (Another source, a placard at Gubeikou, says the brick weighed about 10.5 kilos, but let it pass.) No records have been found that describe the solution, which suggests that no new techniques were required. It was all down to manpower. Teams must have carried stone slabs from quarries in wagons and levered them into position. One worker could carry four bricks on level ground, two uphill. Lines of men could pass bricks hand to hand. There are records, of a sort, however. They are steles (some 200 of them), bricks and tablets inscribed with the names of builders, the army units, the commanders and the sectors they built: someone had to be held responsible if the work was not up to scratch, or if their section of the Wall fell.

By any standard, this was building not only on a massive scale but to the most exacting specifications. Was Qi Jiguang a builder and architect as well as everything else? He left no building treatise, but my guess is that his builders, knowing his standards, found their own ways to translate his high expectations into practice, without thinking to keep their own plans. Qi died in his home town in 1588, but is alive in memory. His wall guaranteed the peace ushered in by the treaty with Altan in 1571. With trade flowing through Kalgan and an impregnable barrier elsewhere, the frontier was secure. Qi's army of guardians, joined by their families, ensured that the Wall lived up to its Chinese name as a 'long city', alive with villages, fields and orchards, many of which survive to this day, thanks to him. Quite rightly, he is there in bas-relief, overseeing tourists at one of his prime creations, the Great Wall at Badaling.

Do you really have to go to Badaling? Must you find a bus or hire a car and join the throngs (4 million a year and rising), run the gauntlet of soft-drink stands and knick-knack sellers and purveyors of 'cultural relics', try to ignore the shouts of 'Hullo, coke!' and 'Hullo, sweatyshirt', fail to ignore them, buy the damned T-shirt with its 'I climbed the Great Wall' slogan, labour up the steps, take the clichéd pictures and drag back into town? Given the choice between all that and missing the Wall completely, yes: *you must not miss it*. Even with the crowds, even with all the dross, there is no better way to see Chinese history made manifest. This will not be unalloyed pleasure. There is a sense of duty about a visit to Badaling. But still, if you can spare an hour or two, you can escape the masses. Badaling is big enough to absorb the millions and remain unspoiled. If you choose your time, it becomes a place not simply of significance, but of beauty and silence.

Tourism has turned Badaling into a little community. The 1,000 workers who run the restaurants and hotels have their own football team. It's a strange community, because everything closes when the tourists leave around dusk. The workers go back to their village. Suddenly the place is empty, a dim pool of a few scattered lights surrounded by mountains of darkness. I was in one of the hotels with my two guides, Cheng and William. There was nothing to do, except have supper and go to bed, so I awoke before sunrise. Hungry for a magical moment before the world stirred, I put on an anorak against the chill of autumn, and pocketed camera and tape-recorder. It didn't look too promising outside, with nothing on offer but a huge, empty car park and shadowy hillsides that entirely concealed the Wall.

The main door was locked, with no one around to let me out. I opened a ground-floor window, climbed on to the sill and, with a guilty glance around, jumped down. Across the car park a path led up through trees – quite a well-worn path, actually, with a scattering of beer-cans and plastic water-bottles; not all tourists followed their groups. For now, though, I was alone in the silent woods, bar a pheasant which rose with a cackle.

I came out on to a high ridge, and found what I had hoped for. At my feet, a tide of shadowed forest lapped over the dark Wall and rolled in ever-fainter waves to a high horizon. A spotlight of sun from the hills to my left touched a tower and the eastern side of the Wall where it zigzagged up the hillside opposite. Shadows fell back, colour emerged. The woods turned a soft green below, while further off the sun picked out the rusty tinges of autumn. It was dead calm. Nothing stirred, not even a single red flag on a tower. As the sun rose, it revealed exactly why Badaling had to be built. To my left, the valley cut eastwards towards Beijing, hardly wider than a chariot. I could see the new expressway, the westbound lane only – there was no room for the eastbound one, which lay out of sight, deep in mountains.

Not far down there to the east was the second line of defence, Juyungguan, a mirror image of Badaling, except for the presence of something much more ancient: Cloud Terrace, the great arch built by the Mongols when they controlled all this and had no need of defences. It spanned the road, forcing every cart into the same ruts, which are there today, deeply worn channels in the old floor-stones.

By now Badaling was coming to life. A noisy little motorbike laboured up the road and through the gate. A lone official began a long climb on top of the wall towards me. I realized I was hearing a faint roar, from the motor-way which runs through a tunnel past Badaling on its way to Zhangjiakou, emerging somewhere unseen, but not unheard. Even at this hour it was busy.

I plunged on downhill through bushes and saplings, across a steep ravine to the Wall, and found a new path leading to a terrace. A plaque in English and Chinese told me this was part of the Badaling International Friendship Forest, set up by the US–China Environmental Fund, sponsored by Conoco-Phillips; in today's China, protection and privatization go hand in hand. Other plaques repeated the usual tourist stuff about 120 million(-plus) visitors and over 400 heads of state coming here. For some reason, plaques and pamphlets quote these here-today-gone-the-next politicians, none of whom have anything interesting to say, some of whom try to express nothing at all, like President Fernando de la Rua of Argentina, whose quote of the day was: 'It is hard to express my feelings with words.' Let's be kind: his mind was probably not on the Wall. This was in 2001, just before his country collapsed into yet another economic crisis and drove him from office. Or what should we make of Emir Mohammed of Qatar: 'I'm sure mankind will benefit from it in the future.' I am tempted to read this through gritted teeth and supply a sub-text: Is this some sort of a joke? You guys drag me out here just to show me something that has been *completely useless* these last 400 years?

Close to me on the forested slope was a watch-tower, into which I climbed. Even with the trees, which would surely not have been there in the sixteenth century, I had a fine view westward over the plain to the distant mountains of the Mongolian highlands just visible through the gathering haze. Any attacking Mongols would have been seen a long way off; and even if they had made it this far, it would have done them no good. The Wall 20 metres behind me was fourteen rows of close-set stonework, topped by bricked battlements. I scrambled to it, imagined myself in the boots of a Mongol warrior, felt the stone rough and cool beneath my fingers and stared up at the battlements. Two people, the first tourists, glanced over, their faces made a blank by the bright sky behind them. They were Germans.

'*Wer sind Sie?* [Who are you?]'

'I am a Mongol!'

'Don't attack!'

Not a chance. No Mongols in their right minds would have a go at this. I waved, and headed back for breakfast.

Soon the tourists came. I joined them trudging up first one side of the pass then the other, trying to root out new fundamental reasons why people come, and why they climb, for once up on the top of the Wall, you feel the urge to move, and there is only one way: upwards. Most, of course, were Chinese, families, kids, grandparents, faces red with the effort of climbing slopes and stairways. I passed a camel on which people sat for photographs. Someone hoping for coins was playing 'Auld Lang Syne' on a penny whistle (this is a popular tune in China, often to be heard spilling mournfully from loudspeakers in lifts and shopping malls). Why were we all climbing? I asked people as I went, and received only the blandest of answers. 'I've no idea . . . to have fun . . . to conquer something . . . to get to the top . . . to prove something to yourself.' An American struggled for a deeper response: 'With westerners, it must be that you've come this far, you better do it to the maximum of your ability.' For Chinese, it is surely to feel part of their history. But when I asked, no one could find anything deep or original to say.

So I guess the appeal is the purity and simplicity of being there on the Wall. You are part of a massive and eminent structure. You can go as far as you like, without feeling the competition that grips runners, yet able to respond to the challenge of the next high point. Once you're away from the huddle of stands down by the car park, no one bothers you. It's not like walking on the shore or through a forest. Here, on the Wall, you are contained, safe, yet free. You share an experience, moving aside, offering a helping hand, smiling at the effort and achievement of others; but because you are free, you can make it your own, admiring the backbone of stone as it twists away over ridges, knowing that, if you wish, you can walk and climb along it in safety. There are not many places on earth with such an easy balance between being a part of the human crowd and apart from it.

I went to see the site's deputy director, Zhang Min, in his office above the museum, and asked him about Badaling's past and future. Speaking through my guide William, he was formal to start with, but as he spoke, he opened up. He looked a fresh-faced youngster with the merest hint of a moustache, but he had been there for thirteen years, and was a man in love with his job, proud of the throng, proud of Badaling's international fame, and proud too of his little community and its football team. 'You know what my internet name is?' He switched to halting English: 'Arsenal! You know Arsenal?'

'I live near the new stadium.'

'Oh! Owen! Beckham!'

That was the limit of his English, but it was enough. Badaling's story poured out. This is a condensed version:

'After the war, the place was a wreck, because the Japanese had fought over it in the nineteen-thirties and then had come the civil war. There were no trees – they had all been cleared by the Japanese. But this was not just an important place. It was on the main road, and it was a station on China's first railway, the one that led to Zhangjiakou. In nineteen fifty-two, with the Communists securely in power, Guo Moruo – poet, historian, novelist, translator, archaeologist [the same man who had saved the Flying Horse of Gansu] and one of Mao's top officials – suggested that the Great Wall at Badaling should be opened for tourism. By nineteen fifty-eight, it was ready. There were few cars then, so people came by train. There were hardly any foreigners in those days. Then came a big change. President Nixon came to China, and the government brought him here. That was the twenty-second of February, nineteen seventy-two.'

I was impressed he knew the exact date. This was a milestone. And Nixon's words of wisdom? 'I think that you would have to conclude that this is a great wall,' he observed, which is where many press reports stopped, much to Nixon's later annoyance, because it made him sound foolish by cutting the conclusion: 'and it had to be built by a great people.' Not the best of quotes, but not as daft as most of the other 419 heads of state, and certainly not as daft as the mischievous misquote – 'This sure is a great wall' – makes him sound. The Badaling Museum, by the way, back-translates Nixon from the Chinese, and has him saying: 'Only a great nation can build such a magnificent wall.' Which is equally bland, but at least not completely dumb.

I have interrupted Mr Zhang. 'Suddenly the eyes of the world were focused on this wall. Many Chinese started to come, because as living standards rose people wanted to see more. Of course they could see the Forbidden City in Beijing, but that is an imperial creation, and cannot represent all the people. Only the Great Wall can do that because it was built by the bare hands of the common people. But still people did not come from abroad. China was very closed until nineteen seventy-eight, when the party leader, Deng Xiaoping, declared an Open Door policy. By nineteen eighty-four, we were getting perhaps ten thousand a day, though they could only go a few kilometres along the Wall. Since then we have been rebuilding all the time. Then in nineteen ninety-nine came the expressway. We suggested the expressway, you know, but insisted that it did not destroy the natural environment. That's why it goes through a tunnel. Now, at the height of the season, in Golden Week in early October, we get sixty thousand people a day. We used to get two million a year. Now it is four million. Do you know how many people have been here? [I thought I did, but didn't want to break his flow.] A hundred and thirty million people! [Ah, an update by ten million.] And four hundred and twenty heads of state! Your Queen, and your Mrs Thatcher, but not yet your Tony Blair.'

It sounds a lot, I said. How many could this section take?

'Our limit is seventy-five thousand a day, all year round.'

A potential of 27 million visitors a year! Almost seven times today's amount. Impossible in practice, of course. But I had seen from the empty car park and the few hotels and the darkened restaurants that the place still had huge tourist potential. So if you are concerned about the numbers today, you may like to worry about what's going to happen in the future. Why, they've hardly started.

Eastward from Badaling, you can track the wall, but can't get close unless you walk it. If you keep clear of the Ming tombs and the hordes visiting them, you find yourself deep in rural charm, a rare commodity in north China. Orchards of apple, peach and persimmon flow up hillsides, giving glimpses of the Wall high above. Poplar-lined lanes lead through villages where farmers use the road for drying crops. This is where Beijing gets its apricots, lettuces and ducks.

And some of its water too, from the reservoir of Huanghuacheng, where the Wall drops from its ridge-top route to meet road and river. This was never an open door for nomads – the hillsides are too steep and the bottom would have been a V filled with a rushing torrent. Now it's a lake, not large but picture-postcard pretty, backed up behind a dam. If you negotiate the village – it was in the middle of an upgrade, with a trench down the only street – and climb the dam, you can force your way up a tangled hillside and then at last reach the Wall, as I did with Cheng and William. It is what is termed the 'wild Wall', overgrown with bushes and saplings, which in high summer are a riot of *huánghuā* ('yellow flowers', in this case marigolds – hence the name of the wall here). I saw no sign of visitors, none of the usual cigarette packets or plastic bottles. The wall's sides are wonderful 2-metre chunks of dressed masonry, twice the size of Badaling's, but in some spots they bulge like paunches, in others they have fallen – torn away, more likely, because they are superb, ready-made building blocks – to reveal a tangled intestine of rubble and earth. A dilapidated tower offered a view of the Wall running like a rusty zip over hill and ridge on its way to Badaling, 30 kilometres away.

'Look, Cheng. No battlements. And all these bricks.' Underfoot, roots twined over a surface that seemed like a hard-core base for a road that was never built.

'Local people take for building, I think. Then no renovations here at all.'

'So this is not natural decay?'

'Yes, natural as well. Wind, rain, frost. And we had a big earthquake in nineteen seventy-six. We felt it in Beijing. Two hundred and fifty thousand people died.' He said it so casually I didn't know whether to believe him. But it was true. The great earthquake of July 1976, centred on Tangshan, 150 kilometres to the east, was the third most destructive earthquake ever recorded: officially, 242,319 people died and 93 per cent of residential buildings were knocked down – a catastrophe largely hidden by the government. Such a shock, 7.8–8.2 on the Richter scale, was enough to weaken any wall. It was a tribute to this one that it had survived so well.

'My God, I had no idea.'

'Yes, very bad.' By now we were climbing back down to rejoin the car. 'They could not remove the bodies or clear the damage. They have rebuilt the city on the dead and the ruins.'

Driving on eastward, I wondered if the locals ever climbed up to the Wall, if it meant anything to them. Why not ask? Swerving around a heap of corn-stalks drying on the road, we turned up a side-lane. A short walk past a group of young men absorbed in a card game brought us to a brick compound, where an old man in a blue jacket and cap was piling chestnut husks for winter fuel. His name was Zhang, he was 83, and he had been living in this compound with its single-storey house all his life, except when he had fought the Japanese in the late 1930s. He was happy to talk about that. As a teenager, he said in a soft but animated voice, he had been in the No. 8 Anti-Japanese Army Group, and had lost his younger brother in the conflict. I pointed to the wall snaking across the hills above the village. He glanced away. No, he had never been there. Nor had anyone he knew. No story of youthful climbs up the green mountainside came pouring out. He was happy to be left to his chestnut husks. I should have known, for it is a universal truth that familiarity with almost anything kills curiosity, unless you earn your keep from it.

This they do a few kilometres further on at Mutianyu, because this is another, if lesser, tourist destination. Here, once you are clear of the T-shirt sellers ('Look, mister! Many colours! One dollar, one dollar!'), a cable-car whisks you aloft to a 3-kilometre section of restored wall – restored in 1989, according to a plaque, with the help of a German company based in Düsseldorf. 'The Great Wall,' it said in German, Chinese and English. 'May it continue to act as a symbol of friendship for future generations.'

Cheng stared at the sign and shook his head. 'This is strange. Great Wall was built for war, and now it is symbol of peace. How is this possible?'

A good question, which I pondered for the next few kilometres, on a little tower-to-tower walk, away from the few stalls and along the crest of crinkled ridges. This bit, rather oddly, has battlements on both sides, as if the defenders expected to be fighting off their own people as well, or were planning for the Mongols to be on their way back from a breakthrough that never came.

At the top of a long flight of stairs, I came to the remains of a tower, and a doorway blocked with broken bricks which framed a notice in Chinese and typically ungrammatical English: 'The front not opened section road, no passing.'

There's a rule about researching: the untrodden road is a challenge that must be accepted. A wild wall of rubble and tussocks, interspersed with some of the old pavings, led on upwards to an arch of cracked bricks, topped by an empty socket where an incised stone had once recorded its number and its builder. From up there, a pretty view turned glorious: a crumpled, shadow-specked landscape of forested ridges and side-ridges tumbling down to the valley where Mutianyu's white-walled houses, turned into toys by distance, shone in the setting sun. To my right another of Beijing's reservoirs glinted in its clasp of green hills. Below me, the wall turned from ageing wreck to restored perfection, from what it was to what it will be.

But the battlements still puzzled me. Perhaps aesthetics played a role: battlements on the right balanced by battlements on the left. But now I came to look at them, these battlements were not serious – smaller than Badaling's, half-hearted. A guide-book hinted at an explanation. Although Mutianyu's main castle was built soon after the Mongols were thrown out (in 1404, actually), the walls either side were the product of Altan's peace dividend in the late sixteenth century. It all hung together: the peace made with the Mongols in 1571, the growth of trade through Kalgan, the building of an impregnable barrier, the villages that arose nearby. This section, like the rest of Qi's wall, could indeed be seen as a symbol of peace. It saw no warfare at all, until the threat vanished and it became entirely useless, good for nothing but tourism and symbolism and glorious views.

*   *   *

Gubeikou is everything that the previous two spots are not. Once on the main route to the Manchu emperor's summer palace, it's a wide open pass on the River Chao which at prime invasion time (late summer) dwindles to a stream between broad and welcoming banks. It proved a soft target for Altan in 1550 when he broke through nearby, so it took all of Qi Jiguang's expertise and ingenuity to seal it, creating a structure that almost dams the river, zooming up into mountains on either side.

Exploration is made easy by a charming hotel, with a wooden bridge over a lily pond leading past red lanterns into a courtyard of lawns, where a friendly, fluffy, white chou licked travel-dust from every exposed part of my anatomy. Restored, I set off up the wall with Cheng, William and our burly, overweight driver. A path led upwards to a guardian mountain, up which the wall made its steep climb from the river. I told my companions we should get to the top, or at least as far as we could by dusk. Why? I don't know. Because it was there. Because I was now in the mood to climb everything I could. Because I was a little obsessed.

Progress was slow, because the path first took us across a park which was punctuated every few metres by placards of text regaling passers-by with snippets of history and legend. There were scores of them, an encyclopaedia of the Wall spread out page by page, in Chinese and the language that in official publications passes for English. I learned I was climbing into the Wohu / 卧虎 (Crouching Tiger) mountains. I could tell you the name of every mountain, all sixteen passes, and all eleven 'famous fighting towers'. I could tell you the how, why and when of every name-change of the park's little temple. I could quote you a poem that urges you 'to seek the agedness for knowledge'. I could write you an essay on the three types of brick-kiln – the dragon-back, the hoof and the horn. It took two placards to tell the story of how the leg of a twelfth-century hero, dismembered in battle, was buried here in a tomb that started to grow, so that his enemy had to build a 1,000-floor tower to weigh it down. Cheng and William began to argue about when this happened, except it didn't happen, because it was a fairy tale, and the 1,000-floor tower – which had apparently once stood here, because the placard said it was 15 metres high – wasn't here any more, so the whole thing was a complete waste of time, especially as dusk was beginning to fall and the tower at the top of the mountain was glowing an enticing orange in the setting sun.

We climbed on past a watch-tower, one side of which dropped sheer to the river-bank below. An opening in the wall framed a strange bumpy landscape of barren brown hillocks, like giant mole-hills, on which stood two towers guarding hidden ways up from the river (they were, I think, towers left over from a vanished section of wall; see Gubeikou in second plate section). Onwards and upwards, the path, rough and hardly used, ran beside the Wall, which had a strange structure here, a double skin – three layers of brick over coarse stone – as if the Ming wall had been built around and over a pre-existing wall. It flattened briefly over a tunnel, the railway line that linked Beijing to Inner Mongolia, then zoomed on up to the dark tower another couple of hundred metres above us. Somewhere along the way we had lost our overweight driver, who would wait for us below. Now we were on the Wall itself, picking our way over rubble, for the surface had all vanished, either into local houses or as detritus littering the slopes below.

Even here there were placards, which I simply could not ignore, any more than one should ignore ancient aunts at a family reunion: they might just have something interesting to say. And so they did, because the placard-writer turned away from information to philosophy and spiritual awakening. The starting point was Mao's diktat: 'He who does not reach the Great Wall is not a true man; and he who does not love the Great Wall is not a hero.' Did love mean restoration? Not a bit. The purist who wrote these texts was all for leaving well alone: 'It should absolutely be prevented from being unnatural and modernized.' For him, the whole point was to accept the decay, the 'broken stone and the incomplete fort', for 'the remnant that endures wind and rain is just like the orderly grey hair on a grandmother's head'. Difficulty and isolation ensue: and in accepting these we strengthen ourselves. The placard-writer sounded as if he were devising slogans for a Californian self-help seminar: 'I like walking on the Great Wall alone. I will sit down for a rest when I am tired. I will develop my potentiality constantly and overcome the dangerous road while climbing.'

The rough slope turned to rough steps, which someone had cut, and then rough rock, which they hadn't. I scrambled up into the broken tower, and turned.

The tower's shattered entrance was a grandstand over a panorama very different from anything I had seen before.

No soft green forests here. It was all bare earth hills or autumnal scrub: a desolate landscape, its silence broken by the wail and clatter of a goods train entering the tunnel. The battered Wall itself was like a scar, where the hills had healed an ancient wound. Close to, all was in shadow, as was the valley of Gubeikou, where distant buildings speckled the river-banks. But just beyond the river the hills were still in brilliant sun, which mixed their dull brown with orange. At first glance they looked like sand-dunes, until I saw that there were small groves of trees cupped by some of the dips. The landscape was craggy and random, as if a giant hand had smacked a glue-covered board on it and then torn it up again. Across this crumpled array ran the Wall. Why the Chinese compare it to a dragon beats me. At that distance, it looked more like a piece of string wiggling away over the rough landscape; but this was no random wiggle that lost itself in valleys. It stood proud and deliberate on ridge-tops, climbing to mountains that ran across the horizon. Beyond them – that was where I would meet the Wall again the following day.

I explored, and bumped into yet another placard. There was just enough light to point me in the direction of something new. Heinrich Schliemann, the German archaeologist who discovered Troy in the 1870s, had come up here in 1863 (the placard said), and wrote a book about the experience called *My Travels to the Great Wall*. It was odd, in this remote place, to stumble on a reference to a westerner, one of the few to come this way in the nineteenth century. The Wall had made quite an impact on him, if his words were quoted correctly: 'This is a mythology created by a giant clan before the era of the Flood.' Why had he come? What did he think of it? I would check up on it when I got home.

I was not yet at the summit. The Wall climbed on up to another tower, a blank shadow against the red of the sunset. But I was not going to risk twisting an ankle, and set off back down. Luckily, as the sun vanished, a full moon rose, turning the path and the distant hills to grey. I walked, gingerly, in the steps of William and Cheng, until we met the anxious driver, and followed our moon-cast shadows back to the hotel.

We turned up a side-road, past tiny fields and terraces that set Cheng talking about coming to this place with his father when he was a child. 'The first time I came it was really cold. I was only eleven or twelve. It was a dirt road then, and the people were very, very poor. The children in the village didn't have shoes, and the houses didn't have glass in their windows, only paper. I remember the dogs. There were dogs everywhere. And eating some cold pie and drinking only cold water. But my father loved it here. It wasn't open to the public, so we were the only ones. It was he who named it, you know, after talking to the village people. The village used to be called Er Dao Liang [Two Mount Ridges]. Now, like the Wall here, it is Jinshanling, Golden Mountain Peak.'

This village, 15 kilometres from Gubeikou, has the odd distinction of being on the 'wrong' side of the Wall, right in the path of Mongols invading up the 100-metre-wide valley. It was yet another hint that Qi Jiguang benefited from Altan's peace dividend when he built the Wall around Beijing. Perhaps villagers first built here to take advantage of Mongols coming with their horses to trade, rather than to fight.

It was Cheng Dalin's attention that brought change to Jinshanling; quite a change, because now it is all one huge car park. In 1980 the village was moved lock, stock and barrel 200 metres up a side-valley, with a small payment to compensate the inhabitants for the enforced change. Their unpaved road runs to a dead end past brick compounds which are homes for 40 families. Reconstruction started in 1985 and took two years. They still have their fields and their chickens and ducks, but they also have tourism. An old woman with yellow teeth as irregular as abandoned tombstones attached herself to me with a toothy grin.

'What should I do?' I asked William under my breath.

'She is your guide. Pay her, but at the end. That is her business now.'

So far, there had been nothing to exhilarate a new visitor, but bear with me.

Cheng, William and I started to walk up the paved road towards the Wall, which loomed high above us round corners and over hillsides. Our crone, Wang Shuzhen, became chatty when she learned that I was with the son of the famous Cheng Dalin. 'There were too many people for the fields here, so we started to sell things to visitors, and take them up to the Great Wall. Our life is much better now. Will you buy a book? It is by someone who was born here.'

The Wall and its pass, which now came into view, was pretty much as I would have expected from Qi Jiguang:

solid, impressive, all that. But you approach from below, with no preparation for what awaits you as you emerge on to the Wall itself. It was like that childhood moment a parent tells you to close your eyes, step this way, and now open them. My universe exploded. In this section, the Wall's watch-towers come every 60–100 metres. They ranged away both sides, on the right towards the mountains I had seen the previous day from Gubeikou, on the left towards a line of hills topped by towers. The whole horizon was one long battlement.

This unappreciated glory was Cheng Dalin's favourite spot, because here you see more of the Wall than anywhere else. 'We used to sleep down there, in the village,' said young Cheng. 'He would wake me up at four o'clock on summer mornings, and we would come up here to wait for the fog.' He meant the mist, which veils and unveils the view until the sun burns it off.

'You know about our flying man?' asked Wang. We were climbing westward, towards the first tower, and she was pointing to a plaque commemorating a strange event. In November 1992 a stunt-man and action-movie director named Ke Shouliang had decided that he would enhance his name by jumping the Wall in a car. He had two platforms built either side of the Wall, to provide himself with a run-up and a landing, and successfully 'flew' from one to the other. 'To show the Chinese spirit!' explained William. 'He specialized in risks. He jumped the Yellow River and many other places in his car.' Apparently, the exploit stood him in good stead, winning him national fame. The internet tells me he was well established in the Hong Kong film industry, directing six films, appearing in

34 and directing the action in another six. It also tells me that on 9 December 2003 in Shanghai, at the age of 51, he died of alcohol poisoning, after attending three dinner parties. *Sic transit* in Hong Kong and Shanghai; but he lives on here at Jinshanling as a local hero, proclaimed as the first Chinese to ride *across* the Wall, rather than along it.

We arrived at the top of a hill, which was guarded by the Five-Eyes Tower, so-called from its five windows. This was the end of the line. A notice declared: 'Please stop. Ahead is military forbidden zone.' Beyond, the Wall zigzagged on towards Gubeikou, but everything was overgrown. The surrounding country looked equally wild, pitted like a First World War battlefield. 'When I was child,' said Wang, 'we used to come here, but no further, because there were guards. We had to come this far to collect wild vegetables. It was all muddy then, and they grew well up here. These are the plants' – she pulled some leaves from a shrub – 'it's called *heng zi ya*. You boil it with a little salt. Now the living standards are higher, no one eats it any more.'

That was then. Now the Wall was her livelihood. Almost every day she took a small group of visitors, mainly foreigners, for the four-hour walk in the other direction, eastward, to the next stop down the line, Simatai, towards which she now led the way.

We topped a rise to find ahead of us an idyllic scene: a small house that was a book-stall supervised by an attractive young woman, who was playing with one of the most beautiful and cheerful of babies. The place was owned by the local photographer, whose book had been offered to me on my arrival by Wang. His name was Zhou

Wanping, and his work is a love affair twice over. The first passion was for the Wall, because the village is almost part of the Wall, and he is a villager through and through. At nine an encounter with a piece of electrical equipment left him crippled, but after graduating he returned to help with the restoration work, gaining a deep emotional understanding of what they say of the Wall round here: it is built with the sweat and blood of the Chinese nation. Recording the Wall in all its moods has become his life's work. As he writes in his introduction, 'I would love nothing better than to walk the Great Wall the year round and take pictures of it for the rest of my life.' The second love affair was with his wife, the woman who was looking after his stall, Li Yafen. Both were locals. 'Look,' she said. 'You can just see the house down in the village. The one with the red roof.' She used to be one of those selling books to foreigners until she met Zhou. That was ten years ago. Now she helped run the business, especially when he was away in Beijing, as he was at that moment.

This is the most beautiful section of the whole Wall – her opinion, Cheng's opinion, my opinion – so beautiful that it formed the background for a daily news programme. It is a wonderful walk, surely one of the best in the world: smooth stone underfoot, no crowds, and raised the height of a double-decker bus over superb, untouched and utterly deserted countryside. There was high drama still to come; but for tranquillity I'll be back here, walking from Jinshanglin to Simatai.

As we approached Simatai, the view ahead was blocked by the sides of a valley dotted with little heaps of white stones, which were not graves but bases for newly planted fir trees. We were following a little river with the charming name of Xiao Tang, Little Soup.

'Tang? Like the dynasty?' I asked Cheng.

'No, different tone. "Tang" meaning "soup" is first tone.' He made a flat movement with his hand to act out the sound. 'In ancient China, it also meant "hot spring". You know, tone can change. We are here at Simatai, which means Commander's Horse Platform, but in old times it was different tone and meant Dead Horse Platform.'

There was more, but I didn't hear the end of the lesson because, as we turned a final corner, the valley opened on to an extraordinary sight. Beyond the Little Soup river and a few slender trees was a low hill, and beyond that a sharp ridge several hundred metres high, a breaking wave, a fossilized tsunami, complete with a foaming crest of bare rock, and along the crest another, smaller crest: the Wall. It defied all sense to build up there. The ridge was itself a natural Wall. If attackers climbed up from the other side, they could surely never climb down that sheer drop, without abseiling gear. And even if they did, how could they possibly return? There seemed only one explanation for this outrageous, fairy-tale creation: Qi Jiguang and his builders took one look at the challenge and said, 'It's impossible. Let's do it.' This had to be an expression of sheer architectural genius for its own sake, the equivalent of Mad King Ludwig's spire-encrusted castle in the Bavarian Alps. I didn't really believe this, because Qi Jiguang was far too practical for such exuberance, but that's what this crest on a crest suggested at first glance.

It's easy enough to check the reality, because you don't

have to climb, unless you want to waste three hours. You can do it in fifteen minutes riding in a rickety cage dangling from a cable. The slow ascent suspends you in time as well as space. You measure progress by the gentle creak of the swaying cage and your shadow's gradual advance over the newly planted trees below. After climbing 400 metres upwards, you transfer to a funicular for a further 150 metres, and then a final staircase that ends at the Wall itself. This was not built for tourists. Stamped into a brick at the top was a record of when it was made and by whom: 'In the 5th Year of the Emperor Wan Li [the reign name of Zhu Yijun, i.e. 1577], the builders were from the Shi Tang [Stone Pond]' (*Wan li wu nian shi tang zao* / 萬曆伍年 石 塘造). Yes, another *tang*. This one is *táng*, with a rising tone.

Then, from 619 metres up, there was the view. Westward, the Wall wove over grey hills towards Jinshanling, four or five hours' walk away. Below, fields and hills were cut by a new road, the Beijing–Chengde expressway, which would be open in time for the 2008 Olympics. And above was the razor ridge itself, leading up almost another 300 metres to the topmost point, known as the Tower for Viewing the Capital because from there, at dusk, you can see the lights of Beijing. Obviously, that was what we should head for.

'But, Cheng, I still can't understand why. Suppose someone gets up there. They just fall off the other side. What's the point?'

'No, no, not fall. Go along wall, attack guards, take next section.'

I began to see the logic, and recalled the ground rule

about not allowing a single weak spot. What a contrast to the Wall in the open immensities of the far west, where the defences had to stop or deflect cavalry. Here the fear was that a small, intrepid group of Mongol mountaineers would take the heights and then advance downwards, clearing the Wall of defenders as they went. Pretty soon, they would have taken lower sections, allowing more attackers on to the Wall, and all would be lost. That's why there had to be guards up there on the highest point.

Do you recall the placards at Gubeikou recommending the spiritual benefits of a walk on the Wall? It's true. Up there on Simatai, on the remains of a fort right at the end of the restored Wall, I met a Frenchman named Franck who had come with the purpose of making sense of his life. He was a photographer and a businessman who had been managing director of a film-manufacturing company which, with the rise of digital photography, was in deep trouble. He had resigned, and was wondering about his future.

'I am going to turn forty in three days. My wife and kids agreed that this trip should be for my birthday, as long as I get back in time to celebrate with them. I have no idea what I am going to do. It is time to walk, to see, to think.'

I told him about Jinshanling, a mere four hours away.

'But for me it is slow, because I must stop every two hundred metres and take photographs. And this is so perfect, is it not? I have been up here for two and a half hours. I just sit, and eat my banana, and contemplate.'

'I envy you. I must go on higher.' I glanced up, beyond the ruined walls, to the Tower for Viewing the Capital.

**The Ming Empire
1368–1644**

MONGOL

Gobi
Desert

Yellow Sea

MING EMPIRE

East
China
Sea

Tropic of Cancer

South
China
Sea

Black Mts.

Yellow River

T h e
O r d o

Jiayuguan

Shenmu

Zhangye

Yinchuan

Wuwei

Sanguan
Pass

Dingbian

Jin

Anbian

Lanzhou

Wei River

Ch

The Ming Wall 1368–1644

—— Modern borders

∿∿∿ Stone walls

-◾-◾- Earth walls

Yangtze Ri

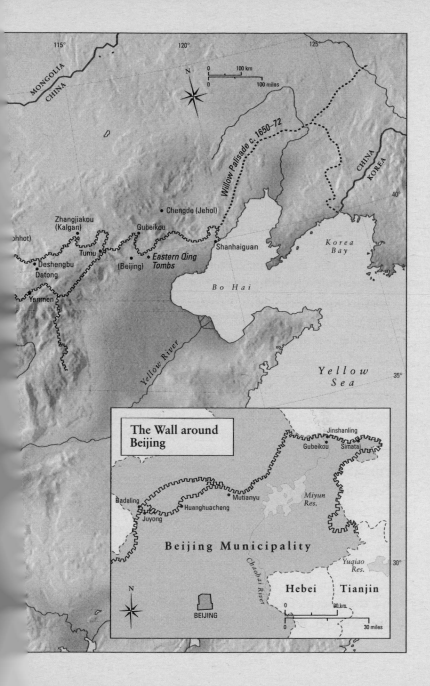

MONGOLIA
CHINA

Willow Palisade c. 1650–72

CHINA
KOREA

● Chengde (Jehol)

Zhangjiakou
(Kalgan)
Gubeikou
(hhot)
Tumu ● Eastern Qing
● Deshengbu (Beijing) Tombs
● Datong
Shanhaiguan
Korea
Bay
Yanmen

Bo Hai

Yellow River

Yellow
Sea

The Wall around
Beijing

Jinshanling
Gubeikou Simatai

Badaling
Mutianyu Miyun
Res.
Huanghuacheng
Juyong

Beijing Municipality

Yuqiao
Res.

Chaobai River

Hebei Tianjin

BEIJING

'It is dangerous. And there is one information I can share with you. The fine is two hundred yuan.'

'But who will catch me?' I said, for there were only three others up there beside William and Cheng.

I left him to his view and went on, past the last guard rail and its enigmatic warning: 'Do not crush and span the rails.' I saw why. Once over the chain, there was nothing between me and a 50-metre fall. But the path, no wider than a shoe, was well worn. Others besides me ignored the notice. I edged forward, with the drop to my right, and to my left, the northern side, another near-vertical slope, but one that was covered in saplings. A Mongol SAS unit could climb up here, but what then?

Further on, both sides became sheer. I found myself sitting on a ledge, with the Wall against my back. Behind it was what seemed an abyss, a circular sink-hole that disappeared into shadow. In front was a precipice. This little saddle of rock was entirely taken up with the Wall – 30 centimetres of random stones – the ledge I was sitting on, and a path the width of my feet, perhaps a metre in all. This was, I think, the Wall at its absolute thinnest. Below, the cable-car was a line of dots. The wind was from the south, holding me against the Wall.

I'm sorry to say I got cold feet. It would take me an hour to mountaineer my way up to the tower, negotiating a series of steps and cross-walls each designed for one man, like a line of brick shields. The view set my imagination to work. This was created by men carrying bricks and stones on their shoulders, edging past each other like New York steeplejacks. I don't normally mind heights, but it did cross my mind that, when I stood up, a severe gust of wind from some other direction would cut my trip shorter than I had intended. William and Cheng were waiting, nervous that I had escaped. I made my way carefully back to them, to find Franck still contemplating. I must remember to ask him how his life worked out.

16

THE END OF THE WALL,
THE END OF THE MING

OF COURSE, IT WAS BARBARIANS WHOM THE MING HOPED TO
keep out by building the far eastern end of the Wall; but
these barbarians were not Mongols. They were Jurchen –
soon to be renamed the Manchus, after whom Manchuria
is named: descendants of the people who had seized
northern China five hundred years before, ruled for just
over a century as the Jin dynasty, and then been overrun
by the Mongols.

What faced the Jurchen, as they advanced from their
mountains and forests in 1644, was pretty much what you
see today in its restored glory: defences blocking every
narrow pass between Beijing and the sea, all of them too
narrow for an invading army – and then, right at the end,
something far more promising: a flat corridor 8 kilometres across, with only the Wall standing between them

When I was there, Yanmenguan was almost hidden by fog, which gave it a melancholy beauty.

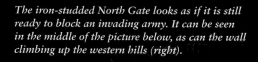

The iron-studded North Gate looks as if it is still ready to block an invading army. It can be seen in the middle of the picture below, as can the wall climbing up the western hills (right).

Taken from the north, this panorama by Andrews' photographer J. B. Shackelford shows how Kalgan (today's Zhangjiakou) blocks the way to Beijing. It was never assaulted, and instead became the prime trade link between Mongolia and China.

Ming: 14th – 17th centuries
GATEWAY TO MONGOLIA

Zhangjiakou (Zhang Family Gate) used to be known as Kalgan, from the Mongolian for 'gate', because it dominates the pass that leads up to the Mongolian plateau. In the 1920s, when the expedition led by the American explorer Roy Chapman Andrews came through, the town still retained its Ming impregnability – mainly to control traders, not armies. Now that China has spread northward it has lost its strategic significance, but the old North Gate is still intact and the Wall still guards the mountainous flanks.

Above: *The Wall on the western hills gives a good view of the pass: a mere 500 metres across, some of which is taken up by the Qing Shui He (Clear Water River). Beyond, the Wall picks up again and heads eastwards.*

Left: *The dry-stone wall, without battlements, and now much restored, still climbs the western hills, as it did in Ming times and Andrews' day. Today, steps lead up to a lookout point.*

North Gate

Dry-stone wall

Ming: 14th – 17th centuries
BADLING: THE PEOPLE'S WALL

By bus, train and car, they come to this carefully restored section by the million from Beijing. This, too, is where the government brings visiting heads of state to pay homage, in effect, to China itself. Yet even at Badaling, the Wall is bigger than all this. Its broad walkway is impervious to the crowds and the officials, and remains stunning. And if you choose your moment right or walk far enough, it can even be private.

In 1972, President Nixon was one of the first heads of state to be taken to Badaling. Here he is with his wife Pat on his left. As China has opened up, over 400 leaders have followed in his footsteps.

Main picture: *Half an hour northward from the main pass, you can look east and see this section swinging round to close off every ridge in the direction of Beijing.*

Below: *A rare view of China's most popular tourist destination just after dawn, with absolutely no one about.*

Ming: 14th – 17th centuries
GUBEIKOU: THE IMPERIAL ROUTE
TO THE NORTH-EAST

The broad valley of the Chao River provided one of the easiest invasion routes up until the late 16th century. Later, during the Qing Dynasty, this was the way to the emperor's summer palace in Chengde (Jehol). It was this road that the British embassy, led by Lord Macartney, followed in the summer of 1792, a visit that produced the first major image of the Great Wall produced by a non-Chinese.

Under a full moon, the Wall drops down to the Chao river, then heads eastward toward Jinshanling.

The Wall at Gubeikou, as seen by the Macartney mission. The engraving was made by the official artist, William Alexander, from a sketch by a young engineer, Henry Parish. This inspired the West's image of the Wall as a curtain of stone stretching across all China.

A beacon tower to the north of the Wall guards the Chao valley.

THE WILD WALL

For almost 400 years there has been peace on the northern frontier, and the Wall has been redundant. Except at the major tourist spots, most of the Wall around Beijing is wild, often hard to climb and sometimes dangerous. But there are entry points, as at Huanghuacheng, where a dam provides access. Here you can see up close what happens to the Wall as frost and rain nibble at its flanks and plant-roots loosen its stones.

Drying crops, against hills where the Wall is just part of the mountain landscape.

A doorway with finely shaped stones on their way to collapse.

A water-spout long since blocked by rubble from the Wall's inner core.

The dam at Huanghuacheng holds back a reservoir, right where the Wall once ran.

Jinshanling: On Golden Mountain

It's hard to get to, with a stiff climb up, so there are
few visitors. Your reward is this glorious place, Golden
Mountain Peak. My adviser, Cheng Dalin, loves it above
all. He first came here decades ago, when it was wild and
virtually unknown. He publicised it, and named it. Now
it is the start of one of the world's greatest walks, the
13 kilometres to Simatai.

Main picture: *Punctuated by towers every hundred metres or so, the Wall between Jinshanling and Simatai ripples over unpopulated ranges, with astounding views in every direction.*

Cheng Dalin, the Wall expert who gave Jinshanling its name and whose photographs brought its beauty to public notice.

Ming: 14th – 17th centuries
SIMATAI: THE FAIRY-TALE WALL

A walker arriving at Simatai from Jinshanling must become
a mountaineer to explore its dizzying heights. You can avoid
a gruelling climb by taking the cable-car and cog-railway. A
further climb takes you to a section of wild wall that induces
vertigo, astonishment and admiration. Tackle it at your peril.
Or simply look, and wonder if those who planned and built it
were madmen, or geniuses, or both.

Above and left: *Like many Wall bricks, this one is stamped with its date and origin. When turned upright, it reads: '[Emperor] Wan Li's 5th year [i.e. 1577], made by the Stone Pond [factory]'.*

Right: *There are places where it feels as if you are teetering along an uphill tightrope, with an abyss on both sides.*

Below: *If you dare get to the tower on the right, at night, you can see the lights of Beijing 120 kilometres away. Hence its name: Tower for Viewing the Capital.*

Ming: 14th – 17th centuries

TO THE WALL'S END

From the border of Beijing Municipality the Wall winds erratically east, over the pass at Huangya, close to the eastern tombs of the Qing emperors, down and round and up and over until it bursts out of the Yan mountains to block a lowland highway from Manchuria into the heart of China. Beyond this 'throat' lies Shanhaiguan (Mountain–Sea Pass). From here a last stone tongue pokes eastward into the sea, and the Wall comes to a full stop.

Left: *In Huangya's cloistered garden, Mao is portrayed in a romantic pose against the Wall he so admired. In one of his poems, 'Mount Liupan' (1935), he urged his followers: 'If [we] fail to reach the Great Wall, [we] are not men.' But there were no pronouns in the original, and now the popular quote runs: 'If you never reach the Great Wall, you are not a true man.'*

Below: *Huangya: the Wall tumbles from impassable heights to a pass once entirely blocked by the fortress and the river Jiu. Now a narrow road runs through it.*

Left: *Hawthorn berries dry in Huangya's fortress. They are used to make medicinal tea.*

Below: *Near the eastern Qing tombs, the Wall is ignored, forgotten, overgrown, and cut through by farmers.*

Below: *From Mount Jiao, the last of the Yan mountains, the Wall plunges down before crossing lowlands to Shanhaiguan, and the sea.*

Right: *Shanhaiguan's East Gate, the only one of four to survive, proclaims its historical importance with a plaque, which reads from right to left: First Pass Under Heaven.*

Below: *Old Dragon's Head, once battered to bits, has been resurrected, with Ming-style iron clamps anchoring the stones to make sure that the Wall's eastern end will last for centuries.*

and the open road to Beijing. Here, the Wall tumbles down from the mountains, freewheels across the plain, gathers itself into a muscular fortress at Shanhaiguan (Mountain-Sea Pass), and then runs on to finish in the Pacific. It was a formidable obstacle, well defended by a Chinese army 80,000 strong. This was the nut the Jurchen had to crack. Yet, when the crisis came, that was exactly what they did not have to do, because the great fortress at Shanhaiguan opened to let them through.

Fifty years before, even twenty years before, no one would have predicted that the Ming Dynasty would perish in an eyeblink. China had some 200 million people, one-third of the world's population, and there was no civilization to touch it for wealth, artistry or military power. It had been stable for almost 250 years (imagine present-day Europe or the United States having been dominated by one ruling family since 1750). No outsiders had been a serious threat to the empire as a whole. True, there were gross inefficiencies. Our old enemies, the eunuchs, had held dominant positions for years. There were 100,000 unemployable imperial relatives to be supported. But inefficiency, corruption and nepotism on a grand scale hardly seemed enough to undermine the empire or the dynasty. Certainly no outsiders could seize power, for did not the Great Wall safeguard peace along the northern frontier? Yet, in the crisis of 1644, it fell without a struggle. Or at least, without a *military* struggle. There were plenty of human struggles, involving a cast of characters fit for an action movie, including a bandit leader known as the 'dashing prince', a feckless emperor, a barbarian chief, a young general and his beautiful concubine.

To see what happened we have to go back to the late sixteenth century, when the Jurchen menace arose.[1] No one saw it as a menace at the time, first because attention was focused on the Mongols, second because the Mongols nearest the Wall were, in effect, Chinese allies, and third because the more civilized Jurchen, mostly farmers, were seen as old vassals, disunited by feuds and kept tame by Chinese trade, gifts and the award of empty titles. But in the late sixteenth century, there arose a Jurchen Genghis, Nurhachi by name, who welded the clans into a nation-at-arms, with squads ('arrows') of 300 grouped in eight 'banners', named for their coloured flags (a term that they would take with them into China, where a 'banner', *qí*, is still used as an administrative unit). The Chinese awarded him a fine title – 'Dragon-Tiger Generalissimo' – and the Mongols acknowledged him as a khan, and an equal, despite the difference in their lifestyles. Princes took Mongol wives; Mongols who joined him acquired their own banners; when Nurhachi (like Genghis) saw that he needed a system of writing to administer his domains, he chose to adapt the vertical Mongol script brought in by Genghis. With peace assured on the Mongol border, Nurhachi declared himself the head of a new dynasty, Jin (Golden), the same name his forebears had used in north China.

Ambitious for empire, Nurhachi looked first to the

---

[1] What follows is almost entirely based on Mote's vivid yet erudite account in *Imperial China*, chs 30–1.

south, to Chinese living in the coastal areas north of the Wall. Although this area, the Liaodong peninsula, was beyond the Wall proper, it was a Han Chinese enclave and therefore designated the first of the 'Nine Defence Areas' that administered the Wall borderlands. There had always been walls of some sort around this enclave, and they are sometimes included on maps as part of the Great Wall. But they really weren't, because they were hardly more than earthworks punctuated by forts. Even the Ming wall here, built in the second half of the fifteenth century, was nothing more than parallel rows of stakes filled in with dirt.[2]

In 1619, an attempt by China to push Nurhachi back failed disastrously, leaving him master of a powerful state that swallowed the Chinese area, lapping right up against Shanhaiguan and all the north-eastern Wall. More Mongol groups submitted to him, giving him authority over all Inner Mongolia. His only major setback came in 1626, when he attacked the walled city of Ningyuan, famous for its hot springs, 80 kilometres north of Shanhaiguan. The Chinese garrison fought him off with cannon, newly acquired from the Portuguese in Macao (the town is now Xingcheng, its walls, historic core and fine beaches still unspoiled). Nurhachi retired, nursing a wound, and never recovered. He died the same year, just before the Chinese emperor, leaving the next round to their respective sons, Hung Taiji and the sixteen-year-old Zhu Youjian, usually known by his reign title as the Chongzhen emperor.

[2] Edmonds, 'The Willow Palisade'.

It was Hung Taiji who in 1635 renamed his people Manchus. No one knows why. Perhaps it sounded similar to the Manchu word for 'brave'; or perhaps it echoed the name of the Buddhist bodhisattva of wisdom, Manjusri, of whom Nurhachi claimed to be an incarnation. A year later, he declared himself ruler of a new dynasty, Qing (*qīng / 清* ('clear' or 'pure')), choosing a Chinese name to reflect his ambitions for conquest. Mongol nobles, once the dominant force, were eager to marry their sisters and daughters into the Manchu royal family.

In China, Chongzhen came to the throne in 1627 with high hopes of reforming the dreadful inefficiencies that clogged his administration. Those hopes soon crumbled. Take the case of the man responsible for defeating Nurhachi, a certain Yuan Chonghuan. The emperor's initial response was to cover this civilian-scholar-official-turned-general in glory, summoning him to court and rewarding him with a precious sword. The court's powerful chief eunuch, jealous of anyone who might challenge him, began whispering in the young emperor's ear. Yuan was in touch with the Manchus; but was he negotiating – or was he perhaps considering switching allegiance? 'Evidence' came when Yuan captured a local warlord and beheaded him, with the emperor's sword, no less. This warlord had been famously anti-Manchu. Perhaps, therefore, muttered Eunuch Wei, Yuan was pro-Manchu. Just at that moment, autumn 1629, Hung Taiji, taking advantage of dissension in the Ming ranks, breached the Great Wall north of Beijing – at Gubeikou, probably – and plundered the countryside. That did it. The victor of Ningyuan was accused on trumped-up charges, found guilty of treason and dismembered, his family killed or exiled.

Enter, stage left, 'the dashing prince' (as he called himself), a bandit named Li Zicheng. He rose to infamy and fortune in the historic but now poverty-stricken regions along the western Great Wall, the Ordos and regions to the south and west. Beijing's attention was on the Wall's eastern end, yet officials wrung recruits and taxes from the west, sparking widespread resentment and eventually rebellion. Warlords arose, or 'roving bandits', as Beijing called them, robbing the rich and giving to the poor – that is, themselves and their ragtag followers. The most famous of them was Li Zicheng, who is still considered hero and villain in equal measure. After many adventures, by 1641 he had gathered an army of 100,000, which included Ming officials and officers. This was a full-scale rebellion, apparently on its way to seize power from the Ming. In 1642 he took the old capital of Kaifeng, flooding it from the Yellow River's dykes and drowning a million people (so it is said). Other rebel chiefs joined him. Wagon-loads of loot were taken from government buildings. Ordinary people flocked to join him, swelling the ranks of the rebel force to 400,000. In early 1643 Li, commanding all central China, declared the imminent arrival of a new dynasty, Great Shun, with himself as king. Sweeping eastwards, he took Datong, and in April 1644 was on the outskirts of Beijing.

In Beijing the emperor, still only 33, was in an agony of indecision – as always: he appointed and fired 50 Grand Secretaries, about one every four months. He had a miserable life. Grief-stricken after the death of his favourite consort and four of his sons, he was isolated in the immensities of the Forbidden City with a bad-tempered wife. Li's advances drove him into tearful self-blame.

Meanwhile, to the east, a general named Hong Chengchou, who had once held Li at bay, had been drafted in to fight the Manchus. But a Chinese assault north of the Great Wall led to catastrophe. An army of 130,000 was defeated and Hong surrendered, so disillusioned by the Ming that he chose to serve the Manchus – to great effect, as we shall see.

Beset on two fronts, the emperor floundered. Should he flee to safety in Nanjing? Should he send his family away? One day he would decide, the next change his mind and throw out accusations of treachery. Terrible lapses came to light. Troop numbers were down, costs up, corruption rife. Some desperate souls suggested using paper currency, a lunatic idea given the lack of faith in anything Ming. The only strong leader in Beijing, the Grand Secretary Jiang Dejing, who had written memo after memo in attempts to combat corruption and mismanagement, resigned and left town in disgust.

In Manchuria, the death of the Manchu emperor, Hung Taiji, in 1643 caused hardly a ripple in his people's morale. Within months, a five-year-old was on the throne, with experienced generals in command as regents, their top man being the late emperor's younger brother, Prince Dorgon.

The main Chinese force in southern Manchuria was an army of 80,000 troops based in the Liaodong peninsula. In command was a young general who was to play a vital role in what followed. His name was Wu Sangui, he was

32 years old, and he had a vested interest in making things turn out right, because his very beautiful girlfriend, Yuanyuan, was in Beijing with his father and the rest of his family. Wu was ordered to bring his men south, behind the Wall. It took ten days for boats, shuttling back and forth 160 kilometres across Bohai Bay, to ferry the men to safety behind Shanhaiguan; but by mid-April they were in place.

A few days later Li Zicheng made his move on Beijing. It was a walkover. Scaling ladders and mines were enough to clear a section of the city walls, and defectors opened a gate into the new Outer City to the south of Beijing's older heart, leaving only the walls of the Inner City between the invaders and the Imperial City, with, at its hidden heart, the Forbidden City itself.

Inside the imperial grounds, the emperor climbed Coal Hill, a 100-metre eminence topped by a pavilion, to see for himself the smoke rising from the south. At this point, failure and indecision seem to have unhinged him. He went back inside, ordered the three princes to seek refuge in the homes of their mother's father, and told his bad-tempered wife to commit suicide. Having downed enough wine to make himself drunk, he decided to save his dozens of daughters and concubines from being raped by killing them. This he would do by stabbing them, a fate which they naturally refused to accept. Lunging incompetently at the screaming women, he wounded several, but failed to kill any of them.

That night, Li's troops broke into the inner city and advanced on the palace. At dawn on the twenty-fifth, the emperor, dressed in golden silk as if for an audience, climbed back up Coal Hill accompanied by a faithful eunuch and hanged himself from the beams of the pavilion, which was called, ironically, the Pavilion of Imperial Longevity. While hundreds of his staff committed suicide, his body was secretly cut down, perhaps by the eunuch and a few others, and hidden under bushes.

Next day Li Zicheng, wearing a broad felt hat and pale blue robes and riding a black horse, led a procession into the palace. Sitting beside the throne to receive the submission of Ming officials, he did not declare a new dynasty, but ordered the emperor's fate to be determined, a mystery solved two days later. By then the three princes, including the fifteen-year-old heir, were almost certainly dead, along with many others who might have carried on Ming rule. This was Li's moment – but he could not seize it. Looting and killing spread chaos, Beijing plunged into anarchy, and his coup rapidly ran out of steam.

The truly decisive events were unfolding at Shanhaiguan. General Wu Sangui was in a quandary. His much-loved concubine Yuanyuan was in war-torn Beijing; the Manchus were pressing on the Wall; and in mid-May Li Zicheng set out to crush him.

His first priority was to save the Ming dynasty, if he could. To do this, he had to have help, and the only help available was that of the Manchus. As it happened, he had many links with them; so he wrote to Prince Dorgon, a lesser evil than Li Zicheng, suggesting temporary co-operation. He larded his proposal with reminders of what the Manchus owed the Ming. Together, he wrote, they could restore peace, with inevitable rewards flowing to the Manchus:

I beg you to consider the loyal and righteous words of a lone servitor of the fallen dynasty, and with all speed select crack troops who can press strongly forward, together with the force under my command, so that our combined forces will be able to strike all the way to the gates of the capital, exterminate the roving bandits who are in the very palace precinct, and in that way make a show of great righteousness ... The gold and treasure accumulated by the bandits are beyond calculation. As soon as your righteous troops arrive it will all be theirs.

Dorgon, of course, had nothing to lose, and an empire to gain. Advised by his Chinese captive, Hong Chengchou, he agreed – just in time, because Wu stopped (or thrashed; judgements vary) Li's army just one day before Dorgon's troops poured through the open gates of Shanhaiguan, joining Wu in pursuit of Li's fleeing army. The fort's massive 2-tonne cannon, cast only the previous year, never saw action, and still stands on the battlements as a memorial to a battle that never was.

That is the way historians tell the story. But there are many gaps and much room for interpretation. Is Wu a hero for opposing Li, who caused the death of an emperor? Or a villain for allowing the Manchus in? Or a hero for the same act – an agent of Heaven, perhaps – given that the Manchus created a new dynasty? And what happened to the beautiful concubine, Yuanyuan? Folk memories and stories fill in the blanks. She became a sort of Chinese Helen of Troy, many things to many people – prostitute, entertainer, concubine of many powerful men, even the emperor himself, and through it all Wu's true love.

Here's one version of the story, which weaves in and out of history like a docu-drama:

The emperor in Beijing has three empresses, each living in her own palace. One jealous empress, wishing to distract the emperor from the other two, orders a search for the most beautiful woman in the land and has her brought to court. This, of course, is Yuanyuan. The emperor is too busy with affairs of state to notice her. So she is sold to a count. At a feast held by the count, Wu Sangui, about to leave to quell the Manchus, sees her, falls in love and asks the count for her hand. The count refuses. After Wu's departure the count regrets his refusal, for Wu is a great general, and sends the girl to Wu's father. Wu hears of the gesture, and sends the count a fair sum. Li Zicheng captures Beijing, takes prisoner both Wu's father and his beloved, and orders the father to write a letter telling Wu to surrender, which as a dutiful son he would have to do. But Wu learns the reason for the letter, and in a rage rejects the father and swears vengeance on Li. That's what drives him into the arms of the Manchus. Together, Wu and the Manchus swoop on Beijing. Li beheads Wu's father and is about to kill Yuanyuan when she points out that to do so would just make Wu wilder. Li releases her, and flees. The lovers meet on a river-bank, and live happily ever after. Thus did the Battle of Shanhaiguan give a general a bride and the Manchus a dynasty.

William told me a very similar version of events. 'So you see, John,' he finished, 'Wu betrayed his nation for the love of a woman. Some people say it was her fault the Ming fell and the Manchus came.' Other versions turn the story into a tragedy, with Yuanyuan rejecting her lover for his treachery. Who knows her end? Some say she entered a Daoist convent to expiate her misplaced love. In any event, she has been a popular heroine, her story being told in two novels, several films and an opera.

The historical account, based on written sources, is hardly less dramatic. Li was now a man driven crazy by the change in his fortunes. To have toppled the Ming only to be toppled himself, all in six weeks, was too much. He declared himself emperor of his Great Shun dynasty, and then set fire to the palace, grabbed what treasure he could, and fled, leaving the shattered capital city to the Manchus.

For Dorgon, this was just perfect. He could ignore Wu and grab the throne, while making self-righteous statements about restoring peace as regent. He came not as a conqueror and an outsider, he said, but as a true Chinese and a force for law and order. Luckily for him, Wu's attention was elsewhere, for he had discovered that his father and the rest of his family had been tortured and killed (though what had become of Yuanyuan the sources do not relate). Set on revenge, he went off in pursuit of Li (or perhaps only his troops, for Li was probably dead by now, having either committed suicide or been killed by his enemies).[3] In any event, Wu left Dorgon to blame the bandits for the demise of the Ming, which was obviously Heaven's way of transferring its Mandate to the Manchus. All would be done peacefully. As his turncoat Chinese

[3] Li has an 8,000-square-metre tomb in Tongshan, southern Hubei, restored by the government at a time when he was considered a hero in the fight against feudalism.

general Hong Chengchou advised him: 'The ordinary people must not be killed or harmed, their houses must not be burned, their possessions must not be taken; if it is done in this way, far and near the word will spread, and on hearing it people will submit.'

So it was that Dorgon proclaimed Hung Taiji's son the new emperor and a regime of foreigners became a dynasty that asserted itself to be more Chinese than the Chinese. Very soon, that was what it became, remaining in power for two and half centuries until foreigners of a different type undermined it and republicans hounded it from office in 1911.

If you want to see what the Manchus were up against, track the Wall seawards from point to point, starting about 100 kilometres east of Beijing. You find yourself in a strange world, where cars are still a novelty and they do things differently. It's on twisting, back-country mountain roads like these that you learn the real highway code. Hard shoulders are for overtaking on the inside. White lines down the middle on corners are no bar to over-taking, because anyone coming the other way will give way at the last moment. Two-wheeled tractors entirely smothered in corn-stalks may wander blind on to major roads. Use of the indicator is a sign of eccentricity. There is no such thing as dangerous driving. We almost brushed a 'dog riding on a rabbit', which is what our driver called a farm-worker on a mini-tractor with long handlebars, but our vehicle was scrupulously following the unwritten rules. It's the unwritten rules themselves that are dangerous.

Crags and ravines and contorted outcrops of pale pink strata opened suddenly into a wider valley, along which a river bubbled over a stony bottom. The Wall sprang down on either side, converging on Huangya, a fortress that was also a small town, a maze of little streets hemmed in by big walls.

It was dusk, and overcast. We found a family in the town who had taken advantage of China's new freedoms to turn their courtyard and few rooms into an inn. This was basic, rural China, where hot water comes from thermoses. It was dark by now, and the electricity would not come on until later, if at all. We unpacked by the light from candles and mobile phones, with William explaining the conditions: the lack of power, the shortage of water, the increase of population, the failure of new-found wealth to filter down. But our driver, the chef, supervised the creation of a superb candle-lit supper, with mountain mushrooms, a local river-fish, slices of pig heart, egg with 'wooden ear' (some sort of vegetable that is 'good for the lungs') and – the *pièce de résistance* – a soup of thirteen fragrances, the crucial thirteenth ingredient of which was a local secret, all done for a total cost of 100 yuan, about £1.50 or $3.00 each.

Morning revealed Huangya to be a top tourist attraction for Chinese, especially schoolchildren. The well-restored fortress-town was a monument to Ming enterprise. Here, as an exhibit in the museum proudly recalled, a workforce under a general called Li Zhao had taken two months to build 42 metres of Wall. Now the Wall and its fortress were one big park, for play, relaxation and contemplation. A Longevity Garden displayed 1,000 forms of the character *shòu* / 寿 (longevity) overseen by a statue of Peng Zu, a legendary Chinese Methuselah who lived for 800 years. William, whose name is Shou, was delighted. 'A whole garden devoted to my name!'

This restoration, complete with a cloistered garden, had been done in 1985 under the Communist Party, which made sure that all visitors knew it. The cloisters were set with 100 plaques immortalizing the handwriting and the shallow comments of 100 generals who had come to this honoured spot. 'Without the Communist Party there would be no new China,' said one, and another, a Tibetan: 'The Great Wall is a masterpiece containing the wisdom and diligence of all the peoples and nationalities of China.'

Well, he would say that, because this was holy ground. The garden was dominated by a fine cast-iron statue of a youthful Mao, in Byronic mode, cloak and hair blowing in the wind, with the Wall and a tower looming on top of a hill behind him. For Mao was with the Chinese in 1985, the date of this statue, and he is with them still, his sins outweighed, officially at least, by his virtues. 'We see today's market economy, and we forget,' said William. 'But we come to a place like this and we remember. We say he was seventy per cent good, for liberating us and changing the world, and thirty per cent bad.' William, Cheng and the driver were suitably reverential before the statue of young Mao and before a large plaque in his own free-flowing calligraphy. It was one of his most famous poems, 'Snow', the one in which he recalls the winter landscape of the north, derides past ages and proclaims his own (this being in 1936, long before he came to power):

North country scene:
A hundred leagues locked in ice,
A thousand leagues of whirling snow.
Both sides of the Great Wall
One single white immensity . . .
This land so rich in beauty
Has made countless heroes bow in homage.
But alas! Qin Shihuang and Han Wudi
Were lacking in literary grace,
And Tang Taizong and Song Taizu
Had little poetry in their souls;
That proud son of Heaven,
Genghis Khan,
Knew only shooting eagles, bow outstretched.
All are past and gone!
For truly great men
Look to this age alone.

'This age' was, of course, defined by him, with a ruthlessness (and literary flair) that he claimed, with pride, outshone any of those previous, unpoetic rulers. But ruthlessness was not on show here; heroism was all.

Then I spoiled it. At my exclamation – 'Young Mao!' – William, Cheng, even the driver broke into gales of laughter, as if I had told them the most brilliant of jokes. They laughed, they suppressed their laughter, and it burst out of them again as they saw my baffled look. William at last managed to explain: *Yángmáo* / 羊毛 means 'wool'. They were laughing at a foreigner with rudimentary Chinese coming out with such an incongruous word. But there was something else in the laughter, like naughty schoolchildren laughing when some inadvertent comment punctures the authority of a headmaster. 'Young Mao, *Yángmáo*. Oh, I'm sorry—' And William was off again, wiping tears of laughter away with his hand.

There's no denying both the power and the charm of the Wall here. It is not massive, since it zooms through terraced persimmon orchards up to cliffs that stop it dead after a few hundred metres ('Some scholars call these mountains another Great Wall,' Cheng put in). There are (as yet) no good hotels, and thus very few foreigners, and a blessed absence of tourist stalls. Instead, there are children, by the hundred. Every child must go to the Wall at least once, so every school organizes two trips to the Great Wall every year. This is the perfect place: wide open spaces, easy climbs, lots to do, no crowds and very safe, with just the one road where horses and camels wait to give rides beneath poplar trees. At the bottom of the Wall, locals dry carpets of bright red hawthorn berries next to kids charging around in dodgem-cars zapping each other with toy laser-guns. When I climbed the smart grey bricks of the restored wall, where children dashed back and forth with the exuberance of puppies, the view laid bare the strategy of building here. The floor of the narrow valley blocked by the fortress; the 100-metre bridge spanning the road and the river; two protective ramparts zooming up either side to prevent attackers outflanking the fortress. With the fort behind them, a few hundred archers on its battlements could have held off tens of thousands. No Manchu commander would have considered bringing his army through here.

*　　*　　*

Twenty-five kilometres eastward, where the mountains fall away in a vast and gently sloping apron, it seems they should have had better luck. This is where the Manchus of the Qing dynasty buried five of their emperors. Ever since the First Emperor had himself interred with his Terracotta Army, there had been nothing Chinese emperors and empresses liked better than a grand tomb. It displayed power; it confirmed Heaven's blessing on their dynasties; it honoured the past; it controlled the future. Every ruler, emperor or empress, spent a good deal of his or her reign planning something suitably extravagant. Mountains to the north balanced by mountains to the south, low hills to right and left as guards, rivers flowing nearby: all had to be in accordance with the demands of *feng shui* to create 'a land of four spirits' through which Sacred Ways would bear the body to its final resting place. So it was for the Ming emperors in their much-visited tombs to the west of Beijing, and so it was for their successors the Qing. This, one of three Qing royal cemeteries, is a necropolis on a scale staggering by all standards except those of the First Emperor. Five emperors, 15 empresses, 136 imperial concubines and one prince, buried in 14 cemeteries with a total of 300 buildings.[4] The tombs are all linked by broad roadways paved with stone and lined with statues of respectful animals

[4] Several official publications (e.g. *Imperial Tombs of the Ming and Qing Dynasties*, Beijing, China Esperanto Press, 1995) and websites claim the site measures 2,500 sq. km. This is half the size of Kent, or the state of Rhode Island, which is obviously nonsense. I measured it on a map. The whole area is about 54 sq. km. Perhaps the site itself is 25.00 sq. km and someone left out the decimal point.

and officials. The roads peel off to secondary tombs from a stone-paved dual carriageway, which itself seems to spring from a distant mountain to the south, making a great double bend around a lake in accordance with the *feng shui* of the location, then running through arches, past arcades of animals and over bridges to the tomb of the greatest of the Qing emperors, Qianlong.

All very impressive. But the roads were sprouting grass, and there were few people around. It struck me that the roads were for the sole purpose of carrying corpses – just once. They had no other purpose. They and the tombs to which they led were as dead as the royals they had carried and housed. I found the experience profoundly depressing. Wandering this immense and useless space, I realized why. I was here to track a section of the Wall, which was called Malanyu after a nearby village.

But it wasn't there.

It wasn't there because the Qing had knocked it down, for the simple reason that it was the creation of a former dynasty and did not belong anywhere near a Qing cemetery. I couldn't wait to get out and track down whatever remnants of the Ming wall might have been allowed to survive.

My map showed surviving bits of the Wall running through hills somewhere to the north. We bumped away up a side-road and re-entered life: fields, the explosive farting of unsilenced three-wheeled trucks, a fork-lift hoisting a dump-truck full of rocks from a ditch. The track got worse. Our sump began to bang against hardened mud. We abandoned the car to walk along a track covered with an increasingly thick coating of grey dust. A farmhand told us it was 'iron ash' from a works up ahead. The roar of a heavy motor drew us on. A few hundred metres later, picking our way past poisonous-looking slurry, we arrived at a plant crushing rocks to get at the iron inside.

Beyond, hemmed in by an orchard of dust-covered persimmons, was the Wall, made of poorly dressed squares of rock piled up without cement to a height of about 3 metres. Somewhere up ahead was the mine from which came the iron-rich rocks for the crusher. Locals had cut a hole in the Wall, and little rock-filled trucks with naked, noisy engines and threadbare tyres thudded through. A three-wheeler full of pigs came by, passing a rock-carrier with a swerve, a shout, the clamour of engines and much squealing. I had fled a luxurious but sterile morgue, and found destruction, pollution and life.

I climbed the Wall, to find its earthen top had been colonized to raise a crop of corn. From up there I could see the purpose of this section. It blocked a small valley, with a small river running along the bottom, which might, I supposed, have offered an opening to an invading army from Manchuria. Commanders would have known that a couple of kilometres further on the mountains ended and the gentle slope on which their own tombs would later stand led down to the very path they would eventually take to the capital. But the thought didn't convince. To get to Malanyu, an army from Manchuria would have had to cross 150 kilometres of mountains, all outside traditional Manchurian territory. There was no road; and if they did break through, Chinese troops would be on them in no time from the open ground beyond. It was never going to happen.

*　　*　　*

The same is true of the dozen little passes between the Qing tombs and the sea. Really, the only place for an invasion in these parts is the corridor at the end of the Wall, at the end of the Yan Shan range. One last mountain, Jiaoshan, forms the side of the corridor, some 6 kilometres inland.

I climbed it for an overview. From the plain, the grey-brick Wall picks up beyond a new turnstile, for this is a park for which you need a ticket. It shoots upwards, past a mock horse and chariot where visitors pose, turning into alternating steps and 40-degree slopes, so steep that even gym shoes threaten to slip. Knee-high steps lead to an iron ladder, which rises inside a series of rings in case you fall over backwards. Now you are on to and over a tower, climbing upwards until you come up against a notice: 'This part of the Great Wall undeveloped! Detour!' It's in English only, so presumably the Wall's guardians assume that only foreigners would be mad enough to continue. Now I was on all fours, climbing in silence, for it was utterly windless. Then the Wall, by now a degenerate mass of stones and dust, gave out, and I was on a footpath deep in trees, near the top of the hill.

Suddenly I stumbled upon an incongruous yet familiar sight: four pink-skinned, bearded men in shorts, staring into bushes. No group could have been more obviously English. One of them was looking through heavy-duty binoculars. The other three had serious cameras at the ready. They were all silent and watchful, and took not the slightest notice of me. I knew the type. I had often seen their like, with telescopes and telescopic cameras, among the dunes and reed-beds of the Norfolk coast.

'Something in there?'

One replied in a Yorkshire-accented whisper: 'Could be a laughing thrush. It's a good area for them.' He was referring to a species of *Garrulax*, which are large, strong-billed, sometimes strikingly patterned song-babblers, according to the *Britannica*. These shy forest birds form sizeable flocks and reveal their presence by cackling and screaming loudly. If this one was there, it was so shy it had forgotten all it ever knew of flocks, cackles and screams.

I whispered too, hoping for new insights into the ecology of the Great Wall. 'Is this place famous for birds?'

'Not really.'

A Welsh accent took over. 'There's a place called Happy Island that's really famous. We were there for two weeks.'

'We came here to see the Wall,' said Birdwatcher No. 1, 'but you never know.' His eyes slid away, back to the bushes. As a mere featherless biped, I merited rather less attention than the shy, silent and possibly absent *Garrulax*.

I wandered away down a winding path, back to the Wall and the view of what confronted the Manchus when they approached in 1644 – the steep, swerving drop to one tower, then another, and on to the three-arched ticket office and out over the plain. The Manchus timed their arrival well. Half a millennium earlier, this was all water. But over time the land rose, dried out and was turned over to agriculture. There were a few early walls and a substantial fort in early Ming times, but nothing like Qi Jiguan's creation of the 1570s, which from that distance was invisible, swamped by the new buildings growing up beyond the Beijing–Shenyang expressway. Across the horizon lay the soft blue of Bohai, the great inlet created by the Liaodong peninsula.

Halfway to the sea, over the expressway, lay the pass itself, the fort through which the Manchu army streamed after Wu had treacherously, or valiantly, opened it to them. Now only the east gate survives. It looks down on a huge square and an appalling model chariot with four model horses. A brick arch supports a painted two-storey pavilion, which displays a giant sign proclaiming the name quoted in every tourist pamphlet: First Pass Under Heaven.

There is an unlikely story about the creation of this sign. It concerns Xiao Xian, one of the great court calligraphers during Ming times. He had resigned his position at court and returned home to Shanhaiguan. There came a time when the emperor ordered the creation of a tablet for the city's east gate. The mayor asked Xiao Xian to do the job. He agreed, but then turned instead to physical exercises, carrying water, hoeing fields, until the mayor could stand it no longer, and upbraided him. Xiao Xian said, 'It is not an easy job to write such large characters well. I have to prepare myself.' He carried on doing so for several more days, and then declared: 'Now it's time to write!' Taking out his brush and paper, he wrote down the Chinese characters Tian Xia Di Yi Guan / 天下第一關 (First Pass Under Heaven), each character almost 2 metres high. The chief official rushed to have the huge characters copied on to a tablet to hang on the east gate. But when the tablet was in place, it was found to everyone's horror that one stroke was missing, the little side-stroke of the character 下 (*xià*, 'under'). Xiao Xian calmly took out his handkerchief, screwed it up and dipped it into thick Chinese ink. He then threw it up at the hanging tablet, hit it in the right place and completed the character. As any guide will tell you, this teaches us that great calligraphy involves the whole man and the whole body.

Incidentally, the sign also teaches us that at that time it didn't matter in which direction you wrote. The phrase actually reads backwards, from right to left.

It was a blustery day at the Wall's end. A wind straight off the mountains tore to tatters the edges of the flags marking the walkway to Old Dragon's Head, and whipped the tops from the waves as they surged over gravel and rocks. The grey-green sea was as cruel as the sky. No Manchu cavalry could sneak round this way because, as the sign says, the Wall stretches 22.4 metres into the sea – not that you could pace it out on a day like this. Choose your angle right, and the end of the Wall looks as it should, tough and forbidding. Its superstructure has been restored, but its foundation is the rock of ages, for all its massive stones had vertical channels carved in them, into which the builders poured molten metal to weld them together.

Along the beach, past pleasure boats waiting for better weather, you get a different perspective. On a pier, a temple to the Sea God gave a view of what lay beyond Old Dragon's Head: wharves, shipyards, cranes. New China has turned an impassable barrier into a minor hurdle between tourist beaches.

17

THE WALL REBORN

THE COMING OF THE MANCHUS IN 1644 – THE BEGINNING OF the Qing dynasty – marked a new phase in the story of the Wall. The Manchus, if you remember, governed the Mongols. So when the Manchus took over in Beijing, Mongol leaders were subservient to the new regime and the Manchus steadily extended their control over the whole of Mongolia, from the Wall, across the Gobi and the grasslands to the north, right up to what is now the Russian border. At a stroke, therefore, the Wall became totally redundant. As an eighteenth-century chronicler put it: 'The Empire was at peace. On the frontiers no more fires were lit in the watchtowers of the Great Wall announcing alarm, the troops and the people enjoyed happiness, and . . . people lived until an old age.' Why bother to preserve the Wall? Why even admire it? It was soon seen not as an architectural masterpiece or a historical relic to be cherished, but as the creation of an earlier and discredited dynasty, the Ming – or, worse, of the Wall's originator, that tyrant, the First Emperor. Physically, of course, it was a presence, and made its way into the occasional painting. But on the whole it was ignored or actively denigrated.

It's true that the Qing did do some work on the frontier, in the east, beyond Shanhaiguan, in the region that had been so easily overtaken by the Manchus on their rise. But this so-called Willow Palisade, built c.1650–72, was only of earth mounds and trees to act as a boundary between Han and Manchu areas. On some maps, this frontier is marked with the same battlemented symbol as the Wall itself, but that's wrong. The Willow Palisade was built much later, and was too slight to count as a wall at all.

That with the coming of the Manchus the Mongol problem had been well and truly solved is an unpleasant truth for Mongolians today, but it is a truth nevertheless. A brief nationalist revival under the western Mongol khan Galdan was crushed by a Qing army in 1697. Thereafter Mongol aristocrats looked to the Qing for status, inter-marriage and official appointments, often doing business at the emperor's summer retreat, Chengde (Jehol, as it was called then), in mountains 150 kilometres north-east of Beijing. What a come-down for the descendants of Genghis! Chinese trading firms trapped Mongols, nobles and commoners alike, in a cycle of debt. Buddhism expanded, under a Mongol 'incarnate lama'. In the mid-eighteenth century, as a further way to limit Mongol aspirations, the Qing emperor ordered that any new incarnation could only be found in Tibet. Despite this, Mongol men increasingly turned to the priesthood – over half of them in the early eighteenth century, with devastating effects on the economy and military traditions.

The results are still obvious today in Mongol archery, supposedly one of the three 'manly virtues' along with wrestling and horse-riding, but in fact a shadow of its former self. There must be, somewhere, good bow-makers, but the only bows I have fired are sloppy things, the arrows far from true. At the annual games and in archery contests, Mongols shoot padded arrows at rows of little baskets. The whole thing strikes me as not 'manly' at all. The Mongols were once the greatest mounted archers in the world, but I have never heard of a Mongol horse-archer in modern times.[1]

The consequence of Mongol impotence and Qing strength – and also, at a greater remove, of the 1571 peace treaty and the building of Qi Jiguang's masterpiece – was that colonists began to move into Inner Mongolia. When the trend was identified in 1748, Qing officials decreed that colonists had to have permission to settle, but 50 years later, when there were over 400,000 Chinese in former Mongol territory, no one was taking any notice of the outdated ruling. Inner Mongolia became China's Wild North, open for land-grabbers, money-lenders, traders, farmers and businessmen happy to be beyond the law.

[1] The tradition has recently been revived in Hungary by a man who has made himself a master of the sport, Lajos Kassai. He looks back beyond the Mongols to the Huns, whose forefathers probably came from Mongolia. See my *Attila*, ch. 3.

Naturally, Mongols resisted the takeover. Tensions built up for over a century and came to a head in 1891 in a violent confrontation in which Chinese peasants attacked and drove off many thousands of Mongols.

At this time, the Qing government was under severe pressure from foreign interests. It had just lost a war with Japan, several foreign powers had imposed massive reparations after they had suffered at the hands of the anti-foreign group known as the Boxers, and in the north Russia was showing rather too much interest in Mongolia. The Qing answer in Inner Asia was to step up colonization. The policy provoked violent protests, which helped inspire Mongolia's declaration of independence in 1911. But in Inner Mongolia, it was too late. Mongols were in a minority in what had once been their own land. By 1912 there were 1.5 million Chinese in the province. A final revolt in 1929 was crushed. By 1937 colonists numbered 3.7 million.

In these circumstances, the Wall played no role at all, except that it allowed Qing officials to monitor the flow of people through some of its gates. It had been built to stop the barbarians moving south, which worked only because it was manned by thousands of troops; empty and abandoned, it was no hindrance at all to Chinese moving north.

Roy Chapman Andrews observed the process in midstream in 1922:

> The Great Wall of China was built to keep the Mongols out and, by the same token, it should have kept the Chinese in, but rich ground for agriculture has lured

the Chinese farther and farther into the grasslands of Inner Mongolia. Thus, when our cars roared through the gateways of the Wall, we entered a farmland region dotted with the brown walls of Chinese mud villages where blue-clad peasants were already at work in the fields . . . For 110 miles north of Kalgan, in 1922, there were fields owned and cultivated by Chinese. The Chinese governor of the district opens a new region for settlement every two or three years, and as soon as the land is sold to colonists more is taken. The average advance is about 12 miles each year . . . As a matter of fact, until the area of Chinese cultivation is passed Mongols are virtually non-existent.

Now Inner Mongolia is fully part of China. Mongolians are few – they make up just 25 per cent of the population – pastures are vanishing and Chinese farms are everywhere. The Great Wall is no longer either a barrier or a border. No wonder that for so long it was ignored, reviled, abandoned, eroded, torn apart for building materials and cut through to make roads.

Yet today the Wall is revered as the greatest of national symbols. Its picture – showing it in ideal, pristine, untouched form – is everywhere. How did the change come about?

The answer is that it took foreigners to bring the Wall back to the attention of China, after a slow start. At the time the Manchus came to power, seventeenth-century Europeans knew of the Wall, but only in a vague way. A map of 1626 shows it, and comments on 'a wall of 400 leagues [2,000 kilometres] . . . built by ye King of China against ye breaking in of ye Tartars'. Several Russian diplomats, trying to establish relations with their neighbour, commented on their entry through the Wall. But nobody actually wrote about it until the late seventeenth century, which is astonishingly late for such a famous monument. In 1676, when the Manchus were still extending their authority northward, a Russian named Spathary arrived on a diplomatic mission. Nikolai Spathary's story, as told by John Baddeley in *Russia, Mongolia, China*, is worth a detour.

Born in Moldavia in about 1625, Spathary gained a reputation both for vast learning – he spoke Greek, Turkish, Arabic, Latin, Italian, French and Russian – and for volatility. He was accused of treason by Moldavia's ruler, who had his executioner slice Spathary's nose either open or off, it's not clear which. The deformity won him a nickname: Chicken-nose. Having taken refuge in Brandenburg in north-east Germany, he found a German doctor who transplanted skin from Spathary's cheek to his nose, which 'grew again in its proper place and was healed'. He then became a top government interpreter in Moscow, and in 1675 was appointed head of the mission to China. He wrote of his adventure in Russian, inserting it into a detailed description of China, brazenly plagiarized from a work by a Jesuit named Martino Martini, published a few years before in Latin, German, Dutch and French. There is no disputing, however, the authenticity of his eyewitness report – the first detailed report in any language – of passing through the Wall, probably at Gubeikou:

The Wall [he wrote, in Baddeley's translation] leads over ridges and lofty mountains and down across the deeps of the ravines. And there are frequent towers, 100 sazhens [212 metres] one from the other. The Wall is built in this way: at the foundation, cut stone of huge dimensions, undressed granite and above that brick. The height is 4 sazhens [8.5 metres], the breadth is 2 sazhens [4.25 metres]. In some places, amongst the mountains, it has fallen down. The Chinese, speaking of it, boast that when it was built there remained no stone on the mountains, no sand in the desert, in the rivers no water, in the forests no trees . . . There, at the first gate, was a great tower, and at the gate stood the governor of the town, counting all who passed, for such is their custom; and not only the people, but the arms they carry; all which is written down, lest any other man or weapon should pass out when these return. And this they do not only at these gates, but at all gates in the Great Wall . . . We passed through the first gates, which were [8.4 metres] wide. There was a guard there and [25 metres] further on we came to the second wall, with similar gates, and beyond that a third. All those gates and towers are very strong, the third (inner) wall being thicker than the others, and all three are built across the stony ravine about 56 feet [17 metres] wide, with a high and rocky cliff on either side. The doors themselves are sheathed with iron.

Slowly the image grew in the European mind of something immense and grand running across north China. Perhaps the image was bolstered by word of mouth from Jesuit surveyors who, after ten years' work, included the

Wall in a detailed map of China presented to the Ming emperor in 1718. Descriptive phrases fell from pens like the words of poor critics, all bombast and judgement and ignorance, like Voltaire's 'superior to the pyramids' and 'does honour to the human spirit'. Dr Johnson told Boswell to visit the Wall, because his children would admire him for it. But the only accounts were limited. No traveller provided a vivid, authoritative, first-hand description; and, crucially, there were no pictures to send minds racing with images of the Wall's true scale. The change came after 1798, when the first good eye-witness picture of the Wall was published – a picture which has its own curious history.

This picture was one of many illustrating the first British mission to China in 1792. Considering that European powers had been trading with China for centuries, this is rather late for a first contact between the dominant powers of Asia and Europe. Why hadn't it happened before? The reasons are rooted deep in China's attitude to trade, which proved highly significant for the mission. They also explain why this picture was the first good one of the Wall, and why it was the only one for many years to come.

China, like much of the rest of the world, had benefited from foreign trade for 1,000 years. Merchants, families, towns, whole regions had become rich on it. The government itself relied on the taxes derived from it. Yet an ancient truth still held: officially, even in 1792, there was no such thing as foreign trade. Logic decreed it to be an impossibility. Trade implied dealings between equals; China was the world's greatest power; therefore no other power was equal to it; therefore there could be no trade, only 'tribute' from inferiors on the one hand, and 'gifts' from superiors on the other. This was an attitude from which foreign traders, like the British, suffered. That they had suffered it so long without trying to do something about it was because trade was in the hands of a private company, the East India Company. Officially, they could trade in Canton, and nowhere else. They were not to sully the emperor by coming to Beijing, certainly not by meeting with senior officials; and the idea of foreign envoys – 'tribute envoys' – meeting the emperor was anathema. If a meeting were to be arranged, there were strict rules. 'For a tribute envoy's entrance of the frontier and the tribute route which he follows, in each case there are fixed places,' said the 1764 edition of the Qing dynasty's *Collected Statutes* (*Da Qing Huitian*). And fixed rituals as well, including the kowtow: three separate kneelings, each followed by a full prostration with the forehead knocking the ground three times, all done in obedience to an usher calling out the movements to be followed. It was a humiliating procedure for foreign leaders, and that was the whole point: to impress them with the truth.

Of all this, George Macartney was unaware. If he had been, he would surely not have agreed to lead the mission which the government had decided, in the name of King George III, to send to Beijing. Not that he lacked international experience. He had taken the Grand Tour of Europe considered vital for the education of a gentleman. At 27, he was envoy to Catherine the Great in St Petersburg. His CV included action in the West Indies during the American Revolution, friendships with the great and some of the good, and the governorship of Madras. Along the way he was made a knight, a viscount and the first Earl Macartney. At 54, he was a good choice as envoy to Qianlong, the greatest of the Qing emperors.

Macartney's brief was to negotiate a treaty of commerce and friendship on an equal footing, extend British trade by opening new ports to foreign ships, obtain concessions near to silk- and tea-producing areas, and pick up as much information about the country as he could. To achieve this, Macartney took along two ships holding 95 people. Fifty-three of them were members of a military escort. The rest included two interpreters (trainee priests from the Catholic College of Chinese in Naples, there being no British speakers of Chinese), seven scientists, five (German) musicians, a painter (Thomas Hickey) and a draughtsman (William Alexander). A young lieutenant, Henry Parish, was also a rather good artist, which was fortunate, as we shall see. The ships were loaded with gifts designed to win over any emperor: telescopes, clocks, watches, Wedgwood vases and three newfangled post-chaises.

It all sounds like an exercise in British imperial arrogance, an embodiment of the rhetorical question: Who could fail to be won over by objects that showed how advanced and civilized the British were? The answer was: The Chinese, who were experts at dismissing the claims of foreigners. Macartney's mission was doomed even before it arrived. An edict rejecting everything Macartney wanted, approved nine days after his meeting with the emperor, was drafted well *before* the audience, on receipt of Macartney's requests. In elegant language, it spells out China's view of foreigners and the proper relationship with them. In the words of the edict's most recent translator, J. L. Cranmer-Byng, 'this is perhaps the most important Chinese document for the study of Sino-Western relations between 1700 and 1860'.

Here it is, in summary:

'We, by the Grace of Heaven Emperor, instruct the King of England to take note of our charge.' Though living so far away, you have at least had the sense to incline your heart to civilization, and come to kowtow, honour the imperial birthday and bring local products. But that's it. You want a resident in Beijing? 'This . . . definitely cannot be done,' because, by Chinese regulations, he would have to enter imperial service and never be allowed home. How could we change our regulations 'because of the request of one man – of you, O King?' It would just open the flood-gates – every other nation would want similar concessions. As for your gifts and trade goods, 'we have never valued ingenious articles, nor do we have the slightest need of your country's manufactures'. 'Hence we have . . . commanded your tribute envoys to return safely home. You, O King, should simply act in conformity with our wishes by strengthening your loyalty and swearing perpetual obedience to ensure that your country may share the blessings of peace.'

Even after 1860, when two wars had opened up China to some degree, there was no real change in official opinion. Given what the British, French, Portuguese, Germans and Japanese did to China in the century following the first of those wars in 1840, the Chinese had a point. They did then, and they do now. As

Cranmer-Byng concluded in 1962, 'The basic ideas expressed in this edict have never entirely lost their power.' Today's diplomats and businessmen, beware.

As you might imagine, neither side gained from the 1792 expedition. The Chinese learned absolutely nothing from the British; the British gained none of their objectives. The whole thing was a complete waste of time and money – except that Macartney and his people were terrific at keeping records. The secretary, Sir George Staunton, wrote an official report in two volumes which is a model of eighteenth-century prose, though somewhat unbalanced, given that the entire first volume is given over to the voyage out. Macartney wrote his own journal, as did several other crew members. In the fashion of 'natural philosophers' of the day, they were interested in everything they saw, from A to Z, from architecture to zoology. And the three artists produced pictures, which, when copied in engravings and printed, became prime sources of first-hand information about China in the 1790s. They include a representation of the Wall – the one and only eye-witness view for many years to come.

The visitors saw the Wall at all only because the Emperor was in his summer quarters in Jehol (today's Chengde),[2] a hot-spring resort in mountains 160 kilometres north-east of Beijing. Here Qianlong had created a huge estate, 10 kilometres in circumference, with a 120-room palace, 70 other buildings and a park carefully maintained to seem wild. Having spent almost three

---

[2] *Rehe* in pinyin, 'Hot River', the final 'l' stemming from the local pronunciation of *hé* / 河 .

weeks sailing upriver to Beijing and a further ten days in Beijing, Macartney's party left for Jehol on 2 September. Their route, paralleled by another, much better, road reserved for the emperor's use, lay through the Wall at Gubeikou, and the prospect delighted everyone – except two. The trouble was that space was limited, and the two artists, Alexander and Hickey, were declared redundant. Alexander was bitterly disappointed. 'This to me was a most severe decision,' he wrote in his journal. 'And to have been within 50 miles [well, more like 100] of the famous Great Wall, that stupendous monument of human labour, and not to have seen that which might have been the boast of a man's grandson as Dr Johnson has said I have to regret for ever.' The only man left with the ability to record images of this week-long journey was Lieutenant Parish, engineer and skilled draughtsman.

Most of the delegation travelled in Chinese carriages or on horseback, while Macartney was pulled over the rough road in a post-chaise drawn by four Mongolian horses. One of three brought from London, this vehicle was of the very latest design, with springs, glass windows that opened and closed, and Venetian blinds. Once Chinese officials overcame their fear of overturning, they accepted Macartney's offer of the occasional ride, becoming in Staunton's words 'inexpressibly delighted with its easiness, lightness and rapidity'. It would, the ambassador assumed, be much admired by the emperor, for whom it was intended. The road ran through a tobacco-rich area, for the Chinese were great smokers, and then into mountains, where the population was half Mongol, half Chinese. 'The Tartar women', Staunton noted, 'were distinguished chiefly by having feet of a natural size' – not bound, as was the excruciatingly painful fashion in China.

Ahead, the British noted a strange line that ran up and over mountainsides, like a vein of quartz. It was, of course, the Wall, in its most dramatic manifestation: running along the ridges of Jinshanling, Gubeikou and Simatai. Here, in his convoluted style and idiosyncratic spelling, are Staunton's words – the first close-up description of the Wall by a foreigner:

> What the eye could, from a single spot, embrace of those fortified walls, carried along the ridges of hills, over the tops of the highest mountains, descending into the deepest vallies, crossing upon arches over rivers, and doubled and trebled in many parts to take in important passes, and interspersed with towers or massy bastions at almost every hundred yards, as far as the sight could reach, presented to the mind an undertaking of stupendous magnitude . . . It was not alone the dimensions of those walls, however considerable, that made the impression of wonder . . . It was the extreme difficulty of conceiving how the materials could be conveyed, and such structures raised, in situations apparently inaccessible, which principally occasioned surprise and admiration.

His open-mouthed wonder fitted well with the fashion back home for wild landscapes and exotic ruins, the very landscape conjured by Coleridge only four years later in his poem about the summer palace of Kublai Khan in Xanadu, a mere 160 kilometres (though more by twisting roads) from where Staunton first saw the Wall:

Xanadu, which boasts a sacred river, measureless caverns and incense-bearing trees, and where

> Twice five miles of fertile ground
> With walls and towers were girdled round.

And only a year after that, Coleridge and Wordsworth together wrote the preface to *Lyrical Ballads*, generally considered to set the agenda for the Romantic movement.

Now, one element in Romanticism is the exploration of the way landscapes work on the imagination, producing a heightened, exaggerated realism. Staunton was more than a staid secretary. He had literary aspirations, and an imagination that went beyond what he saw. Add all walls known to history – Hadrian's, others raised in Egypt, Syria, Turkey, one 'eastwards of the Caspian, by a successor of Alexander, and another in the country of Tamerlane' – and the result, he said, would still not equal this Wall. Parts of it were now crumbling, but on the whole the structure, 'in a course of 1,500 miles', was so well built as to have 'preserved it entire for about two thousand years'. In other words, he made three assumptions: that the Ming wall was also the First Emperor's wall, backdating it by 2,000 years; that the wall was a whole, single wall, not many bits and pieces; and that it was all of brick and stone rather than pounded earth. These assumptions, still widely held today, seem to be backed up by the strongest single image that came from the trip.

On the third day, with the Wall drawing them on from its heights, the party came to a ravine, across which ran a wall capped by a tower. A kilometre further on, they reached the town of Gubeikou (variously spelled by the British as Koo-pe-koo or Ku-pei-k'ou). After breakfast the next day, they climbed the hillside for half an hour until they found a hole knocked in the Wall, which gave access to the walkway above. This allowed Parish to record a tower along with the foundations, brickwork and parapet: 6 metres high, 3.5 metres wide, 'so that there is room for two coaches or five horsemen abreast'. It is an image that remains popular today.

'If the other parts of it be similar to those which I have seen, it is certainly the most stupendous work of human hands,' wrote Macartney, adding that ancient China must have been a very wise and virtuous nation to establish a perpetual security at such enormous expense. He noted that, although some parts were in good shape, 'in general it is in ruinous condition, and falling fast to decay'.

The officials who accompanied the mission were somewhat puzzled by the foreigners' interest. 'The Chinese . . . look upon it with perfect indifference; and few of the mandarines [sic] who accompanied the Embassy, seemed to pay the least attention to it.' But they did pay attention to the way the British paid attention, for it made them highly suspicious: 'They were astonished at our curiosity, and almost began to suspect us, I believe, of dangerous designs,' though it is hard to imagine what these might have been.

Arriving at Jehol on 8 September, the emissaries found themselves billeted in a little town of crooked, unpaved and dusty streets lined with miserable hovels, set humbly below the imperial palaces, temples and gardens: a startling contrast of magnificence and wretchedness. The audience happened a week later, on a chilly day, with Macartney in embroidered velvet, carried in a palanquin at the head of a glorious horseback procession (though not all that glorious, perhaps, considering the presence of several other heads of state, 12,000 mandarins and 80,000 troops). They stopped by a large, round, highly decorated tent, the emperor's nod to his Manchu past. After they had been waiting an hour in the morning cold, the emperor arrived, carried in a palanquin borne by sixteen men, and attended by officers bearing flags, standards and umbrellas.

Now what? It was time for the kowtow. There had been much back-and-forth on the subject of kowtowing. Macartney had refused the three prostrations and the nine head-knockings, to the consternation of officials. He said he was prepared to kneel and kiss the emperor's hand, as he did to his own sovereign. How about two knees, came the reply, and no hand-kissing? The rituals were too far advanced to backtrack, so Macartney got his unprecedented way: a simple one-knee obeisance. The emperor graciously pretended not to notice. With all attendants maintaining a reverential silence, he accepted Macartney's gifts without interest (the carriages, later left in Beijing, were never used, being dumped into store in Beijing's Summer Palace along with other 'tribute trophies'). He handed over a few slight presents of his own, and then presided over a banquet. Through his interpreter, he asked George III's age (55), and wished him a life as long as his: he was now 83, and a remarkably fit 83. He was dignified, affable, gracious, commented

Macartney; 'a very fine old gentleman, still healthy and vigorous, not having the appearance of a man of more than sixty'. It was all pleasant enough, but totally bland. Nothing was agreed.

There followed a tour of the park, which in its contrived wildness reminded Macartney of his father-in-law's estate, Luton Hoo, a creation of the great landscape architect 'Capability' Brown. It included a boating lake, giant willows, virgin meadows, and innumerable palaces filled with works of art, including clockwork figures imported from Europe, of which the Chinese seemed most proud. Other ceremonies followed over the next few days, in honour of the emperor's birthday. In the first festival, when a band struck up to signify the presence of the emperor behind a screen, in Macartney's words,

> instantly the whole court fell flat upon their faces . . . The music was a sort of birthday ode, the burden of which was 'Bow down your heads, all ye dwellers upon earth, . . .' and then all the dwellers upon China earth there present, except ourselves, bowed down their heads, and prostrated themselves upon the ground at every renewal of the chorus.

Another gathering was held later in the vast Potola temple, an imitation of the Dalai Lama's in Lhasa, attended by 800 lamas. Entertainments followed: tightrope walkers, conjurers, acrobats, musicians, dancers; a firework display, ending with an artificial volcano; and a pantomime. And so the celebrations ended, with the visitors all heading to their various homes.

Naturally, on arriving back at Gubeikou, the English travellers were keen to renew their research on the Wall. But something odd had happened. The hole in the Wall through which they had climbed to the top had been 'stopped up with stone and rubbish'. To the obvious embarrassment of the Chinese officials, who tried to divert their attention 'with curious objects of pursuit', they searched out another hole, and were able to check their results. Shortly thereafter the mission left for Beijing, Macao and home, where they arrived on 6 September 1794.

Four years later, Staunton's official account of the mission was published, and along with it a series of engravings which included a version of Parish's drawing of the Wall at Gubeikou. It is clear where he stood to draw it, standing beside the Wall as it runs eastwards towards Jinshanling, looking westward towards Badaling, with the early-morning sun over his left shoulder. The river is in the dip below him, beyond which the Wall rises over the hill I climbed.

It was a view much copied over the next 50 years. One of the copies appeared in a series of engravings by Thomas Allom and G. N. Wright in 1843. But there are subtle changes. Parish's version has a virtually empty foreground, the only people a couple of horsemen. Allom's has a Chinese official being carried in a palanquin, followed by a procession of hundreds, going who knows where, because the road actually leads up the valley, not over the hills. More to the point, though, is the hill in the background. In Parish, the Wall disappears round the summit; in Allom, it goes *over* the summit, has acquired five extra towers, and then picks up again on even more distant mountains. In a way, this serves a greater truth, because it looks rather like the fairy-tale Wall at Simatai. But it's not true to life. I have a photograph to prove it. Along the way, Parish's view has been exaggerated, Romanticized. This is the Wall that became famous in Europe, the wonderful stegosaurus-back of crenellated bricks and stone that supposedly stretched all the way across north China.

This, therefore, was what Heinrich Schliemann was hoping for when he arrived in China in April 1865, ten years before his greatest discovery. This multilingual polymath and self-made man was an extraordinary, complex and paradoxical character: as one of his biographers, Leo Deuel, puts it, 'soft-hearted and ruthless, loyal almost to excess and tricky to the verge of delinquency, enamoured with culture but essentially lacking in taste'. No scholar, he was one of the greatest popularizers of archaeology of all time. He admired himself tremendously, with good cause, yet constantly brightened his image by exaggeration. Here he is assessing himself to his son in 1870: 'I proved how much a person can accomplish with iron energy . . . I performed miracles . . . I was the most able and prudent businessman . . . a traveller *par excellence* . . . the object of universal admiration.' He could pick up a language in a few months – equipping himself with eighteen of them in all – and would learn vast slabs of text, even whole novels, or so he claimed, off by heart (for English, Goldsmith's *Vicar of Wakefield* and Scott's *Ivanhoe*; for French, Fénelon's *Aventures de Télémaque*). In 1863, at the age of 41, he was using the wealth generated by his business interests to explore the world, in a fury of curiosity that compelled him to 'keep moving, to see nothing but new sights, to smell, taste, hear, observe, measure and compare new things'.[3] He saw nine countries in two years, keeping observations in nine languages (though not Chinese).

In May he spent a day in Gubeikou – 'Ku-pa-ku', as he calls it – and made the climb commemorated by the placard I had seen that moonlit night. The placard was wrong on the date – it was 1865, not 1863 – and the title of his book,[4] and it misquoted him; but it was right in spirit. He had been on California's Sierra Nevada, the Himalayas, and South America's altiplano, he wrote,

> but I have never seen anything that could compare with the splendid picture that now unfolded before my eyes . . . a hundred times more grandiose than I had imagined. And the more I gazed upon this immense barrier . . . the more it seemed to me the fabulous creation of an antediluvian race. But knowing from history that this wall was constructed 220 years before our era, I could not comprehend how mortal hands were capable of raising it . . . How is it, I asked myself, that that generation of giants . . . had any real need of it?

How could one conjure up so many millions of workers, marshal so many soldiers to invest 'the 20,000 towers of

[3] Moorehead, *The Lost Treasures of Troy.*
[4] It was actually in French: Schliemann, *La Chine et le Japon au temps présent.*

the wall, which counting all its bends, amounts to a length of no less than 3,200 kilometres?' Well, not so fast. His words are a wild mix of little fact and much assumption and exaggeration. The wall he saw was, of course, only 300 years old, and most of it was of earth, not stone. Yet, on the basis of a few hours' experience and a few kilometres' walk, he sees in his uncritical mind's eye a vast romantic ruin, dating from before the Flood, built by giants, for such was its image in European eyes.

Since so few outsiders had actually set eyes on it, the idea that it could be seen from space was not a huge leap. That idea may have been first suggested by the *Century Magazine*, a US monthly, in January 1893, when a writer and traveller named Romyn Hitchcock claimed that the Great Wall was 'the only work of man of sufficient magnitude to arrest attention in a hasty survey of the earth's surface'.[5] Where did he get the idea? Nowhere, specifically, for it had been in the air since 1877, when the Italian astronomer Giovanni Schiaparelli suggested he could see rivers on Mars, *canali* as he called them, which supposedly carried meltwaters from the frozen poles. Percival Lowell, who ran the observatory named after him in Flagstaff, Arizona, took this suggestion and spun his own theory in *Mars and its Canals* (1906), in which he claimed that it was 'probable that upon the surface of Mars we see the effects of local intelligence'. The famous eleventh edition of the *Enyclopaedia Britannica* (1911) mentions his canals, quoting Lowell's words in a long footnote, and commenting: 'Of the reality of the better

[5] The suggestion comes from Waldron, *The Great Wall of China*.

marked ones there can be no doubt.' The idea seized the imagination of the public and science-fiction writers for the next 50 years, until in 1964 Lowell's canals were shown to be optical illusions by the Mariner 4 spacecraft (though by a strange irony orbiting satellites have since revealed numerous dried-up waterways invisible from earth). In Lowell's time, though, and for decades thereafter, the conclusion was obvious: if we can see them, they can see us. What could they see? Equally obviously, the world's longest structure, as Mr Ripley famously stated in his *Believe It Or Not!* in 1932.

Romantic images, the eighth wonder of the world, the most stupendous work of man: but China was slow to capitalize on the publicity. For almost 40 years after the Qing Dynasty collapsed in 1911, China was in meltdown, in need of leaders and stability and symbols of nationhood. Only when the nation itself was under threat, when the Japanese invaded from their new colony in Manchuria, did the Wall emerge as an image to be nurtured, for it played an important role in several actions. The Japanese fought at Badaling (stripping the trees from the Mongolian side), at Gubeikou and Shanhaiguan, battles that live on in the memory of old men, like the one I spoke to on the way to Mutianyu.

This was why Mao seized upon it as a suitable symbol for the nation, a monument that had no practical purpose any more but could still be coopted to represent an achievement by ordinary, suffering people. That was its purpose in his poem 'Snow'; in the 'March of the Volunteers', which was taken from the 1935 film *Children of the Storm* to become the national anthem; in vast murals like the ones in Beijing airport and the Hall of the People; in the ritual visits to Badaling by foreign leaders (which are, in effect, kowtows not to a leader but to the Chinese people); in the restoration work; in the determination that Chinese children should visit the Wall as part of their education and that the Wall should be open to foreign tourists.

It has not all been a smooth upward course for the Wall. Its prestige sank again during the Cultural Revolution, when anything old came under attack by Mao's Red Guard thugs. Hundreds of kilometres were dynamited, cut through, knocked down, stolen for building materials. But it rose again, although for dubious reasons. Mao kept an iron hold on the country, and compared himself to the Wall's builder, the First Emperor. As he told the Second Plenum of the Eighth Party Congress in May 1958, some 'have accused us of being Emperor Qin Shihuang [the First Emperor]. This is not true [I told them]. We are a hundred times worse than Emperor Qin.' Meng Jiangnu, the ancient heroine whose tears made a section of the Wall collapse, became a counter-revolutionary who dared destroy China's shield, the very symbol of China's strength.

Today, the Wall is attached to any number of products, hotels, resorts, foods and drinks. It is the name given to the company that launched China's first rocket. It appears on stamps. It is the subject of the immense 30-square-metre, 272-kilo tapestry given by China to the UN in 1974. It's a broadband network, a UNESCO World Heritage site, a literary cliché. In August 2006, when Hugo Chavez of Venezuela signed a million-barrel-a-day oil deal with China, he called it a 'Great Wall against American hegemonism'. It is recalled, for better or worse, in the nickname for the cyber-barrier blocking unwelcome websites, the Great Firewall.

The Wall was never the unity its name suggests; it was never the result of a coherent policy, always the least unpleasant option. Now all that is past. The Wall is no longer a border or a barrier, but firmly in China's embrace. Beyond purpose and practicality, it is protected and restored simply because of what it once was. It has risen above the mess of politics, strategy and controversy into an ethereal realm of ideals and symbols: pure heritage.

APPENDIX

DATES AND DYNASTIES: A GREAT WALL CHRONOLOGY

(Many early dates are traditional, and unreliable.)

Period	Dates	Wall-building
	Ancient Times	
Xia (legendary)	2207–1766 BC	
Shang	c.1700–11th century BC	
Zhou (western and eastern, including Warring States, 453–221)	1025–256 BC	Local walls
	China United (1)	
Qin	221–206 BC	First Great Wall, Ordos to coast

Han (Western or Former Han)	202 BC–AD 6	Western extension of Wall
(Interregnum)	6–25	
Han (Eastern or Later Han)	25–220	

Middle Ages

Three Kingdoms	220–65	
Western Jin (brief reunification)	265–316	
Many kingdoms	317–580s	
Sui (reunification in 589)	581–618	Many local walls
Tang	618–907	
Five Dynasties, Ten Kingdoms	907–60	
Song (unified nation)	960–1127	

In north:		
Liao (Khitans)	907–1125	Ditches and ridges, Inner Mongolia
Jin (Jurchen)	1115–1234	
Mongols	1234–	Wall decays
In west:		
Xi Xia (Tanguts)	1032–1227	
In south:		
Southern Song	1127–1279	

China United (2)

Yuan (Mongols, unification 1279)	1234–1368	Wall forgotten
Ming	1368–1644	Building of today's Wall
Qing (Manchus)	1644–1911	Wall ignored
Republic	1912–49	
Communist Party	1949–	Restoration

BIBLIOGRAPHY

The Wall has an immense literature, much of which is embedded in other books about Chinese history. As far as I know, there is no authoritative bibliography devoted to the Wall alone. The best ones are in Waldron and Lovell. The books and articles listed below are the ones I consulted. Researchers should explore (with caution) the Wikipedia and the wide-ranging Travelchinaguide.com sites.

Allsen, Thomas T., 'The Rise of the Mongolian Empire', in Herbert Franke and Denis Twitchett (eds), *The Cambridge History of China*, vol. 6: *Alien Regimes and Border States, 907–1368*, Cambridge University Press, Cambridge, 1994

Andrews, Roy Chapman, *New Conquest of Central Asia*, vol. 1 of 8 (American Museum of Natural History, New York, 1932)

Andrews, Roy Chapman, *This Business of Exploring*, Putnam, New York, 1935

Andrews, Roy Chapman, *Under a Lucky Star: A Lifetime of Adventure*, Viking, New York, 1943

Atwood, Christopher, *Encyclopedia of Mongolia and the Mongol Empire*, Facts on File, New York, 2004

Baddeley, John, *Russia, Mongolia, China*, Macmillan, London, 1919

Barthold, V. V., *Turkestan Down to the Mongol Invasion*, Gibb Memorial Trust/Luzac, London, 1928 and 1968

Bodde, Derk, *Statesman, Patriot and General in Ancient China* (trans. from Sima Qian's biographical essays on Lü Buwei, Jing Ke and Meng Tian, with a commentary), American Oriental Society, Newhaven, 1940

Buell, Paul D., 'The Role of the Sino-Mongolian Frontier Zone in the Rise of Cinggis-Qan', in Henry G. Schwartz (ed.), *Proceedings of the First North American Conference on Mongolian Studies*, Western Washington University, Bellingham, Washington, 1979

Cheng Dalin, *The Great Wall of China*, South China Morning Post, Hong Kong, 1984

Cosmo, Nicola di, and Don J. Wyatt (eds), *Political Frontiers, Ethnic Boundaries, and Human Geographies in Chinese History*, Collège de France (Institut des Hautes Études Chinoises), Paris, 1986

CPC County Committee, Yongchang, *Li Qian Tang Kao Wen Cui (The Roman Legion: Collected Research Papers)*, Yongchang, 2005

Cranmer-Byng, John, (ed. and intr.), *An Embassy to China, Being the Journal kept by Lord Macartney during his embassy to the Emperor Ch'ienlung, 1793–1794*, Longmans, London, 1962

Deuel, Leo, *Memoirs of Heinrich Schliemann: A Documentary Portrait Drawn from His Autobiographical*

Writings, Letters and Excavation Reports, Hutchinson, London, 1978

Dubs, Homer H., *A Roman City in Ancient China*, China Society, London, 1957

Dudbridge, Glen, 'Dubs and the Roman *testudo*', unpublished paper, 2001

Edmonds, Richard L., 'The Willow Palisade', *Annals of the Association of American Geographers*, vol. 69, no. 4, Dec. 1979

Franke, Herbert, 'The Chin Dynasty', in Herbert Franke and Denis Twitchett (eds), *The Cambridge History of China*, vol. 6: *Alien Regimes and Border States, 907–1368*, Cambridge University Press, Cambridge, 1994

Franke, Herbert, and Denis Twitchett (eds), *The Cambridge History of China*, vol. 6: *Alien Regimes and Border States, 907–1368*, Cambridge University Press, Cambridge, 1994

Fryer, Jonathan, *The Great Wall*, New English Library, London, 1975

Han Feizi, *Basic Writings* (trans. Burton Watson), Columbia University Press, New York, 2003

Harris, David, *Black Horse Odyssey*, Wakefield Press, Kent Town, South Australia, 1991

Hitchcock, Romyn, 'The Great Wall of China', *Century Magazine*, vol. 45, no. 3, Jan. 1893

Kierman, Frank A., and John F. Fairbank (eds), *Chinese Ways in Warfare*, Harvard University Press, Cambridge, Mass., 1974

Kwong Hing Foon, *Wang Zhaojun: une héroine chinoise de l'histoire à la légende*, Collège de France (Institut des Hautes Études Chinoises), Paris, 1986

Lattimore, Owen, *Inner Asian Frontiers of China*, American Geographical Society, New York, 1940

Li Yuning (ed.), *The First Emperor of China*, International Arts and Sciences Press, White Plains, NY, 1975. (Includes Hung ShihTi [Hong Shidi], *Ch'in Shih-Huang*, People's Press, Shanghai, 1972.)

Lindesay, William, *Alone on the Great Wall*, Hodder & Stoughton, London, 1989

Lindesay, William, *The Great Wall*, Oxford University Press, Oxford, 2003

Loewe, Michael, 'The Campaigns of Han Wu-ti', in Frank A. Kierman and John F. Fairbank (eds), *Chinese Ways in Warfare*, Harvard University Press, Cambridge, Mass., 1974

Loewe, Michael, *Records of Han Administration*, Cambridge University Press, Cambridge, 1967

Lovell, Julia, *The Great Wall: China against the World 1000 BC–AD 2000*, Atlantic Books, London, 2006

Luo Zhewen and Yan Qiubai, *The Great Wall: History and Pictures*, Foreign Languages Press, Beijing, 1995

Man, John, *Attila: The Barbarian King Who Challenged Rome*, Bantam Press, London, 2005

Man, John, *Genghis Khan: Life, Death and Resurrection*, Bantam Press, London, 2004

Man, John, *The Terracotta Army: China's First Emperor and the Birth of a Nation*, Bantam Press, London, 2007

Martin, H. Desmond, *The Rise of Chingis Khan and his Conquest of North China*, Johns Hopkins University Press, Baltimore, 1950; repr. Octagon, New York, 1971

Menzies, Gavin, *1421: The Year China Discovered the World*, Bantam Press, London, 2002

Moorehead, Caroline, *The Lost Treasures of Troy*, Weidenfeld & Nicolson, London, 1994

Mote, F. W., *Imperial China 900–1800*, Harvard University

Press, Cambridge, Mass. and London, 1999

Mote, F. W., 'The T'u-mu Incident of 1449', in Frank A. Kierman and John F. Fairbank (eds), *Chinese Ways in Warfare*, Harvard University Press, Cambridge, Mass., 1974

Needham, Joseph, *Science and Civilisation in China*, vol. 4, part 3: *Civil Engineering: Walls, and the Wall*, Cambridge University Press, Cambridge, 1971

Needham, Joseph, and Liao Hung-Ying, 'The Ballad of Meng Chiang Nu Weeping at the Great Wall', *Sinologica*, vol. 1, no. 3, 1948 (Basel)

Paludan, Ann, *Chinese Sculpture: A Great Tradition*, Serinidia Publications, Chicago, 2006

Rachewiltz, Igor de (trans. and ed.), *The Secret History of the Mongols: A Mongolian Epic Chronicle of the Thirteenth Century*, Brill, Leiden, Boston and Cologne, 2004

Schliemann, Henry (Heinrich), *La Chine et le Japon au temps présent*, Librairie Centrale, Paris, 1867

Schwartz, Daniel, *The Great Wall of China*, Thames & Hudson, London, 1990 and 2001

Shang Yang, *The Book of Lord Shang* (with Sun Tzu: *The Art of War*), Wordsworth, Ware (Herts), 1998

Shou Hou, 'What is the Origin of "the Wailing of Meng Chiang-nü at the Great Wall"?' in Li Yuning (ed.), *The First Emperor of China*, International Arts and Sciences Press, White Plains, NY, 1975

Sima Qian, *Records of the Grand Historian: Qin Dynasty* (trans. Burton Watson), Columbia University Press, Hong Kong and New York, 1993

Sinor, Denis (ed.), *The Cambridge History of Early Inner Asia*, Cambridge University Press, Cambridge, 1990

So, Jenny F., and Emma C. Bunker, *Traders and Raiders on China's Northern Frontier*, Smithsonian Institution, Washington DC, 1995

Travelchinaguide.com. Comprehensive coverage of the Wall, but of variable quality.

Turnbull, Stephen (illus. Steve Noon), *The Great Wall of China 221 BC–AD 1644*, Osprey, Oxford, 2007

Wakeman, Frederic, *The Great Enterprise: The Manchu Reconstruction of Imperial Order in 17th-Century China*, University of California Press, Berkeley and Los Angeles, 1985

Waldron, Arthur, *The Great Wall of China: From History to Myth*, Cambridge University Press, Cambridge, 1990

Wikipedia.org. Though they are unattributed and should be cross-checked with published sources, the historical articles on Chinese and Mongolian themes, incidents and characters are generally reliable and often extremely useful.

Zhang Xianliang, *Mimosa*, Chinese Literature, Beijing, 1985

PICTURE
ACKNOWLEDGEMENTS

All photographs in the picture sections are by the author except for the following:

First section
Pages 4/5 Huo Qubing's tomb mound: Photo by Victor Segalen, 1914

Second section
Pages 2/3 Jiaya at dawn: © Jose Fuste Raga/Corbis
Pages 6/7 Dingbian in the snow: © Liang Zhuoming/ Corbis
Pages 8/9 Yumenguan on a clear day: Uniphoto/Ancient Art & Architecture Collection Ltd
Pages 12/13 Richard Nixon at the Great Wall: AP/PA Photos

Third section
Pages 2/3 Main picture: © Lin Liqun/Corbis

INDEX

THE TERRACOTTA ARMY
by John Man

In 1974 local farmers digging a well near present-day Xian unearthed parts of clay figures, opening the way to one of the greatest archaeological discoveries of all time. The Terracotta Army was a total surprise – some 8,000 life-size clay warriors and horses buried in 210 BC as a 'spirit army' to guard the tomb of the First Emperor. They had been lying forgotten in their three pits for over 2,000 years.

The First Emperor, the brilliant and ruthless ruler who united China and built the first Great Wall, was beset by paranoia and a desire to dominate in the afterlife, as he had in this one. Around his giant tomb-mound, as yet unopened, other pits concealed a whole spirit world of officials, entertainers, armour, and bronze chariots.

1,000 of the warriors now stand with many other finds in a site that attracts some two million visitors a year. As work continues, there are surely more surprises to come. As John Man suggests, there could even be more warriors still to be discovered. One day, perhaps, the tomb-mound itself will be opened and its legendary treasures revealed.

Weaving together history and first-hand experience from his travels in China, John Man tells the story of how and why these astonishing artefacts were created. In doing so, he sketches vivid portraits of the 'spirit army' and the man who formed the roots of China today.

'One couldn't wish for a better storyteller or analyst
than John Man'
Simon Sebag Montefiore

9780553819144

BANTAM BOOKS

ATTILA THE HUN
And the Fall of Rome
by John Man

'Superb, as compellingly readable as it is impressive in its scholarship . . . the Huns and their king live as never before'
Simon Sebag Montefiore

Attila the Hun is a household name – a byword for barbarism and violence – but to most of us the man himself, his world and his place in history have remained elusive. Until now.

For a crucial twenty years in the early 5th century AD, Attila held the fate of the Roman Empire and the future of Europe in his hands. In numerous raids and three major campaigns he and his warriors earned an undying reputation for savagery, and his empire briefly rivalled that of Rome, reaching from the Rhine to the Black Sea, the Baltic to the Balkans.

Attila's power derived from his astonishing character. He may have been capricious, arrogant and ruthless, but he was brilliant enough to win the loyalty of millions: his own people thought him semi-divine while educated Westerners were proud to serve him. From his base in the grasslands of Hungary, this 'scourge of God' so very nearly dictated Europe's future . . .

Drawing on his extensive travels in the barbarian heartland and his experience with the nomadic traditions of Central Asia, John Man's riveting biography reveals the man behind the enduring myth of Attila the Hun.

'Racy and imaginative . . . sympathetically and readably puts flesh and bones on one of history's most turbulent characters'
Sunday Telegraph

'Meteoric and momentous . . . fascinating reading'
Guardian

9780553816587

BANTAM BOOKS

KUBLAI KHAN
The Mongol King Who Remade China
by John Man

Kublai Khan, the thirteenth-century Mongolian prince who became warrior emperor of China, was perhaps the most powerful man who ever lived.

Grandson of the great Genghis Khan, he inherited the largest land empire in history – and doubled it. Driven to fulfil his grandfather's destiny and ensure Mongol supremacy, Kublai's realm would embrace over half of all Asia: a staggering one-fifth of the world's inhabited land area.

But Kublai Khan was not born to rule. It was his brilliant, scheming mother who placed him in line for the throne. Seizing power when in his forties, he perceived China rather than Mongolia as the key to empire and, after twenty years of war, became the first 'barbarian' to conquer all China. Bringing together vast wealth, military strength and shrewd government, he was to transform his dominion into the prototype of today's superpower.

Drawing on his own travels through Mongolia and China, bestselling historian John Man brings the remarkable world of Kublai Khan to vibrant life.

'One could not wish for a better storyteller or analyst than John Man'
Simon Sebag Montefiore

'One of the great strengths of this book is to rescue Kublai Khan from myth . . . Man knows his subject, and his desire to share it is infectious . . . it is rollicking stuff'
Daily Telegraph

'Man has become a recognised authority on the history of Mongolia and its countrymen. *Kublai Khan* is a worthy successor to his book on *Genghis Khan* . . . a remarkable story'
Times Literary Supplement

9780553817188

BANTAM BOOKS

GENGHIS KHAN
Life, Death and Resurrection
by John Man

'Absorbing and beautifully written . . . a thrilling account'
Guardian

Genghis Khan is one of history's immortals: a leader of genius
and the founder of the world's greatest land empire – twice the
size of Rome's. His mysterious death in 1227 placed all at risk,
so it was kept a secret until his heirs had secured his conquests.
Secrecy has surrounded him ever since. His undiscovered
grave, with its imagined treasures, remains the subject of
intrigue and speculation.

Today, Genghis is by turns scourge, hero and demi-god. To
Muslims, Russians and Europeans, he is a mass-murderer. Yet
in his homeland, Mongols revere him as the nation's father;
Chinese honour him as dynastic founder; and in both
countries, worshippers seek his blessing.

This book is more than just a gripping account of Genghis' rise
and conquests. John Man uses first-hand experiences to reveal
the khan's enduring influence. He is the first writer to explore
the hidden valley where Genghis may have died, and one of the
few westerners to climb the sacred mountain where he was
probably buried.

The result is an enthralling account of the man himself and of
the passions that surround him today. For in legend, ritual and
controversy, Genghis lives on . . .

'A first-rate travel book, not so much a life of the khan but a
search for him . . . a rattling good read'
Independent

'A fine, well-written and well-researched book'
Mail on Sunday

'Fascinating . . . history doesn't come much
more enthralling than this'
Yorkshire Evening Post

9780553814989

BANTAM BOOKS